reclaiming
our
future

reclaiming
our
future

AN AGENDA FOR AMERICAN LABOR

William W. Winpisinger

edited by John Logue

with a Foreword
by Senator Edward M. Kennedy

Westview Press
BOULDER, SAN FRANCISCO, & LONDON

Frontispiece photo by Photo One

Copyright © 1989 by Westview Press, Inc.

Published in 1989 in the United States of America by Westview Press, Inc., 5500 Central Avenue, Boulder, Colorado 80301, and in the United Kingdom by Westview Press, Inc., 13 Brunswick Centre, London WC1N 1AF, England

Library of Congress Cataloging-in-Publication Data
Winpisinger, William W.
  Reclaiming our future: an agenda for American labor / William W. Winpisinger; edited by John Logue; with a foreword by Edward M. Kennedy.
    p. cm.
  ISBN 0-8133-0889-5.—ISBN 0-8133-0890-9 (pbk.)
  1. Working class—United States—Political activity. 2. United States—Economic policy—1981- . I. Logue, John, 1947–
II. Title.
HD8076.W56 1989
322'.2'0973—dc20   89-9121
                                                                                   CIP

Printed and bound in the United States of America

The paper used in this publication meets the requirements of the American National Standard for Permanence of Paper for Printed Library Materials Z39.48-1984.

10   9   8   7   6   5   4   3   2   1

contents

foreword

Senator Edward M. Kennedy

From the workplace, to corporate boardrooms, to the Congress, and to the great international chambers where world leaders struggle to make peace, William Winpisinger has left his mark on every important battle of our time. He has challenged all of us to think beyond today's tasks and to confront the larger issues that will shape our nation's future. And throughout it all, he has kept his eye resolutely on the goal of a society in which each of us has an opportunity to grow, to prosper, and to leave our mark.

Wimpy became president of the International Association of Machinists at a time of extraordinary turmoil within the labor movement and the American economy. It would have been easy, and understandable, for him to lower his sights and narrow his focus, as so many did. That never happened. Whatever the battle—for safer workplaces, for a healthier environment, for corporate accountability, for equal rights for the majority who are women and civil rights for the minority who are not white, and for an end to the nuclear arms race—Wimpy was always there battling in the trenches, urging us to move forward. He reflects and extends the best and most glorious tradition of the American labor movement—a movement fully engaged in every aspect of our civic, economic and political life. Like Eugene Debs, Walter Reuther, and Jerry Wurf, he has left his mark on each of us even if we never carried a union card.

Reclaiming Our Future: An Agenda for American Labor recounts these historic struggles, and the agenda it describes is truly one for the entire nation and our common future. And it is no small agenda.

Wimpy begins, as all progressives must, with the economy, for he understands that a sound economy is America's most important social program. The economy that he describes has undergone vast changes in recent years: Globe-girdling corporations move money and jobs around like pieces on a Monopoly board, technologies change so rapidly that industries become obsolete almost overnight, and competitors now are scattered all over the globe, not just across our country. Adapting to this transformation of the world economy is surely the most important challenge that we face in the 1990s—and the most important message of this book is that while we must adapt, we must never lose sight of our goals. Decent jobs in safe workplaces, paying fair wages—these are the priorities that have animated the American labor movement from its very inception—and Wimpy never lets us forget them.

But for me his singular contribution goes beyond these aspirations. He has always insisted, as he does again in this volume, that it is not enough to merely make products, reap profits, or earn wages; we must measure ourselves by whether or not the things we produce enrich the human condition and improve the world which we will leave to our children. I can think of no one who better represents the powerful biblical injunction that "Ye shall turn swords into plowshares and spears into pruning hooks." For Wimpy, this has meant a tireless campaign to eliminate the excesses in our military spending and turn our attention to meeting fundamental human needs in such areas as health care, education, housing, and the production of safe and inexpensive energy.

In the concluding chapters, Wimpy turns to another of his distinctive themes. He reminds us that wherever we work, we have another job. That job, simply put, is politics. The IAM, under Wimpy's leadership, has helped transform our political landscape. His support for grassroots organizations has helped change neighborhoods throughout our land and has infused our political system with a new generation of citizen activists from every walk of life.

As I reflect on the real message of Wimpy's support for groups like the Citizen Labor Energy Coalition, Citizen Action, and the Rainbow Coalition, I am struck by two points. First is the simple but powerful proposition that the interests of the American labor movement are not separate from or at odds with those of the broader community. His insistence on pursuing a common agenda has helped bring us together and made us stronger.

Second, Wimpy reminds us that passing political victories are worth little if they are achieved at the sacrifice of principle. As he recounts, this has sometimes made him a lonely figure, but it has never stopped him or caused him to pull his punches. In this book, he returns again and again to the issues and the concerns that have driven him throughout his career. This volume is no mere memoir. It is a guide and an instruction manual for those of us who will, with Wimpy's help, continue to struggle to redeem the American dream.

In my campaign for president in 1980, Wimpy was at my side from the first moment and he never left. For me, he was then, he has always been, and he remains today, a pillar of strength and insight.

In these pages, Wimpy carries on the work that brought us together and that we still share. He calls on us to face our problems squarely and to remember who we are and where we are going. Above all, he reminds us that we must join hands to reach our destination.

William Winpisinger and the American labor movement

John Logue

The first act of William W. Winpisinger's tenure as president of the International Association of Machinists and Aerospace Workers (IAM) set the stage for the next dozen years: he convened his initial staff meeting at a minute past midnight, just seconds after he took office on July 1, 1977. Things were going to be different, he told the staff members. "I don't mean to be poetic," he said, "but you might liken this to a new dawn."

As a *Newsweek* writer commented laconically later (October 23, 1978), Winpisinger's dawn "came up like thunder."

Poetic, prophetic, and occasionally profane, William W. Winpisinger has been the most outspoken and most quotable American labor leader of this generation. He has variously been described in the press as everything from "a loud mouth automechanic" and "labor's last angry man" to merely being "brash" and "skilled at capturing the spotlight." No one has ever described him as mincing his words or pulling his punches.

Winpisinger is a machinist: blunt, stubborn, self-educated and proud of his trade. As a spokesman for labor, Winpisinger has articulated the belief shared by millions of Americans that something has gone terribly wrong in our country. The middle class is shrinking. The number living in poverty is growing. The country is being deindustrialized as corporations move their production overseas and engage in what Winpi-

1

singer calls the "corporate cannibalism" of mergers. Technological innovations that displace workers are put into place while other innovations that would benefit millions are suppressed. Social programs have been gutted while the military establishment is glutted. The numbers of homeless increase while construction workers stand in unemployment lines. The low prices caused by agricultural surpluses drive family farmers into bankruptcy while, elsewhere in the world, a billion people are hungry. Something is obviously out of sync.

Characterizing himself as a "belligerent advocate of disarmament" and "seat-of-the-pants socialist," Winpisinger has offered an alternative vision of the United States and the world that is in keeping with the traditions of the labor movement. His issues are the domestic and international economies, war and peace, technology and the workplace, labor relations, and American party politics. These are issues for American labor, but they are surely concerns for other Americans as well. Winpisinger's analysis is iconoclastic, passionate, and genuinely radical in the sense of going to the root of the problem. If you can imagine a combination of Eugene Debs, Thorstein Veblen, C. Wright Mills, and your neighborhood automechanic, you've come pretty close to Winpisinger. Although he is happy to learn from the Europeans and Japanese alike, his proposals all have their roots in American reality.

Winpisinger's radicalism combines traditional trade union militance with a gut-level conviction that something is fundamentally wrong in an economy in which corporations spend hundreds of billions buying each other but don't have the money to invest to create jobs. He mixes a hefty dose of common sense with an admiration for what the Social Democrats have achieved in some European countries, especially Scandinavia, with regard to full employment, occupational safety and health, social welfare, and designing new technology to serve employees rather than vice versa. The consequence is that his vision of the labor movement encompasses both the bread and butter issues recognizable in every union hall and a broader perspective that accords the national and global political spheres a prominence of place. His is a bare-knuckled analysis and criticism of a social and economic system that has gone off track.

The dozen years during which Winpisinger has served as president of the IAM have spanned a fundamental change in the structure of the American economy. The decline of basic manufacturing was promoted by an overvalued dollar in the early years of the Reagan administration. The rise of new, low-wage industrial countries in a globalized economy was encouraged by American multinational firms that moved manufacturing operations overseas. Deregulation of the trucking and airline industries intensified labor conflict there. At the same time, a wave of mergers and acquisitions in the 1980s restructured the domestic economy, loading it down with debt. All of these trends created pressure on the labor movement that was exacerbated by the direct attacks by the Reagan administration on organized labor. The context within which the American trade union movement operates has been transformed. For many unions, it has been a time of retrenchment or retreat.

Under Winpisinger, the Machinists have been under pressure, too, but retreat has not been part of the union's vocabulary. Whether fighting wage concessions, energy price increases, Star Wars, or Frank Lorenzo, the IAM distinguished itself both with its militance and its innovative tactics. The IAM has been quick to demonstrate, not only on the picket line for high wages (or, as has often been the case in recent years, against wage reductions) but also for full employment, social justice, and peace. Although the union movement by its nature organizes producers, the Machinists put themselves in the forefront of the fight for consumers in opposing the deregulation of natural gas prices and the price gouging that followed. It was the Machinists who filed suit against OPEC for price fixing and demanded confiscation of OPEC governments' assets in the United States, embarrassing the Carter administration, which appeared in court as a friend of OPEC to argue that foreign policy had to override American law. It was the Machinists who threw their muscle behind the campaign to bring J. P. Stevens to the bargaining table by pressuring that firm through its banks; it was a novel strategy, and it worked. It was the Machinists, who organize more workers in the aerospace industry than any other union, who beat on the doors of Congress calling for an end to the suicidal arms race and who did the studies that established how many tens of thousands of American jobs were lost by gutting social programs for President Reagan's defense build up. It was the Machinists who have offered a well-documented program for the conversion of America's economy from what Winpisinger characterizes as the "warfare state" into a full-employment, peacetime economy that satisfy the real needs of all Americans. It was the Machinists Union that has pushed Congress to legislate economic conversion. It was Winpisinger as well who broke the AFL-CIO's long-standing prohibition on contacts between American labor leaders and their Soviet and Chinese counterparts. Doctors, lawyers, businessmen, politicians, and even presidents meet their Communist counterparts, he reasoned. Why should labor stay trapped in the Cold War timewarp? Taking office with the slogan "agitate, aggravate, educate, and organize," Winpisinger has done all four.

Convinced that labor has to reach beyond its own membership if it is to achieve its aims in American society, Winpisinger has acted as if he single-handedly could broaden labor's constituency through his own speeches to other unions, community groups, religious groups, Democratic party meetings, farmers' organizations, congressional committees, an occasional business group, and above all else university audiences. While the bulk of his speeches to labor audiences were extemporaneous, most of those he made to other audiences had written texts. This volume is distilled from about 150 of those manuscripts and from his programmatic speeches to IAM conventions and staff meetings (those used are listed in the sources section at the end of the book). No attempt was made to water down the speeches—they are presented with their vigorous language intact.

Winpisinger took over the reins of the IAM resolved to be seen and heard. As a consequence, it often seemed that he was spending more time on the road in local halls or in the halls of Congress than in the IAM's Washington headquarters. Cornering him for an interview there took serious advance planning, even for his editor. It is easier to persuade him to come across half the country to speak to your union local, your community action group, or to a university audience. And when you finally have him seated behind his big desk with your tape recorder running, he doesn't sit still long. Within a few minutes, as he warms to his topic, he is up, pacing, cigar in hand.

THE MAKING OF A UNION PRESIDENT

William Wayne Winpisinger—more commonly addressed within his union and among his friends as "Wimpy"—was born on December 10, 1924, in Cleveland, Ohio. His father was a journeyman printer on the *Plain Dealer*, the city's principal newspaper, and a union member. "That's where my real roots came from," Wimpy told Studs Terkel at the 1988 IAM convention. "I got taught unionism around the dinner table by my father. . . . I guess it was almost a case of osmosis."

His family was one of the lucky ones during the Depression: his father kept his job. Wimpy recollects that the family "lived very decently—not lavishly, but certainly decently" through the period. His parents were Roosevelt Democrats, but rather nonpolitical. "I guess I've got a rebellious spirit, but I can't account for where it comes from. My father was a very mild mannered, even tempered guy. My mother was a lot more volatile, but not in any sense radical. She had all of the Old World values. She lived by them, preached them, and practiced them, and often beat on my head trying to get me to do the same."

But though the Winpisingers lived decently during the Depression, their neighbors fared worse. "My earliest memory of the kind of thing that always disturbed me," says Winpisinger, "was seeing a picture on the front page of the newspaper of bulldozers down in Georgia plowing into the ground an enormous big pile of potatoes which, the commentary said, was being done because there was no market for them. The market price was so depressed that they couldn't sell them at a profit. Yet all around me there were people hungry, in some cases on the ragged edge of starvation. I asked myself why couldn't they give those potatoes away instead of plowing them under? They could take care of an identified, real need and come out just as well as if they plowed them under. Well, I rapidly found out that if you question things like that, you're automatically a socialist."

Wimpy attended Cleveland's John Marshall and West Technical High Schools, during which time he played sandlot football and baseball. He was a good enough baseball player to get a tryout as catcher with a Yankee farm team. Wimpy found school itself less exciting, and his formal education ended early. "I got smarter than the teachers so I packed it in," is the way he explains dropping out after the eleventh grade. In his "short, unsatisfactory employment history" that followed before he joined the military, Wimpy was fired out of a tool company for sassing the foreman, worked briefly in a plating factory that he quit after breaking out all over with dermatitis, and worked in a jobbing machine shop where his employment ended abruptly one day when the boss returned unexpectedly and found Wimpy eating his lunch sitting at the boss's desk with his feet up. Having now reached enlistment age, Wimpy gave up on the private sector and joined the Navy, which trained him as a diesel mechanic. During the war he served in the Mediterranean and the English Channel; he was off Normandy on D-Day.

"I suppose the military made some contribution to my views. I learned in a hurry what happens in an absolutely autocratic environment, and I didn't particularly like it." Winpisinger found himself in conflict with more than one of his superiors when he made no secret of his dissatisfaction. His tenure in the engine room on one ship ended unceremoniously after a dispute with his commanding officer who swore to give him "the first transfer that comes up that's *not* back to the United States of America." That was a blessing in disguise, however, since it landed Wimpy on a repair ship that did engine overhauls and gave him a chance to hone his skills.

His Navy service left Wimpy with the genuine fascination with engines that he still has today. He has a wood shop, auto shop, and machine shop at home, divided between the basement and the garage. He does auto and lawn mower repairs and rebuilds engines for himself and his neighbors. "I don't always build the best, but I get a bang out of working with my hands, creating things. I don't like to have somebody else do it. If I need to machine something, I'd just as soon chuck it up on my own lathe and make it."

Upon discharge, Winpisinger returned to Cleveland where he continued working as a mechanic, rather than starting the lengthy apprenticeship in the printing trades that his father had urged. His first job after he returned was in a shop with a company union. "I joined the union immediately and found out it was a company union. And I found out when I got fired that it really was a company union. . . . I was a big, raw-boned kid in those days, fresh off of a war, in pretty decent shape; and I wound up with the district manager all balled up against the wall . . . which eliminated any grievance procedure. I then went and got a legitimate job. I went into an IAM shop as an auto mechanic and began to earn a very decent living under a very, very good contract, thanks to all of those who came before me."

That debt to past generations of union members remains real to Wimpy. He sees current union leaders as trustees of those past achievements; they are a legacy for the next generation. The current generation simply doesn't have the right to relinquish what was bought by so much sacrifice.

At the time Wimpy joined it, the IAM combined the skilled tradition of the craft union with the breadth of membership of the industrial union. The IAM is one of the oldest of American unions, tracing its origins to a meeting in an engine pit by nineteen railroad machinists in Atlanta on May 5, 1888. The organization that they formed—the Order of United Machinists and Mechanical Engineers of America—had many of the characteristics of the fraternal order and much of the ritual of the Knights of Labor, to which many of its early members had belonged. It was a craft union, with all the skill, pride, and exclusiveness that that conveys. But craft unions faced bitter opposition among employers; it was after the particularly bitter strike of 1901 against the National Metal Trades Association employers that the IAM added a declaration to its constitution affirming its role in the class struggle. It expanded its membership criteria to include "specialists" (i.e., non-journeymen) in 1903, but it was not until World War I brought an influx of the unskilled into what had previously been the sacrosanct province of the skilled machinists that the IAM really opened its doors to organizing the unskilled. It remained firmly in the AFL when the split with the CIO came in 1935–36, but at the same time it embarked on industrial unionism itself in organizing Aeronautical Mechanics Lodge 751 at Boeing in 1935. The IAM grew explosively during World War II, organizing the bulk of the aircraft industry and smaller portions of other war industries. Today it is one of the broadest of American unions, organizing both the highly skilled and the unskilled in railroads, airlines, auto mechanics, machine shops, equipment manufacturing, and a variety of other industries. With 850,000 members, it is the country's eighth largest union. It retains, however, some of the flavor of its origins in its organizational structure—the union has lodges, not locals, and the national organization is the Grand Lodge—and in its substantial decentralization of power inside the organization.

Winpisinger was quickly drawn into active union work in Cleveland IAM Automotive Lodge 1363, first as a shop steward in 1947—"I guess I was gifted with a big mouth" is the way Wimpy explains his first election—and subsequently as local lodge recording secretary in 1948. In 1949, at the age of twenty-four, he was elected president of the 1300-member local. In 1951, he was appointed to the IAM national field staff, handling organizing, negotiations, and grievance and arbitration cases in the Cleveland area.

The McCarthy period completed his political education. "If I had any lingering doubts, they were totally dispelled when I witnessed the outrage of McCarthyism. To brutalize citizens of this country not withstanding our provisions for free speech and free expression just because they wanted to listen to somebody else or speak out on what they viewed as injustice just drove me right up the wall." Wimpy is up on his feet, in motion, stabbing with his unlit cigar to make his point. "I made a solemn vow then that *never* would I shrink from the responsibility to say what was on my mind in any given situation whether I was a worker in a shop, a steward, a local union officer, or anything else. I've pretty much lived by that. I've very seldom buttoned my lip when I had something to say." Wimpy's friends and enemies alike will attest to the truth of that statement.

Wimpy's penchant for saying what he thought and his general rebelliousness fit better into the labor movement than into the military or the workplace. In 1956, he was transferred to the IAM headquarters in Washington as automotive and truck mechanic organizer and handled a number of trouble-shooting assignments in the airline industry. He became the union's automotive coordinator in 1965 and general vice president in 1967 with his responsibility extended to include airline and railroad industries. More than anything else, he owed his advancement to being a hardnosed, but realistic, negotiator who brought home the bacon for the members and to being able to handle crises and strike situations. He followed the discussions of the 1960s, arguing politics in the evenings after handling union matters. When asked about the New York construction workers who attacked an anti-war protest, his comment was "It's hard to tell where the hard hats end and the heads start with those guys." In 1972, Winpisinger became resident vice president, which made him administrative chief of staff for the union. In 1977 he succeeded Floyd E. ("Red") Smith as president of the IAM.

Coming up through the labor movement, Wimpy learned from what he saw and those around him. "John L. Lewis had an influence on me. He was aggressive, had the ability to turn a phrase to fit every situation, tough-minded, and unbounded by all of the traditional horseshit including the national guard. That's what I admired about him: stand your ground for better or worse.

"I admired Walter Reuther because of his social views. I thought the mission of the labor movement ought to be looking out for the guy who didn't have it so good. That's what we're all about. And just because you advance your membership nominally out of those ranks doesn't mean you ought to forget about them. You have to have a social conscience in terms of what you're doing and drag others along with you if you can. There's nobody else to talk for them. Reuther was also very innovative. He always figured out some way to develop some program to take care of a need that was identified among his members. I admired that in him too."

Then there was E. R. White, whom Wimpy went to work for in the IAM in Cleveland. "He was bright, a student of almost everything, and he knew where the union came from and why. He was the only one who put up a fight to keep the 'class struggle' clause in the IAM constitution when all the rest of us were cowed under the pressure of 'Commies talk like that' and 'That's a Commie expression from yesteryear and it ought to come out.' Bullshit! He was right. We're still involved in the class struggle. We're in it up to our eyeballs every day."

NEW STRATEGIES FOR LABOR

When Winpisinger tells the story about his first staff meeting, he often couples it with the old story about the guy who bought a jackass. "He bought it on the basis that it was an educated, obedient jackass. He tried and he tried and he tried giving it instructions and orders and tried to train it, but it wouldn't do a goddamn thing but plant its feet and throw its head back and look at him with its big sleepy eyes. So he finally looked up the guy he had bought it from and complained, 'You represented this jackass as trained and educated.' 'He is,' the guy said. 'I can't get him to do a goddamn thing.' 'Well, I'll be damned,' said the seller. 'I'll be right over.' So he came over, took one look at the jackass, walked over to the woodpile, picked up a four foot long two by four, walked up to the jackass, and hauled off and belted him right between the eyes. Then he told the jackass to do something, and he did it. The buyer says, 'Holy Christ! I don't understand it. What the hell's the point?' 'You want him to do something?' came the reply. 'First you got to get his attention.'"

Winpisinger relights his trademark cigar and laughs. "Well, I got their attention."

He held it at the 1978 IAM staff conference in Cincinnati in which he presented his analysis and charted the union's new course. "Build coalitions," he told them. "Reach out to the churches, students, ADA, DSOC, progressives, farmers, other unions, anybody that can agree with you and help you. Get them in tow, make friends, keep them tuned, and don't be afraid to ask for help." Support public employee unionization, cultivate the media, stop kowtowing to the corporations, demand that politicians actually vote for labor issues when in office rather than just bellying up to the labor bar during the election campaign. The truth was, he said, that corporate America had declared class war on labor. So "forget about being socially accepted . . . don't worry anymore about being mister cooperative nice guy. It won't work because they don't want it to work. It's time, it seems to me, for some good old fashioned civil disobedience and disrespect in labor relations."

Wimpy got the attention of the country at large by his willingness to innovate, even against the odds. Perhaps the most prominent example was the suit brought by the IAM against OPEC. The enormity of the effort to plunder the American consumer through monopoly pricing by dictatorial foreign regimes, aided and abetted by the big oil companies with the complicity of the American government, seemed just overwhelming. How do you fight it? Well, David *can* challenge Goliath. The IAM brought suit under American anti-trust laws against the monopolists to confiscate their American assets to compensate the victims of the OPEC price fixing conspiracy. A similar suit had been pursued successfully against the cartel of Australian, South African, and Canadian uranium producers that had fixed prices. But OPEC was a more sensitive issue diplomatically. The IAM suit brought the Carter administration into court on OPEC's behalf. The lesson? Don't let the bastards intimidate you. Fight back.

A second of Winpisinger's early initiatives involved using capital for labor's purposes: the IAM pressured Manufacturers Hanover Trust to drop the president of J. P. Stevens, perhaps the most notoriously anti-union firm in the country, from Manny Hanny's board. The Machinists had substantial pension funds under the bank's management, and, in what he calls "a fairly simple power play," Wimpy threatened to move them elsewhere. "That money wasn't born in your vaults," he told an incredulous bank executive, who was trying to explain why the IAM couldn't influence the composition of the bank's board. "It arrived in an armored truck from another bank that messed up, and it can leave the same way." He was right. The J. P. Stevens executive disappeared from the bank's board.

What in the long term may be a more significant capital strategy has been the IAM's insistence that it will not grant wage concessions without a quid pro quo, frequently in the form of stock for members. This "wage investment policy" has had mixed success in the airline industry; its flagship, Eastern, which was one-quarter owned by the employees, was captured and looted by that notorious air pirate, Frank Lorenzo. The fight between the Machinists and Lorenzo has had an epic character. But in other firms, such as Republic Airlines and North Coast Brass, the wage investment policy proved more successful.

Wimpy's most popular innovation unquestionably was the union's all-IAM Indy circuit race car program. How, in this television age, were unions to reach the public if they were blacked out of programming and couldn't afford to advertise? "Through the back door," was Wimpy's answer. Sport programming got the biggest audiences. "The most popular spectator sport had just become autoracing. Up to then, it had been horseracing, but we quickly discarded taking that up." Beginning with a small program in 1978, the IAM mounted a serious autoracing effort in subsequent years. The IAM team never won the big money, but it was a good advertisement for the union. "It exposes the union to a whole clientele otherwise prone to view unions as a bunch of Commies. They find out we're human after all. We've organized some people out of it. Race fans, young workers, see you out there and ask 'What union is that? The boss is screwing me over. I got to get ahold of them and find out what's what.'" The racecar program has ancillary positive effects inside the IAM, encouraging social gatherings, picnics, discounted tickets, and an esprit de corps. Besides, Wimpy himself is an unabashed fan of autoracing and a frequent spectator at the IAM big car circuit races.

The autoracing effort was stimulated by the IAM's media monitoring project, another of Wimpy's early initiatives. This study, which trained hundreds of union members in doing media research and the ins and outs of the communications industry, analyzed the presentation of work and workers in television coverage. Their findings confirmed Wimpy's fears. News programming displayed a systematic corporate bias on the major issues—inflation, foreign trade, energy, taxes, and health care— of concern in the monitoring project. Coverage of union activity was limited almost entirely to strikes, violence, and relations to organized crime. Even the presentation of working America was systematically skewed away from productive work. "Monitors counted 44 attorneys for every plumber; nine advertising executives for every electrician; 14 congressmen for every garbage collector; five times as many foreign spies as meat cutters; twice as many pimps as firemen; 16 times more prostitutes than mineworkers. There were ten times more models than farmworkers; and all rabbis, ministers, monks, nuns and priests are outnumbered by burglars," the IAM and other cooperating unions reported.

"Television—the primary source of information, news and entertainment for most Americans—has become no more than an electronic vending machine, offering sweet-smelling bodies; stuffed, satisfied bellies; and great vacant gaps in our cerebral cortex," commented Winpisinger. "What a waste!"[1]

When pressed by the interviewer to cite his accomplishments in office, Wimpy dodges by alleging that accomplishments, like beauty, are in the eye of the beholder. "I am not a yesterday-oriented guy," he adds. "When I finish something, it's finished. I'm on to what we have to do tomorrow. I don't dwell on success or failure, if you can judge things that way." Wimpy prefers to talk about ideas, politics, policies, and plans for the future, not the past.

Still, Winpisinger himself gives primacy of place to two achievements. The first was the acquisition and development of the IAM's education center at Placid Harbor, which is funded by interest earned on the union's strike fund. Wimpy has long been convinced that labor needs more internal education programs, the more so today because of the rising speed of technological change. The second he cites is "playing a role in the transformation of the AFL-CIO at the top level." Wimpy was George Meany's most outspoken critic on the AFL-CIO's executive council until Meany's retirement. Since then, Winpisinger has become what he calls "a team player" in the AFL-CIO leadership in what he habitually refers to as "the marble palace." "The fact is, things did change," Wimpy says. "Kirkland undertook initiatives, and he tried to address what you heard in every union hall the length and breadth of the land while Meany was still around. So I put my load of dynamite away and saved it for another day."

Not for Wimpy the role of "labor statesman" serving as a token union representative on this government board or that foundation-sponsored blue-ribbon committee. He rejected both Carter's voluntary wage and price controls and service on Nixon's wage and price board out of hand. The plan was sure to fail, Wimpy predicted, unless it addressed the problem of "unbridled corporate power." Whether it was pressuring Manufacturers Hanover Trust to throw J. P. Stevens' president off its board, suing OPEC, organizing consumers, attacking Frank Lorenzo, or bashing "Ronnie 'Robin Hood in Reverse' Reagan," his language and views have been those of the labor movement. He has always known which side he is on.

SOCIALISM—AMERICAN STYLE

Press stories on Winpisinger not only describe him as a militant union leader and a maverick in AFL-CIO ranks, they frequently cite his self-description as "a seat of the pants socialist," a phrase he coined as a one-sentence encapsulation of his views. For a generation, he has been the country's most prominent trade union advocate of democratic socialism and of social democracy. He served as co-chair, with Michael Harrington, of the Democratic Socialist Organizing Committee (DSOC), and in various capacities with its successor, Democratic Socialists of America (DSA).

What the media *never* describe, however, is what Winpisinger's home-grown socialism means. It goes back to when he was a kid during the Depression, to those potatoes being plowed under when people were hungry everywhere around him. "I thought to myself—there's something just basically unjust, there's an inequity somewhere in this system of ours that we call free enterprise, and that, by God, if nothing else we ought to give the potatoes to the people that need them," he told Terkel at the 1988 IAM Convention. "And everybody screamed, 'You're a Socialist.' Well, if that's a Socialist, goddamn it, I am one. It's as simple as that."

Wimpy's common-sense socialism has been reinforced over the years as a gut level reaction to what he experiences as a trade unionist. As he put it to an audience at the Boston Community Church in 1986, "in the Reagan era of federal deregulation, deunionization, and the sovereignty of capital, we really haven't had a lot of time to sit around and intellectualize our socialism. We feel it. And we know it when we see it or read about it, and that's generally in places like Scandinavia."

The moral basis of his views is simple: "I have never been able to accept the notion that there ought to be profit engendered on misery."

"Forgive me if I candidly admit that I'm biased in my philosophy," he told one Georgia group in 1982 in defining his unapologetic egalitarian democratic socialism. "To the exclusion of everything else, I am biased in favor of people—human beings—living a life of dignity in fulfillment of economic, political and social democracy. I am biased toward that system of political economy that will enhance and facilitate that fulfillment for all people, not just some or a few. . . . We are talking about people—workers, artists, and artisans—who are endowed with feeling and reason, not mere articles of commerce, assets or liabilities on a balance sheet or chattels in a corporatized caste system."

Winpisinger is still on his feet, in motion. The cigar is out again, but it still can be used to emphasize a point. "The millennium," says Winpisinger, "lies in the marrying of the best virtues of a socialist economy and a capitalist economy, thereby trying to get away from the undesirable aspects of both. I won't live anywhere near long enough to see that, but I think it will come." From the socialist economies he takes planning to make market economies meet the needs of the vast majority; from capitalist economies, he takes the incentives that are missing in the socialist systems. Wimpy's ideal economy would mix public and private sectors. "We would have nationalized, regionalized and/or localized, publicly owned or joint taxpayer and worker-owned enterprises in those industries providing the basic necessities of life, to wit: education, energy, food, health care, housing, transportation. And we would totally nationalize the national defense function including military procurement and production, and thereby remove profiteering from Cold War considerations and foreign policy."

In all but the military and defense industries, Winpisinger would not preclude private enterprise in any industry or sector. Rather, private enterprise would compete with public enterprise. "We as employees want both public and private enterprise. It matters that we have both. From an employee and trade union standpoint, we have long since learned that a single government employer can be just as much an authoritarian and self-serving bastard as any private employer may be. . . ." This is a genuine mixed economy, and Wimpy is first, foremost, and always a trade unionist.

"Until we reach that happy day when employees and their trade unions are actually directing the enterprises in which they exchange their labor, talents, creativity and time for cash and life support benefits and, in selected cases, for a direct share of corporate profits, then we at least would like to have the option of playing off one employer against another."

What do IAM members think about their president being called a socialist?

The reason, answers Wimpy, that "I'm called a socialist—other than my own coining of that phrase—was the fact that I operate in the amphitheater of labor. When you do, you start out with two strikes on you. That's what made the labor movement for too many years so conservative. By being anything else, you ran the risk of being identified as a Commie. Well, that never bothered me. They can call me that all they want. If I'm out there carrying a hod and doing the job, I don't give a damn what they call me. And, I find out, the members don't either."

Wimpy's seat of the pants socialism has an old-fashioned ring to it. Wimpy believes in the intrinsic value of productive work and in making goods to satisfy human needs. "There is no productivity in an unemployment line" is a standard part of his indictment of the way the

American economy has been run by the big corporations. "Minimize welfare, maximize work" is part of his formula for dealing with poverty. It is the responsibility of government to make sure that there are jobs—good jobs—for everyone who wants to work.

Winpisinger also believes in the liberating power of technology. He has no nostalgia for a lost golden age, none of the "small is beautiful" syndrome. He is not a blind believer in technology—war technologies and nuclear power he considers to be innately destructive—but he is convinced of its potential for human liberation. Wimpy preaches the virtues of an expanded space program with space factories and solar power satellites beaming energy back to earth. His requirement, however, is that technology be adapted to human beings, rather than vice versa. Precisely that is the function of the IAM's proposed technology bill of rights for workers.

Wimpy's idea of socialism is a full-employment economy in which the government takes an active role in filling basic human needs, such as medical care, and in stimulating demand, providing for the worst off, and controlling the speculative abuses of capitalism. It owes more to Franklin Roosevelt's New Deal, John Maynard Keynes, and the Scandinavian Social Democrats' social programs than it does to Marx. He is impatient with the academic discussion of the alienation of the worker, lack of dignity or job satisfaction. He has a simple answer to these fashionable intellectual concerns: higher pay and better working conditions. In short, precisely what the union movement has fought for for decades.

A LABOR PARTY?

Throughout his tenure as president of the IAM, Winpisinger has toyed with the possibility of organizing a genuine labor party in the United States. In Canada, where such a party has been created by the unions as the New Democratic Party, the IAM has been a major supporter of independent labor party politics. From time to time when the Democratic Party turned right in the United States, the Canadian course seemed appealing to Winpisinger in this country as well.

But though his view of the Democratic Party has varied between optimism and outrage, Winpisinger has never abandoned hope for reforming the party, returning it to what he considers its historical legacy of the reformism of Franklin Roosevelt and the New Deal which he sees to have been carried on by Harry Truman and John F. Kennedy and in Lyndon Johnson's Great Society before it was hopelessly sidetracked by the war in Vietnam. Winpisinger's involvement in Democratic Socialists of America (DSA) and in its predecessor, the Democratic Socialist Organizing Committee, has been an effort to strengthen that reformist position within the Democratic Party.

It was that legacy that led him to fight for the nomination of Edward Kennedy in 1980, after Jimmy Carter had crossed and recrossed the political spectrum to end up in the pocket of the oil and gas interests. Wimpy judged Carter in 1978 to be "the best Republican President since Herbert Hoover." "One thing that this country doesn't need is *two* Republican parties," Winpisinger said repeatedly. His support for Kennedy carried with it the elements of a crusade for the heart and soul of the party. "It is better," he later reflected, "to have stood and fought and lost with Ted Kennedy for Democratic principles than to have joined Carter in his Pyrrhic nomination victory." The IAM sat out the general election while Winpisinger himself ended up exposing third party candidate Barry Commoner and his views to the IAM political leadership and writing in Edward Kennedy's name on his own ballot.

In 1984, Walter Mondale commanded the loyalty of the labor movement, and the unions could support him with real enthusiasm. His disastrous loss raised the issue of how this honorable friend of labor could have done so badly. Winpisinger's own analysis, which he supports with poll data, focuses on the failure of Mondale, like Carter before him and Dukakis after him, to campaign like a Democrat until after the election was already lost.

Jesse Jackson was another matter. He could be found on the picket line outside election season. He directly addressed the issues of poverty, exploitation, and economic injustice. His message was labor's message. A year before the Iowa caucuses, as the campaign got underway, Wimpy already saw Jackson as "the only candidate who is talking in favor of labor and true union issues in clear and unmistakable terms. He is the one candidate who is putting pressure on the others to stand up for worker and trade union rights as well as for a progressive agenda in general." It was Winpisinger who delivered Jackson's nominating speech at the 1988 Democratic Party convention. He would later comment that, if it had not been for racism, Jackson would have been the party's nominee.

It is Winpisinger's firm belief that in fact a majority of Americans want to enact progressive policies on economic issues, control unbridled capitalism, end the arms race to destruction, restore eroded trade union rights, and improve the situation of those worst off in our society. That majority, however, is to be found among the non-voters, and getting them to the polls requires both a candidate who is not afraid to speak the truth and a massive effort to get the message out in spite of the corporate-controlled media.

TRADE UNIONISM IN THE NEXT CENTURY

Since the Wagner Act in 1935 codified the rules for collective bargaining, the concerns of the union movement have been bargaining wages, hours, and the terms and conditions of employment. That is a relatively narrow focus, far narrower than that of many American unions prior to the New Deal and narrower than the more political unionism of the Western European unions that Winpisinger admires.

Winpisinger's determination to put labor's concerns in a broader perspective stems neither from nostalgia for the more radical American labor movement of the past nor from admiration for the European unions' accomplishments. It is a product, rather, of his understanding of the changing American political economy. The technological transformation of the production process, the growth of speculation as a motor for capitalism in what Winpisinger calls "corporate cannibalism," and the rise of global competition for American industry have fundamentally altered the conditions for American labor and the labor movement. For better or worse, the United States has become integrated in a global economy that is dominated by global corporations. How should the labor movement respond?

The response of the Machinists Union under Winpisinger was to draft a program for reforming the American economy. *Let's Rebuild America*, which the union brought out on Labor Day 1983, is the closest thing to a genuine party program that the progressive wing of the Democratic Party has. It covers imposing responsibility on corporate behavior, channeling domestic investment, reconstructing the foreign trade system, reforming the pension system, rebuilding our decaying infrastructure and central cities, designing an industrial policy, controlling the energy monopoly, restructuring the tax system, and expanding labor rights. It owed some of its ideas to the Canadian, German, Norwegian, and Swedish trade unions and to the policies pursued by the European Social Democrats in office and proposed by the New Democratic Party in Canada. But its principles and its moral indignation about injustice and inequality are as American as apple pie.

At the national level, Winpisinger assumes the necessity for a more active political role by labor to reshape the rules of American collective bargaining, which have become increasingly weighted against unions since the highwater mark of the Wagner Act. But labor cannot achieve its ends alone; it needs allies. Winpisinger's search for allies among community and church groups, environmentalists, the peace movement, and on the university campuses has characterized his term. From the Citizen-Labor Energy Coalition that he helped set up and served as president through the nuclear freeze campaign and the opposition to Star Wars, Wimpy has been the union leader most likely to be found in the forefront of the fight for consumers, the environment, and for peace.

At the international level, the globalization of the economy, the increased mobility of capital, and the escape of the corporation from national control have meant that the traditional tools for managing the economy to achieve labor's goals are losing their effectiveness. Once the rule was that "capital and labor enjoyed mobility that was confined by the boundaries of the United States. Today, that relationship no longer exists. The advantage has been seized by the absolute mobility of capital which deploys its instruments of production all over the globe." Labor, by contrast, outflanked and immobile, is victimized.

Winpisinger has no panaceas for labor in the global economy. Like other American labor leaders, he has preached the need for fair trade to replace so-called "free trade." The concept of free trade in classical economic theory rested on comparative advantage: the relative fertility of the soil, the climate, or natural resources. Today it is a result of political decisions, particularly of governments that prevent workers from organizing to improve wages and working conditions. American corporations, Winpisinger notes, are the primary beneficiaries of the anti-union governments of these export platforms. He proposes to combat this exploitative flight of capital and jobs by requiring American firms to sign *economic and social contracts* that would obligate them to recognize the right of their employees to bargain collectively regardless of where they locate if these firms are to receive U.S. government support, contracts, or the investment of workers' pension funds. It is Winpisinger's expectation that such guarantees would lead to higher wages in developing countries, which would lessen their attractiveness for corporate flight from the industrial democracies. It would also lead to greater domestic demand in those countries, which, in turn, would stimulate their internal economic development. Those effects of the economic and social clause, which seems an attractive alternative to protectionism, point toward Winpisinger's dream: a full-employment economy on a worldwide basis. After years in which pushing the economic and social clause seemed quixotic, the idea caught fire and, by the end of 1988, had been included in three pieces of legislation, including the 1988 trade bill and the Caribbean Basin Initiative.

International collective bargaining, which would permit labor to match the scope of the global corporation through coordinated bargaining across national boundaries, is also one of Wimpy's hopes. It "is clearly a rational solution for many of the problems that have plagued us since the mid-1970s. But it's much easier to say than to do. . . . When you begin thinking in terms of transcending national boundaries, ethnic backgrounds, culture, history, and habits, it's an enormously complex problem. The trouble is that capital has lightning mobility and labor is relatively immobile. We've engaged in international collective bargaining, and it has not been unproductive. It's just the hare and the tortoise syndrome, you know. Once you perfect the mechanism, craft a bargaining position, take care of everyone's grievances and get ready to open negotiations, capital has already moved the plant somewhere else. To get the equation between capital and labor back into balance, you either have to slow down capital or speed up labor." He has had an active role in the International Metalworkers Federation on its executive committee and chairing its World Aerospace Conference.

Labor's declining clout relative to the global corporations in national policy making requires a rethinking of the ideology of business unionism, which combined the acceptance of the premises of the free enterprise mythology with the assumption that militant collective bargaining could increase the share of the workers in the national income. Wimpy, who owed his advancement within the IAM in part to his bargaining ability, has come to recognize the innate limitations of this approach. Business unionism simply produces fewer gains for unionized workers in the new world of global competition and substantial unemployment. Decisions by those in power load the dice against labor, and combatting that politically requires that labor take a more general and more radical position in support of the rights of the downtrodden, regardless of whether they are union members, both at home and abroad.

*   *   *

Winpisinger relit his cigar, which had gone out again while he talked. Other things needed to be done beside being interviewed. But, looking back on a dozen eventful years, Wimpy had a final reflection on that first midnight staff conference in 1977:

"My final exhortation that night was 'I'm going to be gone a lot because my predecessor had sat with his big ass in this chair for eight solid years, and if we hadn't printed his picture in the newspaper every month, nobody would have even known him. . . .' The last thing I told them was, 'When I'm gone, and there's nobody around when something happens and you confront the problem, you think of the most liberal thing you can do and do it. If you screw up, we'll come back and redress it later. But at least we'll be off and running for 90 percent of it.' And by and large they did."

Ninety percent, when you think about it, is not a bad average.

NOTES

1. International Association of Machinists, Union of Operating Engineers, and Bakery, Confectionery, and Tobacco Workers International Union, *Television: Corporate America's Game* (Washington: Union Media Monitoring Project, n.d.), p. 2. The media project was one of the factors leading the AFL-CIO to consider how to affect the media presentation of labor and to the creation of the Labor Institute for Public Affairs (LIPA).

on the threshold
of the future

We are about to enter the last decade of the twentieth century hurtling through the cosmos on our fragile Spaceship Earth, wondering what the ride is all about. We wonder about that point on the navigator's chart where space and time intersect to pinpoint our existence and to prove we are in the present tense. We wonder where we are in the historian's unfinished textbook chronicling the adventures and misadventures of humankind's trip. We wonder what our generation's destination and destiny are. And we wonder, sometimes, if we're even on board, or have been left behind at the docking station.

We look back to see where we came from. No genuine trade union movement—or nation—can have a sense of purpose or a clear-sighted vision of the future, without an appreciation of from whence it came, its roots, and its past.

My union, the International Association of Machinists and Aerospace Workers, or the IAM as we are popularly called, was born in Atlanta, on May 5, 1888. Our organizer was a young journeyman machinist who worked in the roundhouse for the Eastern Tennessee, Virginia and Georgia Railroad. His name was Thomas Wilson Talbot.

Railroads were the cutting edge of advanced technology in that era. And skilled machinists, who, then as now, worked with their minds as much as their hands, were an elite among the craftsmen of the era. Even so, employers abused, mistreated, and attempted to subjugate them to the "Iron Law of Wages," that is, wages that would pay for a subsistence level of living, consisting of the primitive necessities for food and shelter, and nothing else.

The story is told that Talbot decided that machinists needed a union when he realized after twenty years as a highly skilled journeyman, he couldn't afford to send his sons to high school. That was a hundred years ago. Today, there is still a sizable population of wage and salary earners, and, of course the long term unemployed, who can't afford to send their children to high school. And in spite of educational opportunity being one of the keys to economic survival in the current world of technological displacement, unemployment and upheaval, there is a far larger population that cannot afford to send its children to advanced and technical colleges and public or private institutions of higher learning.

In any case, Talbot and eighteen other machinists met secretly on the evening of May 5, 1888, in an engine pit under locomotives being repaired and overhauled, where they were sheltered from company stooges and labor spies. At that first meeting, those eighteen machinists had no resources beyond their own ingenuity and skill, counted no friends in high places, no support in the press, and no sympathy in the courts of the land. If their meeting had been discovered or someone had informed the company, they would have been summarily fired.

Sounds like labor and trade union rights 100 years later, doesn't it?

But when Mr. Talbot and the group came out of that meeting, they had formed the Order of United Machinists and Mechanical Engineers of America. Much of their terminology and ritual was adopted from the disintegrating Knights of Labor, since Talbot and some of his colleagues had been or were members of that organization, too. In fact, Terrence Powderly, head of the Knights, was himself a machinist.

With Local Lodge 1 established in Atlanta, itinerant machinists, called "boomers," who rode the rails in search of work around the country, spread the word and the Machinists Union grew.

While things in our times may be different from those of the days when those dedicated mechanics rebelled in that roundhouse pit in Atlanta 100 years ago, our values remain the same; our objectives remain essentially the same; and, I suspect, the institutional, economic, political and social problems are the same as well.

This is not a book about history, although our history is prologue to our present. It is a book about today and tomorrow. It is a book about common problems, but uncommon answers.

The common answers—the answers promoted by the press, the professors, the politicians, and the corporations—have failed us.

We've had enough of economists, safely employed in their ivory tower universities, who preach to us that the way to restrain inflation is to throw people out of work. We've had enough of companies telling us that, if we don't agree to having our wages cut to Brazilian or South Korean or Mexican standards, they'll pack up our jobs and move them overseas. We've had enough mergers and acquisitions and corporate cannibalism which make a lot of money for a few but do not produce jobs for a single American. And we've had enough of politicians running errands for Big Business, promoting multi-billion dollar corporate tax giveaways.

It's time for a little common sense.

This book isn't going to look like what you read in the morning paper or sound like what you hear on the evening news. The media don't spend a lot of time talking about plant shutdowns and lost jobs and disinvestment and declining income and how corporations rig prices and invest overseas and buy your congressman. A free press is a wonderful thing, especially for those who have enough money to own a newspaper or to buy a television station.

This book is different because I don't work for a big corporation. I don't have a lot of myths to promote or reputations to protect.

I'm a machinist, a high school drop out. I never drew supply and demand curves at the Harvard Business School. I never put together an auto company, but I sure can put together an auto engine. I learned my economics in the real world: the hard school of bargaining contracts for my fellow machinists.

I've learned a lot while doing that. I've learned about the collusion of one company with its competitor to try to beat down their employees' already low wages. I've learned about the collusion between corporations and the government to give the corporations billion dollar tax rebate handouts while the unemployed are stripped of their benefits, widows of their Social Security, and orphans of their school lunches. And when you tell the truth about them, I've seen those politicians wrap themselves in our flag while justifying the most outrageous acts of corporate avarice against us. Show me a reactionary zealot who is raising hell about foreign policy, morality and patriotism, I'll show you a crook damned near every time.

I have also learned that the future isn't somewhere ahead of us. It starts right now as you read this.

We can claim it for our own.

We do make a difference. We are on board and participants in humankind's long journey called progress.

UNDERSTANDING WHERE WE ARE

Where we are in the universe inevitably begins with a description of the political economy.

Economics today is characterized by globalization of the factors of production. Production of goods and services alike is organized into an integrated system of globe-spanning units. For the first time in history the men and moguls who run global corporations and enterprise are able to combine organization, technology, money and ideology in a way that permits them to manage—or mismanage—the world's commerce as an integrated economic unit.

Here at home, it is imperative that we understand what those self-appointed Corporate Rambos in league with business barons in other lands are demanding. It is nothing less than the right to operate outside the rules of, and transcend the sovereignty of, the nation state and to cast the global economy in their own narrow and lustful image.

Fortune magazine (September 26, 1988, pp. 45 ff.) tells us that "globalization will continue to be an inescapable buzzword." With continuing advances in computers and speed-of-light communications, world financial markets will meld. Manufacturing prowess will suddenly appear all over the undeveloped areas of the globe. There will be new Taiwans and new Koreas.

A shrinking world will mean an expanding clock. Electronic fund transfers, financial services and manufacturing production schedules will be spread across global time zones so that, while the United States and Canada sleep, work will go on on the sunny side of the globe. When the sun sets in the Orient, the work will be transferred back to the Western hemisphere, whether that work be in financial services and trade or in manufacturing. For those corporations and firms that have highly developed and integrated global communications and computer integrated production systems, it is possible to get 48 hours of work out of a 24-hour day!

As point-of-sale marketing and supply information becomes available at the speed of light to corporate planners, there will be more decentralization of production. According to *Fortune*, one forecaster predicts that by the year 2000, industrial countries, on average, will be importing nearly 40 percent of the parts used in domestic manufacturing.

The corporate balance sheet and income statement inflate. The national income and balance sheet deflate. So do worker incomes, living standards, and economic and political rights.

By the year 2000, the world will consist of three mega-economic blocs. The first mega-economy will consist of China, Japan and the Asian Rim countries, after Hong Kong is returned to the Chinese in 1997. The second mega-economy will be created on the European continent after the European Community unites in 1992. Increased trade within the European Community and its economic ties with the Soviet Union and the Eastern bloc nations will dwarf the home markets of Japan and the United States. And the third mega-economic bloc is being established in North America consisting of Canada, the United States, and Mexico.

The real significance of the Canada-U.S. "free trade" treaty is to enable private capital to integrate our two economies. And now that the Canada-U.S. trade deal seems safe, the *Washington Post* reports (11/23/88, p. E-1) that President-elect Bush is preparing a free trade treaty with Mexico "with the pact with Canada as a model."

This, in a nutshell is what is happening: the global economy is being restructured into three mega-economies. These are the oceans that the big sharks want the little fish to swim in.

Some observers have suggested that it is *perestroika* without *glastnost!*

Private capital is super mobile and, therefore, super sovereign. Multinational corporate enterprise is shedding all pretense of economic nationalism and economic patriotism. Japanese, German, French, Swedish, Italian and British firms are buying into the North American economy to secure and develop their markets here. Canadian and U.S. firms that have not already gained a foothold in the European mega-economy are moving to do so. The same is true in the Asian mega-economy. And Japanese, Australian and Chinese (especially Hong Kong capitalists) are buying into the North American bloc, too.

All this may seem exciting to the Big Faces with hair on their brains up there in the International Business Roundtable Board Rooms. But we in the trade unions are locked out of the loop. What does globalization mean to us?

It means the Corporate State political agenda, of course.

It means pitting workers in Canada, the United States, and Mexico against each other and against the least common denominator in terms of global wages, labor standards and economic, political, and social equality. Exploited labor overseas cannot buy or consume that which it produces and unemployed labor here at home cannot buy it either.

Globalization means more corporate "downsizing": more personnel slashing and lay offs; more high-tech and new-tech quick fixes; more end runs around trade unions; more erosion of collective bargaining agreements; more weakening of our labor and social laws and legislation.

"Efficiency" and "productivity" are the war cries. "Quality control," "labor cooperation," and "teamwork" are the tactical slogans.

When U.S. companies move capital and technology overseas and produce over there, they become our foreign competitors! What's good for their balance sheets and income statements is not good for America's. This system of unlicensed global mobility of capital is not working in the national interest. It is not increasing the nation's wealth or the people's prosperity. It is a zero-sum game.

It is not winning the international trade war. We in the United States are losing the trade war to the tune of $150 billion a year. Each $1 billion in lost trade costs us 25,000 jobs. We've lost 4.5 to 5 million jobs over the past five years to imports and to the flight of capital.

Foreign interests now own and control more of this nation's private and public wealth and resources, including the federal budget, than at any time in history.

There is very little that is democratic about this global restructuring. Certainly there is not in the United States. Nor is there in Japan or other Asian nations. Those West European and NATO countries that do have economic and social clauses in their national legislation and/ or have co-determination laws and political parties based on trade union membership are also apt to have an industrial policy that gives national economic goals and the public good equal priority with private profit and shareholder dividends.

Even so, except in cases where national legislatures must approve or ratify economic and trade treaties, there is no democratic way to control, direct or otherwise significantly influence those global capital flows.

At this point in time, the most we can do is to press our respective national governments to write into our laws and treaties concerning trade certain defined labor and human rights—economic and social rights—which will prevent exploitation and establish uniform minimum standards with respect to wages, hours, working conditions, freedom of association, and protecting the environment. Through monetary penalties and abrogation of trade deals that violate such labor rights clauses, nations can unilaterally influence the *social* conduct of private capital, but not its mobility.

I see little difference between today's global private corporate sovereigns and the monarchies and colonial powers of yesteryear. If we are going to cope successfully with this international mobility of capital, then we're going to have to look beyond the niches and holes for worker participation in conduct of the individual corporate enterprise and larger political process, toward something much more universal and powerful.

In that context economic nationalism and economic patriotism still have a definite role to play.

Here at home, one out of nine white Americans is poor; one out of three blacks is poor; and one out of four Hispanics is poor. Poverty is on the rise while the middle class is in decline. Real, after-tax income for individuals is at the same level it was in 1967. There has been no real gain for two decades. Household income after taxes and inflation may have risen, but that's because more wives and other family members are working to make ends meet. When two people are required to maintain a standard of living formerly supported by one person, that is not progress.

Nearly 15 percent of the American people live below the government's artificially low poverty line. That's not progress either. Another 15 percent live on the marginal edge of poverty. That means nearly one-third of our people are ill-fed, ill-housed, ill-clad, and have little or no access to decent health and dental care. Inflation in the basic necessities of life—energy, utilities, transportation, food, housing and health care—is twice the inflation rate for non-necessity items. That cruelly compounds inflation's impact on those Americans.

At the top of the pyramid, just 1 percent of the people own and control 35 percent of the nation's wealth. At the bottom, 60 percent of the people own only 8 percent of the wealth, and that primarily consists of consumer durables, such as cars and refrigerators. In terms of financial assets, such as stocks, and bonds, the maldistribution of wealth is even more skewed.

These inequities in income and wealth distribution constitute a social stratification that seriously impairs the functioning of democracy. Wealth means economic power and power means politics. Given our auction block system of campaign fund raising, it is small wonder so many politicians are beholden to so few wealthy people and corporate interests.

Abroad more than half the governments of Third World countries are controlled by the military. Colonel North and the Irangate scandal demonstrate that, even in America, military *coups* are within the realm of possibility.

Human rights, worker rights and trade union rights are purposefully and systematically denied in Canada as well as Central America, in Alabama and Alaska as well as South Africa, in Iowa as well as Indonesia, in South Carolina as well as South Korea, and in Texas as well as Taiwan.

As trade unionists, we are a distinct minority at a distinct disadvantage in the global economy.

So, as we fix our position in the universe, we can too easily see the frailty of the human condition, as well as our own trade union existence, while Spaceship Earth speeds us into infinity's dawn or dusk.

Which will it be? *That* is our ages-old challenge!

TRANSITION . . . TO WHAT?

An often-heard phrase these days is that the United States has "an economy in transition." The critical question we should ask is: "In transition to what?"

There is a long list of changes that impact on our daily worklives; on our wages, hours and conditions of employment; on our collective bargaining contracts; and on our future and our children's futures. The list of major changes underway in our political economy includes:

(1) The change from a manufacturing to an information-based service economy.

(2) The change from industrial hardware interfaced with human intelligence and labor to industrial "thoughtware" and "smart" machines.

(3) The change from metals to substitutes for metal in manufacturing materials and in communications transmission systems. Ceramics, metal composites, plastics, epoxies, and fiber optics are major substitutes for metals.

(4) The change from an abundant and stable supply of natural resources in this country, to exploited and declining resources, and a resulting dependency on global resources, characterized by fluctuating prices and boom/bust economics such as we see in the oil industry.

(5) In the United States, a change from "the baby boomers" and a rapidly growing labor force to a slow population and labor force growth rate, while outside the United States, the global labor force growth continues apace in Third and Fourth World countries. Also here in the United States, as "baby boomers" mature, our population and hence, work force, are going to be dominated by older workers and senior citizens.

(6) In the United States, a change from a limited welfare state to the current dismantled welfare state, and the erection of an aggressive Warfare State that dominates federal budgetary priorities and fiscal and monetary policies.

(7) In consequence of the Warfare State, a change in the United States from a creditor nation to a debtor nation in terms of both private and public finance—typified by the staggering national debt and foreign trade deficits.

(8) Therefore, the change from an insular and autonomous national economy to a dependent and global one, characterized by multinational corporate enterprises that make their own rules and alliances, and that enjoy a unique worldwide sovereignty that no individual nation can control.

(9) In the United States, a change from a gradual, progressive redistribution of income and wealth to a regressive redistribution, from those at the bottom and in the middle tiers of income and wealth, to those at the highest levels.

(10) Therefore, the trend away from the traditional American dream of equality of opportunity toward a polarized economy of a few

"have's" and a multitude of "have-nots." Instead of rising expectations that our parents and grandparents experienced, our succeeding generations are now facing declining opportunities and lower expectations.

The reasons for this polarization into have's and have-not's are basically two. There is a revolution in knowledge and in technology underway. That revolution is independent of the political and economic system, but what impact it has for good or ill is shaped, as we will see in Chapter 5, by the way we organize our political and economic systems and the decisions made there.

The second reason concerns that political economic system.

We have in America today a *Corporate State*, a government that is run and controlled by the large corporations, in tandem with a very carefully orchestrated right-wing political movement. That's the Corporate State. Big Brother from the far right, if you prefer that description. It is not bigness that is the real issue, but it is who government is and who government serves, who controls it and what it does. That is the issue.

If you think this is just idle prattle, remember that in Nazi Germany it was the large corporate custodians of the privately owned wealth, the industrialists, and the bankers, who supported Hitler's rise to power and who helped build the Wehrmacht, the German war machine. They were aided and abetted by—and listen closely now to this laundry list and see if any of it sounds similar to anything you see going around you today—snoop artists and informers, electronic eaves-dropping, violation of individual rights and civil liberties, muffling of dissent, banning of strikes, and destruction of free trade unions. Every one of them was the hallmark of the most vicious dictatorship that has ever disgraced the face of the earth.

Look around and you see the Corporate State in action in every area of our political economy. You see it in the corporate control of the regulatory agencies and how these agencies have been dismantled during the deregulation drive. Often they are staffed with personnel from the industries they are supposed to regulate in the public interest—energy, banking, insurance, you name it.

You see the Corporate State very visibly in multinational corporations. They profess no allegiance to their country or to any community. They respect no flag, they sing no national anthem, and they would rather do business with dictators who demonstrate stability by the ruthless throttling of individual rights and free trade unions.

The multinationals use public funds and money to research and develop a whole new array of technologies—75 cents on the buck, publicly financed technological development, paid for by our members and all other Americans out of their tax dollars. Then they transfer that technology willy-nilly all over the globe for a profit. And they do it in many ways: direct exportation, direct foreign investment, co-production agreements, joint ventures, and a host of other dandy little arrangements.

We see the Corporate State sitting right on the President's Council of Economic Advisors. They have a commitment to a false dogma that says that we cannot have full employment in this country because that will cause inflation. If every American willing and able to work has a job, that's automatically inflationary in their minds. In fact, we have had high unemployment and high inflation at the same time and past evidence shows that the slowest rate of inflation that we have enjoyed in the past thiry-five years has been during periods of full employment during the administrations of Jack Kennedy and Lyndon Johnson.

We see the Corporate State in full control of the media, and corporate acquisitions of publishing houses, newspapers, magazines, and all of the trade press are in abundance every time you pick up the financial page. General Electric, for example, now owns NBC-RCA and Random House, thus controlling the written as well as the spoken word. Only a half dozen major cities in this country have a competitive daily press. Only two wire services feed all of the press there is left, as well as the radio and TV stations around the country. And newspapers are exempted from anti-trust laws.

We see the Corporate State in the Department of Defense. They use a revolving door in Washington to interchange defense contractor firms' vice presidents with majors, colonels, generals and vice versa. It is a constant game of corporate shuttlecock—into industry and back to the Pentagon. As a consequence, Pentagon contractor fraud and scandals are endemic.

We see the Corporate State made manifest in the energy industry, where major American companies were part and parcel of the OPEC Cartel's price gouging of 1974–75 and 1979–80. Big oil, without any shadow of doubt, today means big gas, big nuclear, big coal and big bank tie-ins. We even see the oil company octopus reaching out to buy up the indispensable commodities that contribute to a solar program and to the development of photovoltaics. They bought up copper stocks in the late 1970s to get a strangle hold on copper plumbing and things of that kind that are indispensable to solar installations in the future, so that they can price those out of our reach as we go along. Their aim is to keep them competitively priced with oil to keep their interest forever in the forefront. If they could hang a God-damn meter on the sun, we'd have it today, but they haven't figured that one out yet.

You see the Corporate State day in and day out, in bribes, payoffs, product liability cases, customer overcharges, investor con games, and Wall Street insider trading scandals. I don't care where you pick up the paper, you will find it.

The law does not reach corporate crime in this country the same way that it reaches all of us as individuals. The unemployed or the hungry steal a loaf of bread and they go to jail.

You can't put a corporation in jail, or they say we can't. The executives who call the corporate shots don't bear the risk, because the lawsuits against corporations are "nonrecurring losses" on the balance sheet. Neither the courts, nor the public, nor the stockholders judge the success of management on its criminal conduct, number of lawsuits, or the nonrecurring losses. They judge it only on profits. For what's it worth, in in my humble judgment, in the real economy today there is a genuine head-on collision between ethics and economics, between the values of equity and fairness and the greed of profit and plunder. The free market today offers no priorities, no values, and no human purpose.

We don't have full-blown monopoly; a single monopolistic firm does not rule each sector of industry. But domination of each industrial sector in this country today by a Big Three or a Big Four has become an accepted fact of life. Competition within a concentrated industry (oligopoly) is more a struggle for power to control supply and demand than to win any customers by price competition. And when all American industry today is dominated by 100 corporations which necessarily must rig prices, as they do, then no one else is going to risk the logical results of free competition.

So when the Corporate State and the right wingers raise the banner of free enterprise, all they are really doing is laying down a smoke screen to preserve the system exactly the way it is today. Behind this propaganda blitz of free enterprise and the free market you will find that Corporate America and the right wing are collaborating to control government, pick your pocket, steal your freedom and your economic security. And this system of concentrated ownership and of monopolistic and anti-social behavior has profited neither the public nor the nation.

Taken together, these changes represent a transition "back into the future" of a business climate reminiscent of Richard Milhous Nixon's Watergate era, and before that, of the "Roaring Twenties" in America and the rise of fascism in Germany, Italy and Japan before World War II. Read the history of those eras. The parallels today are disturbing.

HOW WE GOT HERE

The genesis of how we've arrived where we are is not encouraging, though it may well be enlightening. It begins with that infamous American Bluebeard, Richard Nixon, and the conservative revival in politics of the 1970s. True to conservative dogma, it begins with money—Big Money—and preaches "that government is best which governs least."

After World War II and right up until Nixon's time, the system of fixed exchange rates for the world's currencies was negotiated, agreed upon and operated by international rules determined by national governments. Money was regulated in the national and international interest. Fixed exchange rates provided the context for global economic development and reasonably stable growth.

Nixon and the Supermoney Crapshoot

Nixon, in complicity with the conservative international bankers and businessmen, deregulated that managed international money system and changed it into an unregulated global money mart. It's called "floating exchange rates." What it amounts to is an international floating crap game, where a few global banks and corporations speculate on the value of national currencies. By betting in favor of a currency, they can increase its value. By betting for another, or others, they can drive down the value of a currency.

Those economists who are faithful apologists for multinational corporations tell us that this crapshoot is part of the "free market" and of "free trade," too. But we all recognize the crap game is run by a few bank and corporate managers, and it is they who control and throw the dice.

The deregulation of money means that dollars deposited in Europe and Asia are not subject to U.S. Federal Reserve rules, nor to almost any other government policy. There's no deposit insurance, no government reporting or disclosure of where those dollars are deposited, no reserves set aside to cover lost bets or bad loans made with those dollars. The U.S. government doesn't even count them. When that is coupled with computerized telecommunications systems, we have, in the words of Howard Wachtel of American University, a "vast integrated global money system totally outside all government regulation, that can send billions in 'Stateless' currencies hurtling around the globe 24 hours a day."

If we want to learn where all those dictatorial governments and businesses get the capital and credit to launch their own manufacturing and industrialization, here's how:

Most U.S. and Canadian banks are open only six to eight hours a day. During the night, they have deposits that aren't committed to backing credit or loans.

Bankers and gamblers alike fear idle money.

The end of the day in Canada and the United States is just the beginning of the day in Hong Kong, Singapore and Tokyo. With speed-of-light telecommunications, Canadian and U.S. banks send those idle deposits to back credit and loans over there to go to work during the daylight hours there. When the sun sets in the Orient, those monies are returned home, to go to work here, and the process repeats and feeds on itself. The implications of moving billions of dollars from one account to another, from one bank to another, from one nation to another at the speed of light, are enormous.

It takes an irrational faith in the innate goodness of bankers to assume that this awesome power will always be used in the national and public interest.

We already have one known case in point. In 1983 Citicorp was called before the Securities and Exchange Commission (SEC) because it had shifted $46 million in currency exchange profits made from countries with high taxes and parked them in Bahama tax harbors in violation of the laws of France, Italy, Switzerland, and West Germany. Citicorp had been doing this over a period of seven years before it was reported by an inside employee, who blew the whistle. Otherwise, it might never have been caught.

Citicorp's answer to the charge was a shocking display of arrogance. It contended that "because Citicorp had never represented to stockholders or investors that its senior management had honesty and integrity, it had no legal duty to disclose breaches of basic norms."[1]

The SEC itself, whose charter responsibility is to enforce basic standards of honesty in corporate behavior, excused Citicorp by arguing that pursuit of profits it knew to be probably unlawful was "reasonable and standard business judgment."

How's that for good corporate citizenship? And where does comparative advantage that economists talk about figure in this scheme of capital mobility, if Citicorp's behavior was "reasonable and standard" and its senior management has no duty to represent honesty and integrity?

The absurdity can be seen in the proposition that lying, cheating, dishonesty and law breaking are comparative advantages!

The multinational corporation has become a new sovereign entity in international trade and finance, capable of operating quite independently of national interests—whether those interests be economic, humanitarian or social in nature. National regulations don't reach the multinational corporations. They are supranational, and the world simply isn't prepared for this new order of things. Some call multinational corporations the "hollow corporations" where money for money's sake reigns supreme as opposed to real production. Why bother with the messy details of manufacturing and production, when there's bigger money to be made in the computerized international crapshoot?

If, in the meantime, sales and profits from production go sour and cash flow is slow, they can spin-off the loser, or borrow Eurodollars or Asiadollars and acquire or merge with another "cash cow" enterprise. Between 1984 and 1988, some 13,130 takeovers were carried out at a cost of $1,035 billion, according to IDD Information Services. You read that right. Over $1 trillion in mergers and acquisitions occurred in just five years! Mergermania replaces real production in this scheme, with no new productive assets created and many jobs lost.

Couple this with astronomical and mismanaged corporate and government debt. That leads the crapshooters to bet against the dollar and lower its value. Then we have foreign firms buying Canadian and American businesses at bargain-basement prices. Interest rates are then raised to entice them to invest further in our bankrupt economy and prop up the sagging dollar. The United States is now dependent on foreign capital.

The upshot of this new international supermoney system is—and it's fundamental to what's wrong with world trade today—that there no longer is any national sovereignty or control over our money or our economic destiny.

The global moguls owe no allegiance to country, flag, tangible production, or things like economic growth and full employment, let alone worker rights. U.S. corporations are investing billions every year in our trading partners. If it had a mind to do so, Corporate America could well say, "We have met the foreign competitor and we are it!"

Need I remind you how seriously this system compromises our political democracy? Our political system is organized on the ideal of one person, one vote—equal and universal suffrage. Globalization and the supermoney system is based on the inequality of one dollar, one vote, because it is deemed necessary to provide private individuals with incentives to become more than equal. It removes the government's public role in the economy and replaces it with the influence of private economic values based on greed and fear—fear of losing the crapshoot.

It produces international political schizophrenia, domestic economic sclerosis, and declining living standards in Canada and the U.S., without raising standards in other exploited nations where workers are also hostages to the supermoney crapshoot.

Carter, Reagan, and the "3 D Economee"

Then came the energy crunch—grand larceny on a colossal scale— which robbed us at a time when we were just beginning to balance our income and expenses with slight annual gains in real wages and incomes. We paid dearly for that in the 1970s in the form of double-digit inflation and with our jobs in the form of double-digit unemployment.

As the Vietnam intervention staggered to a halt, the war machine quit generating plunder, profits and death. At about the same time, that obnoxious villain Nixon was caught trying to rape the Constitution and implement a police state in America.

In the aftermath of Vietnam and Watergate, Jimmy Carter promised honesty, disarmament and populism, but gave us frustration, defeat and resurgent militarism instead. He ran back and forth across the political center, and finally settled on the right wing, serving the very conservative and corporate interests he'd vowed to control. His about-face on natural gas deregulation and misfeasance with Labor Law Reform, plus his initiation of airline deregulation, were more than this trade unionist— and several millions of others as it turned out—could swallow.

We challenged the Democratic Party establishment from within with Senator Kennedy in 1980. It didn't work for reasons beyond our control, but I said then, and say today, I'd rather have stood with Ted Kennedy on Democratic principles in defeat than with President Carter and his corporate and Republican principles in his Pyrrhic victory.

In any event, the failure of Kennedy and the defeat of Labor Law Reform showed us that the employer/right wing axis was in high gear.

Ronald Reagan's election cemented the assault. The drive for what we have called a "3 D Economee" began in earnest. The three D's are Deregulation, Deindustrialization, Deunionization. Add to these the move to privatize publicly owned enterprise, such as Conrail, and the move to contract out federal wage board jobs, and we see that the Reaganomics equation became $3 D + P =$ the Service Economy. It features low wages, part-time jobs with no life support benefits, and a "union free environment."

The Reagan government took the hard line approach. Breaking the Professional Air Traffic Controllers Organization strike in 1981 was the first big salvo. At the same time, Reagan began stacking the National

Labor Relations Board with Right-to-Work Committee ideologues and corporate lackeys. A dozen or more long established precedents in labor law were reversed or otherwise turned on their head. Prospects for a fair hearing at the Reagan NLRB became so bad that we had to advise our people to cease utilizing its services wherever possible.

The Department of Labor became a representative of employers and the Occupational Safety and Health Administration became a cruel joke, as the director gave employers license to lie, cheat, kill and maim at our job sites. The lousy occupational health and safety standards that resulted in the workplace amount to murder by another name.

As Reagan began making judicial appointments to the federal bench, the courts backed up the assault. Injunction judges restricted our picketing rights. Federal judicial appointments are for a lifetime, and Ronald Reagan appointed over half of all federal district court judges, a squad of appeals court judges, three Supreme Court justices and the Chief Justice.

They're nearly all anti-union right-wing ideologues. They're all brainwashed in the application of the engineer and economist's "cost-benefit analysis" to human problems. And they're all committed to the free trade/supermoney religion. As a result, Reagan's antilabor sword is going to be twisting in our wounds well into the next century.

Paralleling the Reagan government's hardballing has been employer hardballing. In industry after industry, we have experienced the breakup of master contracts, the imposition of two-tier wage schemes, and the massive subcontracting out of our work to nonunion operators, including out-sourcing overseas. Concessions in wages, health benefits, retirement plans, and little freebies like wash-up time and lunch breaks have been demanded and, all too often, granted.

The threat of job blackmail is that the employer will go belly up or will move where it's cheaper to operate nonunion. It always accompanies concession bargaining. We've learned by bitter experience that, even if we make those concessions, the employer is apt to shut down, pack up and move out anyway. If an enterprise is mismanaged, it'll go broke with or without our concessions.

In Canada, the employer and government assault on unions seems to be orchestrated with that in the United States. Whenever flannel mouth Mulroney and the President of Forgetting hatched a hair-brained deal like the Canada-U.S. Free Trade Treaty, then we *knew* they were waltzing together!

Union bashing became so broad and systematic in Canada that the International Labor Organization (ILO) made an on-site investigation of union rights violations. The only other country investigated by the ILO at that point was Poland.

The Conservative Mulroney government intensified its attack on unions, particularly public sector and transportation unions. Under the Public Service Labor Relations Act, strikes are nearly impossible. If the government deems the strike action an "interruption of an essential service," it can invoke back-to-work powers. That back-to-work legislation carries heavy fines for both the union and individual members and can bar union officers from holding office, if they resist back-to-work orders. Sounds like Poland.

When I analyze such legislation, I am always reminded of Samuel Gomper's comment: "Show me a land without strikes, and I will show you a country without liberty."

Here in the U.S., employers have also taken a soft line approach to weaken our unions. The tactic is also spreading into Canada. It is done in the name of "competitiveness" and "less adversarial labor relations." It's called by a variety of names: "Quality of Worklife" (QWL) programs, "Quality Control Circles," "work teams," or "participatory management."

Whatever it's called, it is an iron fist in a velvet glove. It circumvents the union or turns us into a company union. Its promise of workplace democracy is betrayed by manipulation from above. We remain confined to the mini-environment of the immediate workplace, where shop floor workers may have some say in small-scale decisions in the immediate work setting, but we have no part to play in decisions on where and how management invests or disinvests capital, or how it deploys equipment, technology and jobs.

Here's what the U.S. Catholic Bishops have to say about the QWL soft-line approach and other such schemes: "Workers rightly reject calls for less adversarial relations when they are a smokescreen for demands that labor make all the concessions."

We couldn't even get our employers to agree to give us advance notice when they're going to shutdown or sellout and move out on us. They've spent untold resources fighting hammer and tongs against us in the Congress on that pitiful plant closing prenotification bill that finally became law in 1988.

Economic plutocrats do not suddenly become economic democrats. If our employers want our cooperation and a love-in on the shop floor, then why do they rape us on the fainting couch of job blackmail and concessions, and make book with the right wing outside in the political economy at large? *Why* do they?

Put it all together, and the right-wing attack on the working people and their unions has given us a polarized society characterized by class privilege.

The arrogance and meanness of the upper class can be found in a new idolatry among them for the sights, sounds and symbols of the 1920s and in their contempt for anything that smacks of egalitarian principles.

It all becomes low burlesque, though, as a train of officials in both the Reagan and Mulroney governments slip from snob to slob status in a crime wave of misusing public office for private gain—which is a polite way to say they habitually lie, cheat, steal and plunder the public treasury and resources. At the close of his administration, Reagan had over 100 of his top officials either under investigation, indictment or already convicted. Mulroney in his first term had seven of his Ministers or officials driven out of government for breach of the public trust.

Nevertheless, Flannel mouth and Feelgood perpetuated their fraudulent conduct by joining together in promotion of the Warfare State's production of Star Wars. Military contractor hogs on both sides of the border will really be feeding at the Pentagon trough if that Mad Scientist's scheme gets off the ground.

There's a Red Alert to be concerned about, all right. But it's not that the Commies or Russians are coming. It's the danger of the collapse of the global financial market from speculative excesses.

The warning alarm was sounded in 1987, when Black October paralyzed Wall Street. The supermoney crowd lost faith in its own system. Now it's struggling with a green depression of paper profits, debt, deficits, devaluation and tight money.

Only time will tell when a few of the Big Boys cash in their winnings and take off for the Cayman Islands or stash them in secret Swiss bank accounts. If the going gets rough on insider trading deals, greenmail and poison pill defenses, then we can bet the slicks will cut and run.

It all makes for a gray and very uncertain future.

One economist—Ravi Batra—has it figured that there's a severe economic depression on the North American Continent every sixty years. His evidence shows that it happens when the distribution of wealth and income pyramids excessively toward the top.

The last depression occurred in 1929. According to him, we're due for another.[2]

So we must prepare for worst and hope for the best!

Labor in the Global Economy

In a global political economy, labor cannot and must not tolerate isolation. American unions' international education comes for the most part through our affiliations with the International Trade Secretariats—which are international federations of national unions in similar crafts or industries—and from our interactions there with our foreign brothers and sisters. We in the Machinists, for example, are affiliated with the International Transport Workers Federation, headquartered in London, England, the International Union of Food and Beverage Workers, head-quartered in Geneva, Switzerland, and the International Metalworkers Federation, also headquartered in Geneva, and its World Aerospace Conference, which I have been privileged to chair for the past six years.

It is through those Trade Secretariats that we exchange information and map tactics and strategies to deal with our global employers and the global economy. More and more, we're finding recognition of the fact that while we come from diverse countries and cultures, we must now deal with the same employer. The problems we encounter, whatever country we live in, are inevitably the same. I'll return to the issue of how to deal with these problems in Chapter 3. Our role in international trade union relations and education is going to grow at an accelerating pace, too. We have to be prepared to accommodate that relatively new dimension.

Some time ago I became adventurous enough to ignore the long-standing AFL-CIO ban on Federation officers having any contact with our counterparts in the Soviet Union and China. I visited both of those countries and shook hands with a great many warm and seemingly sincere trade unionists—or at least what pass for trade unionists—in those lands.

Please note that my hand did not rot off, and I wasn't duped by Communist propaganda, nor was any attempt made to the best of my knowledge to make me an instrument of their propaganda. What I learned was that those citizens, individually, are remarkably like Americans and Canadians. They love their countries, will fight for them if it becomes inevitable, but at the same time they share our overriding desire for peace. They manifest a genuine concern for the good of their populations and fellow workers, yearn for a permanent peace accord between East and West which would permit realistic arms reductions, and above all, push for an Economic Conversion program in their countries, so that resources currently dedicated to the military can be diverted to domestic production and improve their standard of living.

Quite frankly, those findings didn't particularly surprise me. Workers the world over have pretty much the same desires and aspirations. The first-hand knowledge that I gained makes me the only one so equipped when the cold warriors of the AFL-CIO gather in their periodic Executive Council meetings. I have grown weary of the endless "red baiting" that goes on, in view of the fact that our institution is the only one in American society that finds it necessary to impose on us the requirement of being super-patriots. Business, the clergy, academics, scientists, engineers and others all have on-going contacts with their Soviet counterparts. It is therefore offensive to me that a trade union representative should somehow be viewed as being more susceptible to the Communist doctrine than anyone else in any other walk of life, including American tourists. I have, since indulging in that experience, urged anyone and everyone from our movement who has the opportunity to do the same.

TECHNOLOGY IN OUR FUTURE

We stand today on the threshold of a technological tomorrow that is beyond the dreams of Buck Rogers. It holds the promise of economic bounty sufficient to feed and clothe everyone for the first time in human history. And it holds equally the threat of a technological Armageddon that will end human history. If we can avoid that threat, and we've got some ideas about how to do that in Chapter 4, the technological revolution will have profound impact on our lives and livelihoods. Today that technological transformation, as we will explore in Chapter 5, is destroying skilled, well-paid jobs and replacing them generally with less skilled and poorly paid work.

There is no automatic high-tech fix. Quite the contrary. The Department of Labor has projected where the jobs will be in the next two decades. And the results have been verified by many other independent studies including our own. Janitors, dishwashers, fast food servers and nurses aides were in the top five, along with secretaries.

Computer programmers or computer operators and technicians do not even make the top twenty list. Only seven percent of all new opportunities over the next two decades will be in the high-tech category. Even of those, damned few will pay decently, while most will be poorly paid, unskilled jobs and apt to be shipped off to depressed countries.

At this point, the introduction of new technology almost across the board, from computerized machines, materials substitution and robots, to video quality control, is just another job blackmail threat to workers that is resulting in the weakening of collective bargaining, the undermining of labor and living standards and eroding social values in the political economy.

Yes, technology is certainly changing economic conditions. But is it improving them? And, if so, for whom?

Engineers and scientists like to tell us technology presents us with the "gift of leisure time." Hell, unemployment for any reason does that. The key questions we must ask in light of the new technology are:

- How do you compensate leisure time?
- Who gets to work and who does not?
- Who decides?
- And who gets the wealth created by the new technology's increased productivity?

New technology not only changes jobs, it is bound to change our work habits and our communal patterns of behavior. It will force a restructuring of our economic system. In the process, it will wrench the values built into our constitutional democracy.

If we do not wish to become the Luddites of the Twentieth Century, then our immediate task, as trade unionists representing the best interests of our members, will be to challenge and, ultimately, to share with management control over the workplace. We must share control not only of wages, hours, and working conditions, but control of investment decisions, production priorities, and the full range of personnel administration policies. The scope of bargaining, restrained for nearly fifty years must now be expanded if the institution of free collective bargaining is to survive.

One obvious step is to reduce the work week from forty hours—set half a century ago during the Depression—to thirty hours. Some of our European friends and colleagues, like the West German unions, are already on the road to a thirty-five-hour week for forty hours pay.

The forty-hour week inhibits the fair distribution of wealth and income created by the introduction of labor-saving technologies. If we are going to share the income and wealth derived from labor displacing technologies, then we have to share the work, and that means abolishment of overtime, too.

That is what it will take to provide job opportunities for minorities, women and young entrants into the labor force, if we want them to play a productive role in our society and the economy. Otherwise, they, joined by a hell of a lot of us in the blue-collar ranks, will remain non-producers instead of producers.

The thirty-hour week with no loss in pay and no overtime should be our rallying cry.

New technology also impacts our political environment. Theories of a technological Corporate State are already being spun by corporate and military think tanks. Their corporate and elitist theories are devoid of human emotion and flesh-and-blood relationships. They put total emphasis on productivity, unit costs, and optimum profit pay-offs. Since competition in these frigid systems is to occur between human beings and robots, the normal and traditional measurements of worth of the individual will be discarded. The error-free humanoid will become the darling of corporate and military planners.

In this system, tears and laughter have no place. Creativity and inventiveness are perceived as obstacles to progress, rather than requisites for peace and prosperity for all.

Technology becomes an end in itself.

The political ramifications are appalling. In order to recruit conforming and malleable workers, psychological screening tests that invade personal and family privacy and spying on workplace activity will replace experience and skill qualifications. These insidious practices are already being adopted widely.

Methods of thought control and manipulation of the mind's processes will become standard on-the-job training techniques. Powerful media will be employed to sedate, seduce and motivate blind and unquestioning obedience to corporate and military authority.

Whoever controls the technology will control the means of production and, hence, the destiny of our lives and our nation. At the moment, control of the new technology in this country is shared between the corporate planners and military planners. In neither case, is there room for democratic decision making or consideration of democratic values. The technological revolution then poses the specter of an insidious, creeping technological fascism.

Ask yourself: If this is the future, who do I want at the controls? Corporate executives and Corporate technocrats? The military? Media and mass psychology manipulators? That is the recipe for Orwell's *1984* with its militaristic, sterile scientific totalitarianism.

WE CAN CHOOSE BETTER ALTERNATIVES

That bleak picture of an Orwellian world doesn't have to be our future. We can control science and the new technology and the power derived therefrom, for human betterment rather than human destruction. We can make choices that realize technology's potential and our potential as human beings, instead of crushing it. But those choices require that we set different goals for our political economy. "Greed," as Robert Lekachman says, "is not enough."

In a nation and a world of finite natural resources, it is clear massive numbers of people are now and will be in the future in desperate need of the basic necessities of life. The depletion of our resource base, primarily by narrow and powerful private interests, backed by military madness, is undermining our productive capacity and our democracy. The deliberate exclusion of great numbers of people from access to the opportunities and rewards of our political economy is changing the nature and content of our value system.

We can no longer rely on the private interests to act in the people's interest. It is time to restructure our political economy and begin redistribution of employment opportunity, income, goods and services, and decision-making authority—all on a basis of a shared materialism. This may require a leveling of the economic pyramid and making the crooked straight, along a route to global peace and prosperity.

When I look across the time line into the Twenty-first Century, I see a reregulation of the world's monetary and economic system that will close down supermoney gambling casinos.

I see a reindustrialization of Canada and the United States that will direct the unfettered flow of capital, technology and trade away from dehumanization of the global economy to the higher plateaus of economic and social justice, with equality.

I see a reregulation of vital public services in the public interest.

I see reunionization of the labor force as trade union rights are treated as human rights all around the globe.

I see a redistribution of wealth and income away from the snobs and slobs precariously perched atop their towering pyramid, down to where the builders live and toil.

In the next century, I see a mobilized effort to enact new initiatives for full employment because this nation—and this global economy—cannot survive 1/10 privileged and 9/10 deprived.

I see in the next century national, regional and world government forums to contend with the three mega-economies and dedicated to peace and prosperity in the interest of humankind, rather than the current war and poverty in the interest of the greedy kind.

I see a rewarding experience and future for our children and grand-children in a beautiful blast-off from our mother Spaceship Earth into the sylvan galaxy of the universe for purposes of civil and peaceful exploration, not military exploitation. I see a space program that will create—and not destroy—new wealth and work and progress for posterity.

That is the American Dream. It is also more than that; it is the dream for all humankind.

If we are going to get there, if we are going to get where we want to go then we can ill afford playing the fates and the future by ear. From here on we must make those decisions which propel us into a new dawn at the head of society, and we shall do it in our own self determined way.

To do that we need our own liberation theology which will extend this precious thing that we call democracy from the political to the economic sphere.

The roots of our present moral outrage lie not in the disappointment of narrow personal gain itself but in the frustrations of encountering the new phase of power in America; a phase of Fascism that mocks and smiles at us and manipulates us; that divides us one from the other and plays to the basic instincts on prejudice, self-righteousness and greed. Those are all the ugly hallmarks of the dark forces of the right wing encroaching upon our dignity and our rights as free citizens.

The seeds of our discontent are sown not by our failures as workers or as citizens, but by those in power who insist on undermining our humane and democratic values, while hypocritically paying homage to sacred symbols of patriotism and religion.

They would despoil our flag with the blood of our sons in strange lands for unknown reasons, while here at home they set strange Gods before us.

Behind their masks of authority, religion, morality and economic demagoguery is found the false paradise of fool's gold.

We must free ourselves from the sinister forces of the right because we are all hostages in their quest to plunder our lives and pillage our constitution.

We shall not be deceived. Our mission is to expel the money changers from the temples of government and to scatter the kindling sparks that will reignite the fires of compassion, humanity and freedom that smolder within the bosoms of ordinary men and women the world over.

Our liberation will come from the virtue of subordinating any narrow selfish interest to the over-all good of our union, our countries and the world as a whole.

Our liberation champions not only equal treatment before the law, but the elimination of the vast disparities of personal wealth and economic opportunities that divide us into a society of haves and have-nots.

Finally, our liberation will operate, not on the jungle ethic of competition and survival of the fittest, but on the civilized ethic of cooperation—cooperation to provide an economic growth that will produce social harmony, equality and a shared material abundance for all.

From this time forward, we can prepare for that new dawn, which will enable us to achieve the solidarity, the sisterhood and brotherhood, the peace and the secure prosperity, which has eluded us most of our lives, but which we still crave.

NOTES

1. *New York Times,* February 18, 1982, pp. 1, D6.

2. Ravi Batra, *The Great Depression of 1990* (New York: Simon and Schuster, 1987).

mismanaging America's economy: paper entrepreneurs and corporate cannibals

We have known that heedless self-interest is bad morals: now we know that it is bad economics.

—Franklin D. Roosevelt

Just as war is too important to leave to the generals, the economy is too important to leave to economists. The economy generates the jobs and the earnings that pay the mortgage and put meat on the table—when it works right. But how the economy is structured makes a difference. The economy can generate rising living standards and growing prosperity for everyone or it can generate great wealth for the few and poverty for the many.

Which course the economy takes is a political decision. The United States government chose the wrong course in the 1980s. It chose to turn the clock back on economic policy toward the free market of the period before the New Deal—albeit with a mammoth government give away of tax breaks to big corporations. Supply-side economics was supposed to unleash a wave of investment in plant and equipment. Instead, it unleashed a wave of speculation in mergers, acquisitions, stock index options and futures.

Before we buy the free marketeers' myth that government intervention in the economy is bad except when the government is giving away the store to the rich and to the big corporations, let's look at the record of government intervention in the free market crapshoot. Divide the nation's modern economic history into two periods: the pre–World War II period and the post–World War II period. We'll even give free market faithful an advantage by excluding the Great Depression years. (If we included those, the comparative advantage of government intervention would be overwhelmingly positive.) The postwar period, of course, marked the end of laissez faire economics and the beginning of a slow, tortuous welfare state liberalism—a liberalism, which, by the way, saw businesses and corporations tapping the government till to a much greater extent than welfare mothers or their dependent children.

Economist Walter Heller reported that, with respect to *economic stability*, the prewar economy spent about one year in recession for every year in expansion. In the postwar period, he found four years of expansion for every year of recession. Moreover, he found prewar recessions longer and deeper than postwar recessions. As he graphically depicted the difference, prewar recessions were a deep V, while postwar ones have been a shallow check mark—until Mr. Reagan's 1982–83 skid produced another deep notch.[1]

In terms of comparative *economic growth*, the prewar period had an average annual real growth rate of 2.8 percent (1909 to 1929); 2.3 percent (1929 to 1948); and a hefty 3.8 percent 1948 to 1973. Since the Reagan retrenchment, economic growth has once again retreated to prewar rates.

The poverty rate fell from 33 percent in 1947 to 22 percent in 1960 and finally to 11 percent in 1969, when the Great Society's limited war on poverty reached its zenith. After Mr. Reagan declared war on the poverty-stricken, the poverty rate rose again. Between 1981 and 1985 the Reagan budget and tax policies shoved one million families into the ranks of poverty. The Census Bureau reports that, in 1987, about 32.5 million people were living beneath the official poverty line, up from about 24.5 million in 1978. That was 13.5 percent of the population, or about one American in seven. Two out of three poor adults are women, and they head half of all poor families. Children and elderly women were particularly disadvantaged. Almost one quarter of American children under 5 and one fifth of elderly women living alone live in poverty.

There's more to this brief historical and statistical sketch than I'm reporting here, but the quantitative data demonstrate the nation has prospered much more with an activist government than it has with the free marketeers' "invisible hand."

Democracy has always implied a measure of equality and economic freedom for the many, not just the few. Consider Thomas Jefferson's view that democracy had its economic base in the independence of farmers who owned their land and artisans who owned their tools and businesses. The maldistribution of wealth and the regressive decision-making power vested in the hands of wealth has plagued political economies throughout history. That includes the American political economy, even when directed by liberals. Still, that degree of inequality has been seen as a problem, and we have tried to redress it.

From the New Deal to the 1970s, we made modest progress. Franklin Roosevelt, Harry Truman, John Kennedy and Lyndon Johnson never attempted to strip the wealthy elite of their fortunes. Nor did they attempt to nationalize or socialize monopolistic and oligopolistic corporate entities. They each did strive to rein in the licentiousness of wealth and the self-assumed sovereignty of corporations. They provided some minimal rules of decent economic behavior and conduct.

Those liberals, who were capitalists themselves, sought to have wealthy individuals and corporate entities pay their fair share for maintaining and defending the system from which they profited. These business and privilege taxes were recycled, in part, to give those floundering at the bottom of the economic pyramid the means to buy boots, so they might pull themselves up by their bootstraps. That seemed to be a humane and sensible thing to do. It also was quite consistent with our society's commitment to democracy, economic and social justice and equal opportunity for all.

Over the long run, the system worked slowly but measurably. The percentage of people living in poverty was reduced by half. Malnutrition and starvation among infants and children were practically eliminated. The nation's housing stock increased quantitatively and qualitatively, with low-income people gaining access to the homeowner's badge of respect and security for the first time in our history. Education facilities were greatly improved, and educational opportunities for millions of middle and low income people also increased. Senior citizens were assured retirement income and access to medical care.

I defy anyone to say that that effort was a failure. Roosevelt's New Deal, Truman's Fair Deal, Kennedy's New Frontier, and Johnson's Great Society produced measurable gains for all Americans. Those programs are far from perfect. More could have been done. More should have been done. But that commitment to economic and social justice will stand out for generations to come as one of the most brilliant chapters in American history.

That commitment to economic and social justice always had its opponents. They were the ones Franklin Roosevelt called "economic royalists" and "malefactors of great wealth." The progress of humankind and democracy has always required a fight against those who fear a loss of their power or pecuniary interest, when the benefits of the political economy are distributed more broadly and more evenly across society.

Their fear is not founded in fact or reason. The empirical evidence of the last five decades tells us unmistakably that as the population as a whole prospers, so do those at the top of the pyramid.

But the movers and shakers of commerce, industry and finance have opted for retreat in the 1980s.

Let us chart the theory and the practice of how our economy works and analyze some of its problems before we turn to those remedies that ought to be on labor's agenda.

THE POVERTY OF ECONOMICS

The essential question is not what's wrong with the economy. It's pretty obvious what's wrong. Just drive around town and see the boarded up plants and the slums. The essential question is why it went wrong. Why do we have a planned diseconomy, rather than a functioning and rational economy?

The fundamental reason why the economic sky is falling is the Free Market dogma. It is the Holy Trinity of Free Private Enterprise—in the name of supply, demand and the Mystical Marketplace. Amen.

The High Priest of Free Enterprise, of course, is Milton Friedman who wants to take us to Friedman's Paradise.

But he isn't alone. Every economist of repute in the country whether conservative or liberal, Republican or Democrat, worships at the Shrine of Free Enterprise. When the going gets tough, when the economic machine goes out of whack and its engines stall, even Paul Samuelson and Lester Thurow fall back on supply and demand analysis to explain why things are malfunctioning and how we can save the ship.

That's ironic. What their free market equation of supply and demand tells us is that not only will we *not* have a recession or depression, but also that a recession is impossible. Their litany says that if demand decreases, then prices will come down. If prices come down, then inflation will recede, demand will pick up and so will employment. At full employment, demand will intersect with supply, whereupon suppliers will be induced to (1) increase prices or (2) increase supply, or both. In any case, supplier behavior will put the equation into equilibrium and we will all live in Friedman's Paradise of price stability and full employment.

Obviously, the economy doesn't behave that way.

Since the peak of the Vietnam War, we've had neither price stability nor full employment. We've had inflation, unemployment, and recession simultaneously.

Orthodox economists try to blame this on government regulations that interfere with producers and suppliers and keep them from lowering prices. "Just keep the government out of the marketplace," they say, "and the interaction of supply and demand and competition among suppliers will bring us to the land of milk and honey."

That prescription is hogwash. Here's why:

First, we had an unregulated economy prior to the Great Depression. Far from producing Friedman's Paradise, it gave us economic disasters with mass unemployment and soup lines. That's a historical fact today's free enterprisers choose to ignore. Ignoring the Great Depression is a pretty good trick, but some of these guys have spent their entire lives trying to disassociate themselves from the real world.

Second, if all federal regulations in the business sector were scrapped, the inflation rate would recede by less than seven-tenths of 1 percent according to reputable researchers. Government regulation is simply not a plausible explanation for our long-term stagflation between 1973 and the early 1980s.

So much for the free marketeers' pure gospel.

The Phillips Curve: The Modern Shrine of the Golden Calf

The free marketeers adulterated their own gospel with a particularly pernicious variation on the pure free market theme. This variation has it that supply and demand cannot bring us into equilibrium and Friedman's Paradise. Rather, we must make a choice. We can have either full employment or price stability, one or the other, but not both. The "Phillips Curve" is the esoteric term which economists use to designate this supposed trade-off between full employment and price stability.

Nowhere is the bankruptcy of current orthodox economic thinking more revealing than with respect to full employment and inflation. They want us to worship at the shrine of the Phillips Curve which the Nixon Administration built, at which the Carter Administration prayed fruitlessly, and where the Reagan Administration found the wellspring of its economic policy. Their commitment to the Phillips Curve dogma prevents a full-employment economy. Fear of inflation dictates their priorities. Like much of the rest of orthodox economic theory, the Phillips Curve dogma serves well those who have, but amounts to *triage* for have-nots and slow economic strangulation for those in the middle.

How can the Corporate State extol the virtues of the work ethic and promote a policy of chronic unemployment? It's hypocrisy of the worst kind!

But the policy makers persist. The President insists that high unemployment is required to combat inflation. The Council of Economic Advisors (CEA) insists that inflation can be cured by putting people out of work. The Brookings Institute—the Corporate State's "liberal" think tank—insists that bringing down inflation means raising unemployment. And the Bionic Economists, who call the Corporate State's economic shots with their little black boxes and computerized econometric models, automatically assume we must have high unemployment to achieve price stability.

For too long the U.S. government has used unemployment as a means to control price inflation. It has used restrictive monetary and fiscal policies with full knowledge they will cost millions of people their jobs and livelihoods.

Any policy which consciously sacrifices the economic well-being of millions of human beings is morally indefensible. The moral offense is compounded when employers and government officials preach the gospel of the work ethic while concocting and implementing programs and policies to put people out of work or to underemploy them at part-time jobs with half-time wages and no life support benefits such as health care or retirement.

The High Costs of Unemployment

Official American statistics systematically understate the scope of unemployment. They exclude the entire category of "discouraged workers"—those who have been out of work so long that they have given up looking for work. All part-time employees who want full-time work are counted as fully employed, in spite of the fact that they aren't. If we adjust the official unemployment numbers to reflect the *real* unemployment, as the National Committee for Full Employment does, in 1987 when the official rate of unemployment was 6.2 percent, the real rate of unemployment was 11.2 percent. That 11.2 percent translates into 13.5 million Americans out of work in 1987—a year that the government told us was an excellent year for the economy.

That doesn't mean much, if you were one of the millions out of work.

Policies that promote and perpetuate unemployment are even more heartless when we examine the treatment of unemployed people in our country. Besides the scorn heaped on those out of work by those who put them there, and often by those others who are more fortunate, unemployment brings economic castigation, too.[2] Conservative and right-wing myths notwithstanding, far less than half the unemployed receive unemployment compensation. In fact, in 1987 only 25 percent of the unemployed were receiving unemployment compensation.

Those who do receive unemployment compensation get between 25 and 66 percent of their average weekly income earned while working, depending upon which state a worker lives in. Unemployed workers and their families lose access to medical and health services. Unless they have a union contract, most of the unemployed receive no job transfer or relocation assistance. They lose unvested pension credits. Unemployment diminishes workers' Social Security payments in future years, particularly, if it comes toward the end of the older worker's career. And remember unemployment compensation runs out after 26 weeks.

There are severe human and social costs attendant upon unemployment: increased homicides, suicides, mental breakdowns and family breakups. Dr. Harvey Brenner, of John Hopkins University and the nation's leading scholar on the social consequences of unemployment, reported to the Congressional Joint Economic Committee in 1979 that a 1 percent increase in unemployment causes

- a 5.7 percent increase in murders,
- a 4.1 percent increase in suicides,
- a 4 percent increase in prison admissions,
- a 3.5 percent increase in mental hospital admissions, and
- a 1.9 percent increase in overall mortality rates.

The plain fact is that unemployment kills.

Any government policy or company policy that is based on unemployment is a killer policy, a policy that induces crime. A policy of promoting unemployment is a crime against the individual unemployed and against society as a whole.

If you want to stop crime in the streets, you have to stop crime in the suites first. That means scrapping all the economic claptrap of the past decade and committing this nation, once and for all time, to guaranteed full employment, to education, and to job training and retraining to provide people the means to survive and prosper.

On purely macroeconomic grounds, planned unemployment is indefensible. Each one million unemployed workers costs the U.S. Treasury $30 billion in lost tax revenues, subsistence unemployment compensation and welfare payments. Simultaneously, the private sector is robbed of $100 billion in goods and services not produced, as it loses the purchasing power of those millions unemployed.

The effect of high unemployment is a *de facto* incomes policy. High unemployment reduces aggregate income, drags down productivity, and limits negotiated wage catch-ups with the cost-of-living squeeze. Union-ized workers are more timid in their collective bargaining demands when they are aware of a large surplus labor pool outside the plant gates. The sociological phenomenon of social stratification then comes into play as each kicks the one below on the social and income ladder, while those at the top are able to maintain their self-interest and status by appearing to rise above it all through a business-as-usual attitude.

In short, unemployment is costly in every way. Federal, state and local governments pay out billions of dollars every year in unemploy-ment compensation, welfare relief, food stamps, and the like. Manage-ment spends millions of dollars in support of collectively bargained supplemental unemployment benefits and severance payments. Society as a whole and the affected workers in particular pay the indirect costs related to alcoholism, family breakups, crime, suicides, mental illness and the other by-products of unemployment. Every element of society would benefit if we could divert a portion of this national expenditure into keeping people on the job, rather than merely to help them survive being off the job.

Confronted with our indictment of their bankrupt dogma, the or-thodox economists shriek "what about inflation?"

Well, What About Inflation?

That argument is a smokescreen. According to data from President Reagan's own 1985 economic report, appendix B, pages 271 and 296, as calculated by Professor Lloyd Dumas of the University of Texas at Dallas, since 1950 the average annual rates of inflation, over both five and ten-year periods, were lowest when unemployment rates were low-est; inflation rates highest when unemployment rates were highest.

Thus, in the ten-year period 1950–59, average annual inflation was 2.1 percent with average annual unemployment 3.4 percent. In com-parison, the 1970–79 period saw average annual inflation of 7.1 percent with average unemployment of 6.2 percent. The first five-year period in the 1980s (1980–84) showed a 7.5 percent average annual inflation rate with 8.3 percent average annual unemployment. History, then, gives lie to the orthodox notion that the way to control inflation is to increase joblessness.

The trade-off between unemployment and prices doesn't exist.

So why not turn it around. Why don't we opt for full employment, then see what happens to prices? Historically, whenever we've had price stability, we've been at near-full employment levels.

We achieved full-employment economies in 1955, 1966 and 1973 with relative price stability. But each time the monetary experts and the Federal Reserve Board, with acquiescence of the Council of Economic Advisors and fiscal experts, tilted at the inflation windmill. They enforced a credit squeeze, and interest rates soared. That raised the cost of production and prices for nearly all goods and services, since price of money is basic component of cost of production for nearly everything. Note that raising real interest rates also transfers income from borrowers who work for a living to lenders who own capital.

Apparently, it never has occurred to current "experts" that the only times in history when this system of ours achieved price stability was when we were at full employment.

But, it is argued, those were during wartime.

During World War II and the Korean War full employment economies and price stability featured across-the-board controls on rents, profits, dividends, executive salaries and bonuses, as well as wages. (Those policies differed fundamentally from Nixon's so-called "incomes policy" which applied effectively to wages only. That was a scheme to redistribute income and wealth to the top of the economic pyramid.)

This nation needs to substitute peaceful pursuits for war. Economic Conversion is one answer. Frankly, I never understood why we were able to convert our entire economy into an awesome war machine in the 1940s, but we never have been able to convert our peacetime economy into a similarly efficient, smooth running system. The possibilities for conversion are almost legion: renovating and refurbishing our inner cities, building mass transit systems, research, development, production and mass marketing of solar heating units and systems, along with the development of other alternate sources of energy; continued space exploration and promoting peaceful exploitation of space; and undersea food and mineral mining production.

What is lacking is *planning*.

To those who may shudder at the mention of economic planning, consider this: what we have today is a *planned diseconomy*. This is what the trade-off of full employment for so-called price stability has given us.

It is expensive, wasteful, inhumane, and it doesn't work.

The Myth of the Free Market

The reason why free market dogma doesn't work is because it is far removed from reality.

It is founded on the assumption of competitive behavior among firms in the marketplace. That's what the Mobile ads extol: competition. Smug and safely exempted from the anti-trust laws, editorialists across the land spout the line from their monopolistic perches of the press, and Corporate America reinforces it in expensive full color ads and canned editorials.

Competition? Crap!

Outside of flea markets, garage sales, laundromats, restaurants and sex shops, perfect competition doesn't exist in the United States.

Once we get off Main Street in Small Town America past the ten million Mom and Pop shops that gross less than $10,000 a year in receipts and that have a life expectancy of from 1 to 5 years—once we look beyond those last vestiges of economically insignificant petty capitalism—where do we find competition?

Not in aerospace or airlines.

Not in autos.

Not in banking or breakfast food.

Not in chemicals.

Not in lumber or light bulbs.

Not in minerals or steel.

Not in utilities.

And certainly not in energy.

A free market does not operate in any one of those fields. It is a controlled market—a market controlled by suppliers.

In these and many other sectors of the American economy, there is no free market. Instead there is oligopoly—the economists' term for the control of supply and prices by a very small group of producers. They, not the market, determine how much gets produced. They, not the market, set the price.

The concentrated market power of those giant firms protects them against the market. When sales go down, they don't cut prices. No, these leading firms cut production and put prices *up* to maintain profit margins. The free market, supply and demand and all that free enterprise jazz we hear so much about simply doesn't pertain. Prices are controlled all right, but not by the market or the government. They're controlled by the price leaders, the oligopolistic corporations.

Fortune's Five Hundred, plus a couple hundred more giant, quasi-sovereign corporate entities conduct 70 percent of all economic activity in this country. Less than 1 percent of American manufacturers control 90 percent of all industrial net profits. It is those oligopolistic firms that bestride the American economy like giants crushing the family-owned firms and Mom and Pop stores beneath their feet. It is those firms that make up Corporate America.

Supply-side economics

Orthodox economics was so far from reality that even conservatives recognized that something was wrong. Let's take a minute to look at "supply-side economics," the very peculiar theory that the Reagan Administration embraced as an alternative to the poverty of orthodox economics.

Supply-side economics and monetarism, that other pillar of conservative economics, are to economics as the flat earth theory was to geography or as the geocentric theory was to physics and astronomy.

Supply-side economics, stripped of its esoteric flourishes, rests on Say's Law: that supply creates its own demand. The only possible validity of Say's Law in contemporary America may be as it relates to the military industry—supply of military hardware unfortunately historically has created a demand for its use. But Say's Law has been discredited regularly in domestic economics. The most conclusive and disastrous time was in the Great Depression.

The fallacy of Say's Law is perhaps best demonstrated by applying it to the labor market. If supply creates its own demand, why don't we have full employment? Or more than full employment, since we have an oversupply of labor?

The problem with "supply-side" economics runs even deeper in an economy dominated by a small number of mammoth corporations. Like water seeking the path of least resistance, capital prefers to invest in capital rather than in the production of goods and services.

This explains the failure of billions of corporate tax cuts in the early 1980s to result in a capital goods boom. Why take a risk on a 10 percent return building roads, streets and bridges, or producing steel and safe renewable energy systems, when a simple phone call yielded, as it did in the early 1980s, 12 to 15 percent risk free by buying a piece of the federal debt required to fund the largest peacetime military build-up in the history of the world? Why go through the trials and tribulations of researching, developing, testing, producing and marketing a new product to help meet unmet human needs, when you can cannibalize another firm, puff up your balance sheet and the market value of your stock, too?

None of this activity—capital investing in capital, money investing in money, and money investing in politics—adds anything to the nation's wealth. Not one unemployed worker is put back to work. Not one dollar is added to consumer purchasing power. And that is the second economic truth which supply-side economics ignores: purchasing power.

Before corporate executives commit money to new investment in plant and equipment, to produce cars, refrigerators or widgets, they should see signs of effective demand on the part of consumers. Effective demand means consumer *desire plus the ability to pay* for goods and services. Unemployment restricts and curbs effective demand. No jobs, no income, no effective demand, no investment or production. It's that simple.

The decline in the average household's demand has been cumulative since 1973. Even if supply-siders were building new plant and equipment, even if they were producing goods and services at capacity, they couldn't sell them because there would not be enough effective demand. So they didn't invest in new plant, but they did buy the bonds the Federal Government issued to cover the deficit that the supply side cut in corporate taxes helped cause.

To make matters worse, the supply-siders mixed their economics with religion. They argued that the government should stop anti-trust enforcement with respect to noncompetitive pricing and market domination; eliminate regulation for product safety, and consumer and community health hazards; cease requiring environmental protection standards for air and water; lift safety and health protections for workers in the workplace; and stop public expenditures for Social Security, unemployment compensation, food subsistence, the sick and handicapped, the uneducated, and the poor. No one, they argued, is entitled to employment or even to subsistence wages or income maintenance, to health and dental care, or to legal representation. Reagan's economic program was based as much on this long list of social negatives as on pure economic theory.

Supply-side economics by any name is a crass declaration of class war. It is striking how many supply-siders are dead set against the importation of any of the successful democratic socialist measures and programs from our NATO allies in Western Europe or from Japan, but seem ready at the drop of a hat to import Argentinian, Brazilian, Chilean, South African or Korean anti-democratic ways of doing business.

As we know, an economic "recovery" finally began under Reagan. It was a "recovery" that bypassed much of manufacturing and the industrial heartland of America. It wasn't a supply-side recovery. Quite the contrary: the hundreds of billions federal deficit spending annually during Mr. Reagan's eight years made his policies fiscally Keynesian, albeit a militaristic Keynes.

But military Keynesianism didn't and isn't delivering us the goods or full employment.

Professional economists like to say they are neither moral or immoral in making their diagnoses and prescriptions. In fact, they are amoral. They neither make value judgments nor consider what is right and wrong in assessing the economy and implementing national economic policy. Professional economists say they merely describe and demonstrate the effects of various causes, given the assumptions of free market doctrine. And there's the rub.

It's those assumptions that need to be challenged.

Those assumptions don't stand the test of reality. They are a sterile dogma that serves one purpose only: justifying the inordinate wealth and power of the few and the growing powerlessness of the many. Orthodox economics is not science but *status economics*: economic theory designed to justify the social and economic status of the well-to-do and the poverty of the unemployed.

Remember that slave economies had their economic theorists, too, who justified the plantation owners' power and the slaves' slavery. The interests of the economically dominant class are always wrapped in the flag, fortified by law, protected by the police, taught in the schools, blessed by the church, and rationalized by economists.

It should be abundantly clear that the time has arrived for our national policy makers to establish a new era and ideology of moral economics—Humanomics—that declares the opportunities, privileges and rights of people are to be considered over and above the assumptions and rights of property, orthodox economic theory and those who sit at the apex of the pyramid.

THE CORPORATE STATE

Not only is our economy dominated by huge corporations, there has been fusion of the big corporations and the government into what can only be called the Corporate State.

Simply put, the Corporate State means a government and a political economy owned and controlled by a few powerful private corporations that have no sense of moral or ethical duty to the nation, to the state, or to the communities in which they operate and do business. In the Corporate State, there is only one guiding principle: maximize profits. What the Lord giveth, Corporate America stealeth away.

The Corporate State is characterized by an extreme degree of concentration of wealth.

Imagine a vast pyramid of wealth made up of blocks of balance sheet assets: material wealth and financial intangibles and tangibles. At the top of the American economic pyramid are the very rich. In 1987 the 400 richest Americans, *Forbes* reported, owned $220 *billion* in wealth. Number 1 on Forbes's list was retailer Sam Walton, whose fortune was estimated at $8.5 billion, more than the total gross national product of many nations. Federal Reserve Bank figures demonstrate that, in 1983, just ½ of 1 percent of American households owned 28 percent of the total wealth in the country, up from 25 percent in 1963. One percent of the people own and control 35 percent of the nation's wealth. At the bottom, 90 percent of the households own only 31 percent of the wealth. Yes, you read that correctly. The richest ½ of 1 percent of Americans own almost as much as the bottom 90 percent of their fellow citizens.

In terms of financial assets, such as stocks and bonds, the maldistribution of wealth is even more skewed. Just 2 percent of the households owned 39 percent of all the corporate bonds, 50 percent of all corporate stocks, 71 percent of all tax-free municipal bonds, 33 percent of other business assets, 20 percent of the nation's real estate, and 30 percent of the nation's liquid assets (i.e., cash, checking accounts, certificates of deposit and the like). The top 10 percent of the households in this country owned a total of 70 percent of the corporate bonds, 72 percent of stock, 86 percent of the municipal bonds, 78 percent of other business assets, 50 percent of the real estate and 51 percent of the liquid assets.

This is the nation's economic elite. The top 10 percent—the rich, very rich, and superrich—own fully 69 percent of the wealth in the nation, more than twice what the other 90 percent of us own. The superrich—the top 1 percent—are the coupon clippers. They constitute that tiny but powerful class that lives in large measure from unearned income.[3]

Today after Ronnie Robin-Hood-in-Reverse Reagan has taken from the poor to give to the rich, that distribution is surely even more skewed to the rich. The top tenth probably owns closer to 75 percent of the wealth while the bottom nine tenths of us suckers dogfight over the remaining quarter.

It is not by the sweat of their brow or even the ingenuity of their mental powers that they have come to own and control America. They are the inheritors of wealth and power—inheritors in perpetuity. And they maintain their hegemony by hiring a professional class of corporate managers to parlay their assets into combines, acquisitions and mergers throughout the economy. Interlocking business directorates, as well as flesh and blood intermarriages, make it all one happy powerful family.

Now consider the personal income pyramid. In 1987

- the top 5 percent of income receivers got more than the bottom 40 percent;
- the top 20 percent of income receivers got forty-four cents out of every dollar of personal income in 1987, up from forty cents in 1967; but
- the bottom 20 percent of income receivers got less than a nickel out of every dollar of income in income in 1987, down from almost six cents in 1967.[4]

In a rare deviation from orthodox economic doctrine, economist Paul Samuelson recently depicted the maldistribution of income this way: "If we made an income pyramid out of children's blocks, with each layer portraying $1,000 of income, the peak of the pyramid would be far higher than the Eiffel Tower; but almost all of us would be within a yard of the ground."

Or better yet, use an American analogy. If blocks representing the individual income of each American were stacked against the 853-foot high Transamerica Pyramid in San Francisco, 98 percent would lie around the base, less than one foot off ground level.

The remaining 2 percent would stack to the tip of the spire.

If the blocks represented assets—wealth—rather than individuals, then we would perceive the mirror image of a giant inverted pyramid. That's what we mean by "The Pyramiding of America."

While the select few at the top of the pyramid manipulate sales, prices, profits, dividends, and governments, the rest of us are apt to kick, gouge, and envy one another over a tiny block in the income pyramid. Economists call it the economy of scarcity. I call it contrived scarcity and economic and social injustice. Maldistribution of wealth, income and economic opportunity are the root causes of much of the anger, fear, frustration, hostility, prejudice and discrimination which divide us as a people. In an economy of scarcity, where a few percent of the people sit at the top of a vast, multi-trillion-dollar pyramid of wealth, the rest of us are apt to be perceived as nothing more than a pack of wild dogs, snapping and snarling at the pyramid's base for the last scrap of meat.

There can be no human dignity in that kind of system.

In the marketplace the free enterprise dogma is based on the assumption that competition forces profit-making companies to serve the public and restrains unbridled corporate profiteering. However, the concentration of corporate control over markets and prices in the Corporate State has eliminated effective competition. At the end of World War II, the 200 biggest manufacturing firms had 45 percent of U.S. industrial assets. By 1983, they controlled 61 percent. In 1982, the top 270 manufacturing firms—1/10 of 1 percent of the country's industrial firms—controlled 66 percent of the nation's manufacturing assets, and, through astute use of the tax code, parlayed 61 percent of the pre-tax manufacturing profits into 71 percent of the after-tax profits. Less than 1 percent of American manufacturers control 88 percent of all industrial assets and receive over 90 percent of the net profits of all industrial firms in the United States. As short a time ago as 1960, small and medium sized businesses controlled 50 percent of the nation's corporate assets. That figure had dropped to 30 percent by 1976. The continuing wave of mergers and acquisitions—$1 trillion between 1984 and 1988 alone—has further increased the concentration of industry since those studies were done.

Thus, we have pyramid building in the business world, too. At the broad lower base of the business world we find eleven million business establishments half of which have annual gross receipts of $10,000 or less. The assets and sales of *Fortune*'s 500 are ten time greater than the assets and sales of the second 500 largest firms. (These figures also predate the merger and acquisition wave of the mid-1980s, so they understate business concentration.)

The pyramiding of America, then, provides the dominant, overwhelming economic fact of life in America today. For the pyramiding of America means, simply and starkly, a tremendous concentration of wealth and power in the hands of fewer and fewer individuals. And the reality is that economic power means political power.

The Corporate State is bringing about a disequilibrium in the balance of power of a magnitude never before experienced in American history. Calling the shots is the Business Roundtable, an exclusive group of 140 corporate chief executives. It meets in strict secrecy. If a chief executive officer cannot be present for a meeting, he (there are no women on the Roundtable) cannot send a substitute.

In the past, topics of discussion by the Business Roundtable included how to defeat the Labor Law Reform Bill; how to defeat the minimum wage increase; how to gut the Occupational Safety and Health Act; how to undermine Social Security system; how to speed-up nuclear power plant construction; how to cover-up the dangers of radioactive waste; how to create a "union-free environment"; how to beat the federal consumer agency bill; how to dismantle the federal regulatory agencies; how to select Congressmen and Senators; how to select a President of the United States; and how to select and elect governors and state legislators. The Business Roundtable's agenda is a subversive and secret plot to overthrow our democratic system—or what is left of it—and seize control of our political economy.

When the Business Roundtable's chief executive officers fly into Washington in their sleek whisper jets and go calling on the Congress and on the President, they don't waste time in Congressional hearings airing their views in the public forum. They don't roam the halls of Congress looking for their Congressperson or Senator. They don't cool their heels in the President's outer office, waiting to see him. They get right in—often through the back door.

And when they talk, the politicians listen. Sitting across the desk from those hired guns of industry and finance is just like looking down the barrel of the Gross National Product.

One hundred forty corporate chief executive officers can bring America to its knees by locking out workers and breaking strikes, by buying politicians through their Political Action Committees (PACs), by exporting capital, technology and jobs overseas, by running away to anti-union, cheap labor areas and countries, or by selling out to foreign firms.

Think about it.

If 140 Italian Americans met in such secrecy and had these designs on the American economy, the FBI would be infiltrating them and rounding them up.

If 140 black leaders met in these circumstances, undercover agents would be taking names and notes and hurling charges of communism, treason and revolutionary plots.

If 140 student leaders from around the country gathered in secret conclave and discussed control of the government, you wouldn't be able to tell the students from the spooks. Mace and tear gas would be at the ready.

If 140 trade union leaders behaved the way the Roundtable does, we'd have the FBI, the CIA, the DIA, the local police and investigative reporters tunneling through us like termites.

But the Business Roundtable gets away with it, while the President and a majority in Congress dance to its tune.

The pitiful paradox in our political economy is that we have nearly full blown political democracy but precious little economic democracy.

And without the latter, the former often is meaningless. That may help explain why fewer than half the eligible people vote in presidential elections. The candidates do not speak to their concerns or interests.

CORPORATE AMERICA MISMANAGED

If the corporate elite ran the American economy for the greatest good of the greatest number, to ensure full employment and prosperity for all, it would be carping criticism to complain. But they don't. Those currently running the American economy in the board rooms of Corporate America as well as in Washington have failed us. Chronically high levels of unemployment persist; the number of people forced to dwell in poverty is rising; chasms are widening between the rich and poor; gaping differentials in income, wealth and opportunity among the sexes and races are hardening into rigid class lines. There is a growing body of empirical evidence to show the beginning of the decline of the broad middle class.

Behind this disintegrating economic fabric are the forces of capital flight and mobility, of the rapid introduction of labor displacing tech-

nology, and their ultimate combination in a self-centered, macho corporate management. These new managers are not winning the trade
wars nor are they contributing to peace, security and stability here at
home or around the world.

The evidence is that capital is being squandered through poor management, bad decisions, and non-productive speculative schemes, such
as spinning the international exchange rate roulette wheel, buying up
land and leases, and fattening the corporate balance sheet through
acquisition, mergers and other forms of corporate cannibalism. None
of this "paper entrepreneurialism" produces goods or services which
add to the Gross National Product or help the U. S. compete in the
international trade sweepstakes. None of that adds a single productive
job in the economy.

Why produce steel, bridges, washing machines or houses, when you
can use your cash to buy-up a faltering firm and use its losses to
increase your tax take?

Why produce a new line of products, or develop a new market for
safe alternative energy systems, when you can use your tax largesse to
merge with or acquire an oil company, a copper company or a competitive firm?

Why produce anything for a 10 percent return on investment, when
you can pick up the phone and buy a piece of Ronald Reagan's record
smashing federal deficit, and get as much or more guaranteed by Uncle
Sam?

And why spend a million to research, develop, test and market a
better mousetrap in an economy characterized by declining demand,
when for a few thousand bucks you can join with other members of
the Business Roundtable, buy the White House and a majority in
Congress and cut your tax bill, get rid of regulatory costs, and social
responsibility and put a damper on labor costs, too?

The real investment incentive of Reagan's corporate tax giveaway,
which is explored below, was the incentive to invest in politics. The
Reagan plan clearly demonstrated to corporate America that the rate
of return—in the form of tax subsidies and other benefits—on its
relatively modest investment in campaign contributions and lobbying
expenses is far greater than any they can obtain by exercising their
entrepreneurial skills in the market place.

American managers are developing an international reputation for
their preoccupation with paper profits instead of quality products.
"Profits without production" is what Columbia University Professor
Seymour Melman calls it. Their expertise consists of managing paper
assets and directing legal machinations. Why should we be surprised
when they go for the short-term profits, through mergers, take-overs,

spin-offs and international finance, instead of long-term investment in our industrial base. "So what if that raises unemployment?" they ask. "That keeps the wage bill down. Use your political clout to cut taxes, deregulate, and bust unions—not to get public investment in education, training, and research and development. Subcontract out the work. Send it overseas. The business of business is money." Sometimes it seems that Corporate America's logo is a skull and crossbones flag of convenience.

We have a serious and growing problem with management culture in America. Those insider trading racketeers like Ivan Boesky—and a couple dozen others cut from the same silk cloth—are the illegal tip of the iceberg.[5]

The Boeskies of this world are just an exaggerated form of the "profits without production" syndrome. Too much of American corporate management is industrially illiterate. That's why it is so easy for so many top corporate executives to abandon key sectors of our industrial base. If they don't have hands-on production experience in steel, rubber, machine tools, ship building, electronics and a host of other so-called smokestack industries, then they don't know what they are discarding. In pursuit of profits, these corporate executives are great paper chasers for things like acquisitions, mergers, spin-offs, unfriendly takeovers, and playing the international exchange roulette wheel and honeycombing the tax code for safe harbors, shelters, credits, deductions and exemptions. They are great paper entrepreneurs, fearless free enterprisers with golden parachutes, manning deadly desk top computers in daring unfriendly takeover assaults or defending their corporate honor by constructing harrowing poison pill defenses. But the ability to design and produce a product, durable goods and the hardware necessary to preserve our industrial integrity isn't within their grasp.

If the business community is seriously interested in restoring dynamism to our economy and increasing our international competitiveness, it had better look a little closer to home.

First, look at productivity. There are far too many people in the office, instead of on the factory floor when we compare the United States to Japan. American firms are over-managed and over-supervised, and the managers get paid much more than their Japanese or European equivalents.[6] There is a limit to expecting the high productivity blue collar and skilled worker to make up for the low productivity white collar worker. Blue collar productivity in manufacturing in the United States is quite competitive with Japan and the other major countries beating our socks off in the trade game. It is declining white collar productivity, particularly in the service sector, that makes us uncompetitive.

Frankly, I've never accepted the notion that the responsibility for productivity be placed squarely on the shoulders of wage-and-hour employees. How about the productivity of energy? How about the productivity of capital, especially when management chooses to sink capital into junk bonds, mergers, leveraged buyouts, or other nonproductive investments?

How about the productivity of a corporate executive? How about the productivity of Chrysler's management before Iacocca or Penn Central's, or any other mismanaged firm? Or a preacher, or a professor of industrial relations, or a management consultant? How about the productivity of the Bionic Economists, those who call the economic shots for corporations and government alike with their computerized econometric models, who maintain we must have high unemployment to achieve price stability? By *any* definition and measurement of the term, *their* productivity is zero.

Productivity is a function of management and capital, as well as labor.

Second, look at rampant corporate cannibalism. Giant corporations with more loose cash than they know how to use are busy gobbling up the small, dynamic, innovative firms that provide most of the jobs and most of the new ideas, products and services that keep this country moving.

They buy them up not to advance and accelerate the economic contributions of the small companies, but to control them, to make sure that potential market threats to their vested interests are neutralized or killed off. Solar energy systems, for example, aren't being mass marketed, because Big Oil interlocked with major banks, doesn't want solar competition until they own it and can hang a meter on the sun.

Third, look at a management out of touch with the marketing and production processes, and often unable to recognize, to anticipate or to respond to the need for new products, designs or processes.

Don't take my word for it. The situation is so bad that even the *Harvard Business Review* pointed it out back in 1980 in an article by Robert Hayes and William Abernathy called "Managing Our Way to Economic Decline."[7] In that article, Hayes and Abernathy made a cogent case that unlike the past, when senior executives rose through the production and marketing ranks, today our dominant corporations are run by managers schooled and proficient in financial manipulation, mergers and anti-regulatory litigation. Is it any wonder they try to focus your attention on short-run bottom line yardsticks, or government regulatory procedures? That's the only world they know.

It's always struck me as a cruel irony that companies will spend many millions of dollars litigating against government regulations that they could have complied with at a fraction of the legal cost, and often saved money or made money in the process. If the auto moguls had read the market right and not wasted their time contending against federal gas mileage and pollution standards, during the second energy crisis in 1979–81 we'd have had a decent supply of American-made small cars, fewer workers unemployed in the auto and supplier industries, lower import penetration, and probably lower car prices, because of the benefits of large scale production.

Instead we had none of those.

This nation cannot afford any more managerial myopia.

Fourth, look at government's contribution to corporate mismanagement through its bloated tax subsidies. It's time to scrap the counterproductive business tax subsidies which hurt our economy. We need to restructure depreciation so that it makes economic sense. This means cutting out the favoritism for some investments over others. Such favoritism actually reduces our productivity and our national income growth. The members of my Union want the best tools to work with, not the ones that are the most heavily subsidized by the tax code. And they don't want to lose their jobs to less efficient machines that are bought only because of their tax advantages. Such tax-induced distortions undermine the productivity of both capital and labor. Unless tax subsidies for unproductive investments are repealed, other efforts to use the tax system to encourage productive investment will fail.

American industry is not suffering from a lack of capital, but from the inefficient use of the capital it has. Repealing wasteful tax subsidies which divert resources away from productive uses in the American economy will contribute far more to increased productivity than all the billions of dollars in new subsidies provided during the Reagan Administration. If we are serious about improving our nation's productivity, let's shut down the tax shelter industry and put foreign tax havens out of business.

Last, and certainly not least, is the question of labor relations. American labor relations are bitter and adversarial relative to those in Japan, Norway, Sweden, West Germany, and many other European democracies. That's one of the reasons why their economies perform well. The reason why their labor relations are less adversarial is that they have found socially acceptable solutions to unemployment, inflation, stagnation and decline. They have arrived at those solutions democratically through compromise with a vigorous and active labor movement.

The success of our West European trading partners and Japan in beating our socks off is a testimony to the success of that course.

We'll look at this issue more closely in Chapter 6.

REAGANOMICS, OR THE ECONOMICS OF POVERTY

There's not much political mileage these days talking about the poor, the weak, and the declining middle class. They're "losers," after all. Behind Ronald Reagan's genial personal and aw-shucks rhetorical style was an inflexible ideology of raw power that exalted "winners," while heaping contempt upon "losers." That might have been Mr. Reagan's most lasting legacy: the psychological damage he did to the charitable and cooperative spirit of the people and the sense of failure and self-blame he instilled in those who dropped through his riddled safety net and who did not share in his economic recovery. His legacy has a mean, and demeaning, streak of "I've-got-mine-to-hell-with-you-and-your-kind" sneering in it. It is producing a society divided between callous and smug haves, and increasingly alienated dispossessed and dislocated have-nots.

Let's start with the Reagan Administration's stated economic program of supply-side economics. The rationale was counterrevolutionary. It went something like this:

(1) If you put enough new money into the hands of the well-off by cutting their taxes, and by "freeing" them from government regulation, such as environmental protections, safety and health regulations, and worker and trade union rights—in other words, absolve them of their socioeconomic responsibilities—then something tantamount to economic orgasm occurs.

(2) The well-to-do beneficiaries of this reverse federalism, flush with money and inspired by the prospect of keeping more of what they get, rush to put that new largesse into productive investments. New businesses, new industries and new jobs would be created.

(3) So much economic activity would be generated that the taxes the wealthy beneficiaries pay would exceed the cost of the original tax cut, thus producing an increase in government revenues.

(4) Voila! A balanced budget within two years.

(5) Meantime, the economic floodtide of new goods and services to the deregulated and free wheeling market would keep prices down.

That was the script. The movie turned out differently.

Need we recall that the economy went into a nose dive that was the steepest and lasted longer than any economic decline the nation has experienced since the Great Depression? After the mirrors and smoke of a bankrupt economic theory was tried and failed, the Administration pursued a disoriented attempt to stay the damage by using orthodox means for some very unorthodox and even repugnant objectives. Before the plunge was over, unemployment swapped double digit places with inflation. It's no great accomplishment to put inflation in retreat by throwing 12 to 15 million people out of work. Business bankruptcies reached Great Depression levels. Farm foreclosures and farm forced liquidity sales were reminiscent of the Farm Holiday era. Welfare assistance applications exploded. So did unemployment benefit claims. And as we now know, those joining the ranks of poverty did so by the platoons. Soup lines dredged up the ghost of Herbert Hoover. Homeless citizens began roaming city centers in search of shelter, beds, and food.

The wealthy beneficiaries of all this didn't put their tax cuts into basic industry. In the metalworking industries, they actually pulled out. Plant shutdowns became endemic. Corporate sovereigns went on a binge of leveraged acquisitions, mergers, and unfriendly takeovers. In the auto industry, sales plunged, except for luxury class cars, which were paid for with the wealthy's tax cuts. Government revenues, needless to say, didn't increase. They dropped. The deficit skyrocketed.

The supply-side fantasy became an economic nightmare. It was scrapped.

The Administration resorted to Lord Keynes, after a decade of right-wing economists had heaped scorn on him. It primed the pump and stimulated demand with some good old fashioned federal spending. Lots of it. Only it didn't go into the civilian side of the economy. It went into the military budget. The Reagan Administration presented the people with a five-year $1 trillion military buildup. Gold plated armor was substituted for leaf raking of WPA days. By God, the Russians were coming. They were overpowering NATO, landing in Central America, and, hell, they were invading the United States through a wave of illegal aliens coming across the Mexican border. Red Dawn was here. Praise the Lord and Jesse Helms and pass the ammunition!

Fears of inflation and a demand-pull overheated economy, not to mention the embarrassment of the balanced budget theory gone bust, and the new contempt for welfare "handouts" to the economically disenfranchised led to the Administration's forced austerity program. Monetary policy featured traditional conservative tight money and high interest rates. Fiscal policy featured right-wing attacks on government spending and on social programs. That helped to disguise military pork-barrel spending, and to keep the promise of a balanced budget within grasp.

Mr. Reagan's economic and fiscal policies inflicted much suffering on the most vulnerable members of society. It isn't chic to recant the statistics of economic failure, but let's do so anyway, in the name of truth and justice.

Between 1981 and 1984 administration budget cuts alone shoved a half-million people, most of them children, into poverty. A half-million fatherless families were terminated from AFDC rolls. According to the General Accounting Office, between one-third and two-thirds were left without any kind of health care coverage, half ran out of food at some point after being terminated, more than one-fourth had heat or electricity or gas cut off, because they couldn't pay the bill.

At the same time, the 1981 Reagan tax privilege bill shifted paying the cost of government from the rich to the poor. To hear Mr. Reagan and corporate media tell it, the Reagan tax plan was the greatest thing since grapenuts. They called it tax "reform." We called it tax robbery.

It was Robin Hood in reverse.

When you figured the Social Security tax increase and bracket creep caused by inflation, plus state and local tax increases, here's what you got out of Reagan's so-called "tax reform."

The 34 percent of all taxpayers who earned $10,000 or less got $33 off their federal income tax but $133 added in Social Security and bracket creep. They had a tax increase of $100.

The 14.7 percent of all taxpayers who earned $10–15,000 got a Reagan tax cut of $149 but Social Security and inflation added $319 to their tax bill. They had a net tax increase of $169.

The 12.1 percent of all taxpayers who earned $15–20,000 had a net increase of $176.

The 18.9 percent of all taxpayers who were in the $20–30,000 bracket had a net tax increase of $225.

The 15.2 percent of all taxpayers who earned $30–50,000 had a net tax increase of $300.

But if you made $100,000 to $200,000 a year, you got a net tax cut averaging $989. And if you were in that 1/5 of 1 percent who made over $200,000 your average tax cut was $18,024. Over the first three years of Reagan's tax cut, it was estimated the Chairman of Exxon got a $495,000 tax savings, while the Chairman of Boeing got a $180,000 tax cut. Mr. Reagan's tax privilege bill of 1981 gave the $200 grand-and-up crowd an average tax cut of 16 percent—enough for each of them to buy a Cadillac or Continental, but they probably bought a BMW or Mercedes; or two Toyotas for their kids. The average tax cut for the rich was more than 60 percent of the people in this country *earned* a year!

Between 1980 and 1984 the top fifth of families in the country gained 8.7 percent in real disposable income, while the bottom fifth lost 7.6 percent. The Urban Institute calculated that there was a transfer of

$25 billion from the bottom four fifths of households to the top one fifth. Subsequent Reagan tax changes further skewed the tax system to the advantage of the well to do. A 1987 Citizens for Tax Justice study demonstrated that in the decade between 1977 and 1987, the poorest 10 percent of Americans had their federal tax bill *raised* by 20 percent, while the richest 10 percent had their taxes *reduced* 20 percent.

But that's only half the tax cut story. The other half was the corporate tax cut. When Reagan took office the corporate income tax rate in this country was 46 percent. Not surprisingly, through loopholes and tax shelters, the *effective* corporate tax rates—what corporations actually pay—had never been 46 percent. In the 1950s the effective corporate tax rate was 40 percent; in the 1960s it was 35 percent; and in the 1970s it was only 25 percent. In fact, according to the *Atlantic Monthly*, nearly half the country's corporations were paying no taxes at all when Reagan took office.[8]

But Reagan said corporations needed a tax break so they could invest more in plant, equipment and production—and get the economy moving again. So he gave them the Accelerated Cost Recovery System and the Investment Tax Credit, too. That virtually eliminated the corporate income tax.

The result: of the 250 largest corporations on the Fortune 500 list, at least half of them got off the tax hook altogether in 1982 or 1983. GE, Boeing, and DuPont—global giants—were among them. Dow Chemical, Transamerica, General Dynamics, Greyhound, Grumman and Lockheed made billions in profits, but paid not one red cent in federal corporate income taxes.

Some of the largest tax-dodging, and tax-using corporations actually received tax refunds. Among them were big defense contractors, which are almost wholly tax supported anyway, like General Electric which received a $283 million tax refund on top its $6.5 billion profits between 1981 and 1983. Boeing got a tax refund of $267 million in spite of $1.5 billion profits. The list was a long one. It included chemical, oil and gas companies; telecommunications and machine manufacturing; and conglomerates. Some forty of the 250 top firms surveyed by Citizen for Tax Justice paid no federal income tax at all between 1981 and 1985 despite earning a total of $43.7 billion in profits; instead the federal government paid *them* in tax rebates totaling $1.9 billion.[9] No small companies need apply, however. Fully 80 percent of the tax handouts under Reagan's accelerated Cost Recovery System went to the largest 1,700 firms in America. That was just one-tenth of 1 percent of all businesses!

As David Stockman, Reagan's first budget director, put it in his shocking confession in the *Atlantic Monthly*, it was ". . . a coast-to-coast corporate soup line . . . the hogs were really feeding at the trough."

Research by one of our senior citizen organizations showed that individuals paid $1.50 in taxes for every corporate dollar paid in taxes in the 1950s. In the 1960s, individuals paid $2.50 for every corporate tax dollar paid. In the 1970s, individuals paid $3 to every corporate tax dollar. And in 1982, after Mr. Reagan's first corporate tax cut, individual taxpayers paid $7 to every corporate $1.[10]

The real corporate tax rate for most of the Fortune 500 by 1984 was lower than the 12 percent paid by the average farm and working family. What a return on Corporate America's investment in his election campaign! The big boys didn't rent him. They bought him!

When Corporate America isn't paying its fair share of taxes and is dipping into the tax till, too, guess who makes up the difference and pays for things like the national defense, highways, harbors, farm price supports, and the like?

We do!

We pay for Corporate America's tax cuts and tax handouts.

The poor, the sick, the elderly, and the handicapped pay for Corporate America's tax cuts and tax handouts through bloody budget cuts in Medicare, Medicaid, child support and food stamps.

It's the long-term unemployed people who pay for it, people whose unemployment benefits have expired, who have to sell their cars, furniture and even the china out of their cupboards for a few lousy bucks to buy food or pay a god damned utility bill! Or to buy a kid a school lunch that used to be free. And if jobless workers get sick or hurt, they can't go to a doctor or a hospital because they don't have health insurance!

While the poor stand in line for surplus cheese, Corporate America lines up to raid the Treasury of cold cash!

While those of us fortunate enough to be working worry about sending our kids to college or getting them decent jobs or helping them find a place to live, Corporate America worries about places to send its money so it can get the biggest and quickest return on investment. It scans the globe for cheap natural resources and cheap labor in search of greener, more profitable pastures. Every $1 billion invested abroad costs 26,000 jobs at home. The Foreign Investment Tax Credit, deferred taxes on foreign income, and Overseas Private Investment Corporation were all used to encourage U.S. multinational corporations to shut down, pack up and leave home for foreign shores for three decades.

Federal corporate tax changes in 1986 narrowed some of these loopholes and generally raised tax rates for the worst corporate freeloaders but incentives still remain for U.S. corporations to ship out and set up shop overseas.

Corporate America spends billions investing in plant and equipment overseas each year. It invests in West Germany, where workers have higher wage levels and cradle-to-the grave socialism—everything conservatives and our employers tell us we can't have. It buys into Japan, Inc., where workers have comparable wage levels, guaranteed jobs, and all sorts of socialist subsidies from child care to health care to housing. And Corporate America invests in those countries in spite of the fact that they have to pay higher corporate taxes than they do here at home!

For nearly three decades, Corporate America put three-quarters of its foreign investment in the industrialized nations. Then they bitched about declining productivity here at home!

The other one-fourth of Corporate America's foreign investment went to the less developed and undeveloped countries with low wages and servile labor. U.S. and Canadian workers are told that we've priced ourselves out of the global job market, that we have to compete with workers in Africa, South and Central America, and Southeast Asia. We have to sell our labor, our skills, to the lowest bidder based on the lowest common denominator in countries where there are no free trade unions and no economic, political or social democracy.

That's where part of the corporate tax windfall money in the 1980s has gone: building up the productivity and industrial bases of our trade competitors. Hell, U.S.-based multinational corporations *are* our foreign competitors. They shut down their plants here, build plants abroad, and ship the products back to the United States. No other nation in the world permits its corporations to so disregard national economic and security interests.

Corporate managers and their stooges in government say they have a natural right to such license and mobility, in the name of the free market and free trade. They fiercely resist democratic controls and restrictions on their investment and production decisions. Yet Corporate America is not winning the trade war. Those industrialized countries which are winning the trade war are those which require their corporations to look after the national and international interests first, and their private profit-making interests last.

As a consequence, the U.S. economy is beginning to take on a Third World pall. Like most developing and underdeveloped countries, we now export raw materials in the form of agricultural products and timber, raw minerals and materials, and we import manufactured goods. We run a huge trade and balance of payments deficit—$170 billion in 1987 and $150 in 1988. Every billion dollars in the trade deficit costs about 25,000 jobs here in America. That's more than four million jobs in 1987—enough to put half the unemployed back to work.

We have to finance that trade deficit by borrowing abroad. In 1985, the United States became a debtor nation; and in 1986, we passed Argentina, Brazil and Mexico to become the world's largest net debtor. If that debt continues to grow, it is just a matter of time before foreigners stop lending to us and start dictating our economic policy just like we dictate South and Central America's.

We also have to finance the federal deficit at home.

One man's debt is another man's income. And when the federal government borrows money, it has to pay interest to lenders, too, just like car buyers and home buyers do when they borrow money. It took the first 39 American presidents 192 years to run up $1 trillion in federal debt. Ronald Reagan, the 40th president, tripled the debt to over $3 trillion in his eight budgets.

According to the unwritten rules, interest accruing on the federal debt has first call on the federal budget, even if nothing else in the budget gets paid. And the interest costs on the current federal debt amount to $170 billion in fiscal 1990. The daily interest on the federal debt in fiscal 1990 is budgeted at $465 million a day! And who are the lenders to our federal government? Who gets the interest paid on the federal debt?

Banks, insurance companies, domestic and foreign corporations and superrich individuals.

No wonder all those corporate PAC people running the Reagan/Bush government soft peddled the big government spending issue. Hell, they're getting rich off it. The federal debt is not only their bread-and-butter, it's their lifetime guaranteed annual income. It is their estate for their heirs and progeny into the next millennium, while working people's sons and daughters and their sons and daughters will be expected to pay for it, *if* they have jobs and incomes.

The Vanishing Middle Class

The principal factor making the United States resemble a third world economy has been the growth in economic inequality. The overall distribution of jobs and income in the United States has begun to shift dramatically toward greater polarization and inequality. The broad middle level of decent-paying jobs is being substantially eroded. The bulk of new jobs is toward the bottom of the present income ladder, while only a far smaller number of technical and managerial jobs is being created at the top. What is developing is a two-tier society. The growing inequality that results threatens to make America a very different place to live, as families struggle to maintain living standards by having more members work and by incurring more and more debt. As noted elsewhere, those factors create their own tensions and problems.

Measured in constant 1977 dollars, the Bureau of Labor Statistics reported that, in May 1987, average real earnings of non-supervisory workers bought 10.3 percent less in goods and services than they did in May 1978. If it seems the wage and earnings differential between men and women is closing a little, it's not because women workers are catching up with male earnings; it is because male earnings are moving down toward women's lower wages. Today it takes two people or more working in a family to maintain the standard of living that one breadwinner could sustain before 1973. Despite the additional wage earners, median household income had fallen by 6 percent over the 1977–1987 decade.

In 1970, nearly two-thirds of all families could afford to buy a home, and it required only 21 percent of their gross monthly income to pay the mortgage. By 1986, less than one-third of families could afford to buy a home and, if they did buy one, the mortgage took 44 percent of their monthly income. In 1980, there were 28 million people without some kind of health insurance. By 1986, that number had grown to 38 million people without health insurance. Those aren't just kids and the unemployed; half those without health insurance are employed!

A study of census data by Stephen Rose noted an enormous erosion in the broad central segment of middle-income families from 1978 to 1983. In 1978, 55 percent of the U.S. population lived on household incomes of between $17,000 and $41,000. By 1983, only 42 percent lived on these middle incomes in constant dollars and the decline has accelerated since. This shift out of the middle class saw only about one household out of five moving into an income bracket higher than $41,000. Nearly four out of five dropped below the $17,000 level. Much of the reason lies in what the new jobs in the 1980s pay: during the 15 year period 1963 to 1978, one out of four new jobs created in the economy paid $4 an hour or less. During the six year period from 1978 to 1984, two out of five new jobs paid $4 an hour or less; that's below the poverty line for a full-time worker.

The sources of income were also changing in this period. Between 1979 and 1986, income from capital—from owning stocks, bonds, securities, real estate and the like—rose by 26 percent, while income from labor—from wages and salaries—dropped by 3 percent. The proportion of the population profiting from income from capital was not, however, growing. Between 1977 and 1983, the portion of American households owning stock declined from 25 percent to 19 percent.

The erosion of industrial jobs and the dominance of service jobs can be captured in one set of statistics. Of the 31 million net new jobs added in the last 25 years, only 1 million were in manufacturing. The trend away from manufacturing has been worsening. Between 1958 and 1968 manufacturing added over 3.8 million jobs. From 1968 to 1978 the manufacturing gain was less than 600,000 jobs. And in the economic slide from March 1979 to the end of 1982, U.S. manufacturing lost more than 2.8 million jobs, nearly one job of every seven, while in the same four years U.S. service industries were gaining 3.7 million jobs. Manufacturing did not share in the subsequent recovery. By 1987, after five years of "recovery," there were still 1.9 million *fewer* jobs in manufacturing than there had been in 1979; by contrast, there were almost 14 million more jobs in the service sector.

The Reagan-Bush crowd likes to crow about the number of new jobs that have come into existence during this so-called "recovery" of the past three years. What they don't tell us is that job growth has fallen by nearly a third in the 1980s compared with the 1970s. New jobs per year average 2.7 million in the 1970s but only 2 million in the 1980s. Moreover part-time jobs have increased more rapidly than full-time jobs; since 1979, part-time jobs have increased by 23 percent while full-time jobs have increased by only 16 percent. The average median wage for part-time work is $4.42 per hour, as opposed to $7.43 per hour for full-time work. Furthermore, most part-time jobs provide no health insurance, no vacation pay, no sick leave or other life support benefits.

Unfortunately, the major problems of industrial job loss are not by any means behind us. Indeed, they are continuing even in the midst of "economic recovery." Over the longer term the erosion of industrial jobs and the displacement of production workers can be expected to accelerate further, for example, with the rapid infusion of new technology into industry, the continued loss of jobs to offshore production, and the shutdowns of manufacturing firms through acquisitions, mergers, and leveraged buyouts.

Because of the press coverage, many people believe that most of the new jobs being created involve computers or take place in a sterile, white laboratory. This is simply not true.

While "high technology" occupations are experiencing rapid percentage growth rates, that rapid growth is on a relatively small base of current jobs. The result is that the numbers of new jobs that will be created over the next decade in "high tech" occupations are actually quite small. In fact, the U.S. Department of Labor projects that between 1984 and 1990, only 671,000 jobs will be added by the six out of eight occupations which show the fastest percentage growth rates and which are also generally high tech occupations. This growth in jobs precisely equals the number of jobs expected to be added by the single occupation with the largest net growth—building custodians. Stanford University researchers recently found that the number of janitors needed by 1995 will be 14 times greater than the number of computer service technicians. The only occupation which is growing rapidly both in percentage terms and in the number of jobs being created is workers in fast food restaurants—number eight on both measures of new job creation. The fastest growing occupations are the service sector jobs over there behind McDonald's Golden Arches.

Anyone reading this book may very well wake up one day within the next ten years and find out his or her job is emptying the boss's waste basket, cleaning his latrine, parking his limousine, or emptying his bedpan as a nurse's orderly. That's where the greatest number of job opportunities will be between now and 1995.

The most shocking contrast, however, is the difference in income levels. In 1984 average weekly earnings of production workers in the 20 fastest declining industries was $310, whereas in the fastest growing industries earnings were only $210, or one third less. That translated into an earnings gap of over $5,000 per year. With the exception of professional nurses, none of these rapidly expanding occupations reaches as high as 75 percent of the current national median wage. Of the top ten occupational categories for job opportunities projected by BLS over the next ten years, only two—elementary school teaching and nursing—have the prospect of paying an income that exceeds the poverty level!

The disappearing jobs pay much better than those being created. In 1985–86, good jobs lost averaged $444 per week. New service jobs gained averaged $272 per week. That's an annual difference of $8,800. Look at it another way. Union jobs pay on the average over $100 a week more than non-union jobs. And it is the unionized jobs that are being destroyed.

The change from a manufacturing economy to a service one is creating a colossal economic gap between generations of our people. It is a gap that not only threatens to impoverish us, it threatens to impoverish our kids and grandkids.

Prior to the year 1973—the year of the first OPEC oil price squeeze—young men going from age 25 to 35 could see their real earnings grow by about 125 percent, because they were enjoying the good effects of a good economy balanced between manufacturing, service and basic industries. The unionized workforce was stronger then, too. But in 1983, the young worker who was thirty-five had seen only a 16 percent increase in his earnings since he was twenty-five years old. That's a 16 percent increase in ten-year earnings for today's thirty-five-year old, compared to a 125 percent increase in ten-year earnings for the thirty-five-year old worker a decade ago.

The situation for middle-aged workers is even worse. Before 1973, the average working man passing from age forty to fifty saw his earnings increase in real money by 25 to 30 percent. Wages were growing throughout the economy. But in 1983, the average fifty-year old working man was actually earning 14 percent *less* than he had when he was forty in 1973.

What we are witnessing is the passing of a relatively high-wage generation and the coming of a low-wage generation. Economist Barry Bluestone calls it "the great U-turn in wage growth."

These shifts toward greater inequality have been accentuated by the skewed impact of this Administration's tax reductions and cuts in support for low-income families, by high real interest rates, and by higher unemployment.

The changing industrial structure provides them little or no hope for escaping their deprivation. Along with blue collar male workers displaced from the manufacturing sector, those who do find menial jobs in this high unemployment economy are destined to constitute the ranks of the working poor.

"Statistics," as one sage put it, "are people with tears wiped off." We need to remember that.

The massive restructuring of our economy and of working people's lives which is underway has not been debated in Congress or in the election campaign. Our elected representatives in government have never had a chance to vote on it. For the most part, this economic restructuring has been decided behind closed doors in the boardrooms of Corporate America.

The legacy of the Reagan Administration, the growth of the Corporate State, and the sovereign power of multinational corporations mean that the American dream no longer seems to be embodied in the solid virtues of hard work, production of hard goods with high utilitarian value and value added, or provision of the basic necessities of life and services of civilization. The American dream is no longer enunciated in terms of full employment, or even rewarding employment for those who are permitted to work. It is instead transferred into the maniacal desire to escape from rational and responsible economic and social behavior, by throwing the dice in one do-or-die crap game after another. Winner-take-all and devil-take-the-hindmost are the stakes of intellectually and morally bankrupt economic handicappers. And that's the name of the game in today's cynical economic and social polity.

A long time ago, John Maynard Keynes, who was certainly no Marxist or leftist, analyzed a global economy characterized by massive unemployment, famines and rising poverty on every continent, intensive concentrations of capital on national and global scales, and a paralysis of international trade and uncontrollable protectionism. All of that was in an environment of escalating arms spending and encroaching militarism. It was the 1930s, but it sure sounds familiar.

Here's what the venerable Lord Keynes said about that situation: "The decadent international but individualistic capitalism in the hands of which we find ourselves . . . is not a success. It is not intelligent. It is not beautiful. It is not just. It is not virtuous. And it doesn't deliver the goods."

That's precisely what we can say today.

ALTERNATIVES FOR THE 1990s

You know what the No. 1 growth industry is in this country?

It's not home computers or silicon chips—it's garage sales and yard sales!

You know which stores are experiencing record sales?

Used clothing shops!

You know what kind of "enterprise" is on the rise?

Theft, burglary, armed robbery, homicide and white collar crimes in the suites.

American trade unions and American workers have to realize we no longer enjoy the highest standard of living in the world. Our bosses do, but we don't.

Our employers have to realize they are mismanaging our nation into a state of perpetual decline. They cannot be trusted to manage in the best national interest or international interests. We have to show them a better way.

Our politicians have to realize there is another way to run an economy. It is not the supply-side, trickle-down, "free" market way. It is the West European way, and partially the Japanese way, where full employment is given top priority; where trade unions are strong and central to economic decision making; where the public interest and common good take precedence over private greed; where short-term profit maximization gives way to long-term planning and investment priorities; where economic democracy is as much an ideal as political democracy; where the human factor of production—labor—counts for more than land and capital; and where technology serves the workforce and society, rather than abuses or annihilates them.

How can the United States achieve those goals?

We say look to the Western European democratic socialist countries which match or beat our performance on almost every economic front.

While they now have problems with slow growth and unemployment, their people don't suffer the way most people in similar circumstances in the United States do.

First, those democratic socialist systems have unemployment pay plans and job training and retraining programs that are virtually without limit and are automatically activated when workers become jobless.

Second, employers—many of whom are the same employers we have in the United States—can't fire workers willy-nilly. They have to get permission first, and in some countries that permission must come from the workers themselves, their trade unions, the government, or all three.

Third, employers can't just close their doors, shut down, and pack up and leave town, stranding workers and entire communities in their wake. They have to get permission to do that, too, and they have to cooperate with workers, their trade unions and the government to construct a viable economic alternative to unemployment and economic dislocation.

Fourth, employers in democratic socialist countries don't waste energy and resources fighting and busting trade unions, resisting beneficial economic, health and social regulations. There are no right-to-work-for-less laws in those countries—except one recently enacted by Margaret Thatcher's government in England, but England is in the same bad shape as the United States.

There are no cheap wages or cheap labor in those countries. Six of the top ten countries have higher wage and compensation levels than we do in the United States. Among the top fourteen democratic industrial nations, the United States ranks 13th in annual real wage increases.

Those countries also have all the things that conservatives in government and Corporate America say we can't afford such as national health insurance, paid parental leave and child care, good public housing programs, strict environmental and pollution control laws, and strong trade unions. So if we're looking for a way out of the mess we're in, look to our friendly competitors in Western Europe.

Maybe the reason why our multinational corporations are investing so heavily in democratic socialist countries in spite of their higher wage scales—and 72 percent of all U.S. direct foreign investment goes to already industrial developed countries—is because things like health insurance, retirement income, housing costs, and job relocation and retraining costs are all paid for by those taxpayers. In democratic socialist countries, our employers don't have to pay fringe benefit costs. They only have to pay wage costs. Maybe that is why they love doing business in democratic socialist countries.

And maybe a little democratic socialism would go a long way toward evening things up in this country!

Consider health care. Health care clauses have long been one of the major issues in collective bargaining and have become one of the most expensive components in any collective bargaining package. We can make a significant cost reduction in total compensation simply by getting health insurance off the bargaining table by replacing it with legislation establishing a comprehensive system of national health security like they have in Europe and Japan.

The Japanese approach and the Western European approach are different. We prefer the latter. Western European attitudes and traditions have far more in common with ours than the Japanese do. But there are many similarities between the Japanese and European models. Both prefer specific business subsidies over tax incentives, and they are targeted for special purposes and into selected industrial sectors. Government, banking and finance, and enterprise management sit down with trade unions to discuss, develop and plan investment and production decisions. These joint decision-making and strategy sessions may take place at the enterprise level, on a regional level, on the national level, or on a specific industrial sector level. The object of all such planning is to not only minimize costs, increase productivity, and secure a favorable share of world markets; the objective is also to achieve full employment. There are, therefore, extensive job training and retraining programs and the governments constantly survey, track and design training programs for new and displaced workers.

Excluding Japan, where a two-tiered labor force exists—one in highly unionized basic industries and the other tier found in nonunion subcontracting and supplier industries—most employers in the Western industrial democracies don't waste time or money busting unions or preventing unions from forming. In all the West European industrial democracies, with the exception of France, respective labor forces are anywhere from 50 to 90 percent organized. In Scandinavia, West Germany and the Benelux countries, workers have higher wage levels, and more government-provided fringe benefits, as well as a higher quality of life and standard of living than we have here in the United States.

For those who say this nation cannot afford to base its economic activity on the itemized principles of an economic and social contract, then we say take a look at those mature countries which are beating us in the trade game. We don't believe the people of this country want to buy into the notion that American workers must reduce their level of living to the world's least common denominator in order to compete in world commerce. Raising living standards, not exploitation of cheap labor, creates markets, provides economic and social stability, and ensures peace and prosperity. That's just as true here at home as it is in the Third and Fourth Worlds.

So how do we get there from here?

The first step is to establish what our real goals for the economy are:

- that every American has a right to a job and employment and a full-employment economy;
- that every American has a right to a fair share of the nation's income and wealth;
- that every worker has a guaranteed right to organize and through collective action the right to participate in private and public investment policy decisions; and
- that every American has the right to enjoy the pursuit of and the fruits of peace.

We believe the most acceptable, effective and ethical means to achieve our ends is through social control of the nation's economic resources.

The second step is to begin to take practical measures to achieve those goals.

First, we don't give in at the bargaining table. We don't indulge in concession bargaining without checking the facts first: without checking the tax handouts our employers may be receiving, without checking the boss' books, and without setting up technology control committees.

Second, we don't rely on the Democratic Party to do our job for us. Remember, it was all but a handful of Democrats who made Reaganomics possible. Boll Weevil Democrats brokered Reaganomics and, when the fight began, too many liberals left the room. Left to themselves, too many Democrats try to be more Republican than Republicans or give us the same old economic baloney, sliced a little thinner. The last thing this country needs is another Republican Party.

What this means in political terms is that the trade union movement has to push the Democratic Party onto a progressive path—a path toward peace and prosperity, not war and poverty. We have to begin to rebuild America, not continue to destroy it by selling it short on the altar of the free enterprise mythology.

Rebuilding America's economy is as much about economic democracy, freedom, control and fairness as it is about profits, losses, efficiency and the hard facts of economic growth. We can judge the success of economic policy by how well it preserves and strengthens the people's democratic values; by how much it extends the democratic process from politics into economics; by whether it provides economic and social justice for all; by what amount it redistributes the nation's income and wealth, and hence political power, toward equality; and by whether it does these things in the context of repairing millions of busted dreams and fulfilling unfulfilled dreams or whether it plays to the basest instincts endemic in current social Darwinism.

There is a tremendous backlog of unmet economic and social needs in this country. They include energy conversion, low cost housing, airport construction, urban mass transit systems, rapid rail transportation, water, sewer and street systems, child and day care centers and programs, and special services for senior citizens, the handicapped, and shut-ins. There are dozens of unmet needs in our severely distressed cities, particularly those that are designated hardship cities.

God knows there is enough work that needs to be done in this country to provide full employment for everyone. And there are already more than enough workers with skills lying idle.

Yet, we throw away the resources to meet those needs. We discard the labor power of the millions who are involuntary members of the standing army of the unemployed and underemployed. A full-employment economy will not only benefit our unemployed brothers and sisters, it will enable us to meet those desperate social and economic needs.

Full employment would mean more than that. The three million working poor would have to be paid more than the minimum wage. The 32 million people in poverty could cast off the stigma of welfare, food stamps, unemployment compensation, and social scorn. Potential union members would not fear loss of their jobs for union activities. We in the unions could demand something more than modest contract settlements that do not keep pace with inflation and we could halt the skid of real wages, that is, what we have to spend after taxes are deducted and inflation is accounted for. The flight of runaway plants from the unionized areas of the country to right-to-slave states and nations would not be based on cheap labor. Our working people would not be afraid to speak against environmental, health and safety hazards and violations on the job. Class, ethnic and racial conflicts would disappear in a full-employment economy. In short, full employment would mean an end to keeping workers, unions and minorities "in their place" and at each other's throats.

A full-employment economy would mean that the selected few at the top of the pyramid would have to relinquish or share some of their wealth and power.

No wonder the quasi-sovereign corporations and their political friends panic when full-employment programs and policies are proposed. The select few at the top of the pyramid have a vested interest in maintaining chronic and high unemployment. No wonder their hired guns in the universities' economics departments and business schools and in the Corporate State's wholly owned subsidiaries, the so-called "mainstream" economic think tanks, tell us that full employment cannot be achieved.

They are dead wrong. Full employment can be achieved. It *is* achieved in democratic socialist countries like Norway and Sweden. It can be achieved in the United States too.

NOTES

1. Walter Heller, "Activist Government: Key to Growth," *Challenge* magazine, March/April 1986.

2. Reagan's policies had their costs here too: periods of unemployment have grown longer. In 1979, it took the average worker who lost his or her job 10.8 weeks to find another; in 1987, at the height of the so-called boom, it took the average worker 14.5 weeks to find another job.

3. The statistics on the distribution of wealth are derived from "Survey of Consumer Finances, 1983," *Federal Reserve Bulletin* (September 1984), Table 13, p. 689, and U.S. Congress Joint Economic Committee, "The Concentration of Wealth in the United States," by James D. Smith, July 1986, Tables 4 and 5, as cited in Lawrence Mishel and Jacqueline Simon, *The State of Working America* (Washington: Economic Policy Institute, 1988), Tables 55 and 56. The figures in the JEC report have been adjusted to account for survey error.

4. U.S. Department of Commerce, Census Bureau, Series P-60 (*Money Income of Households, Persons, and Families in the United States* and *Characteristics of the Low Income Population*), no. 97, table 22, p. 43, and no. 161, table 4, as cited in Lawrence Mishel and Jacqueline Simon, *The State of Working America,* Table 14.

5. Consider the question of Boesky and justice for a minute. Boesky got a week's notice so he could make a cool $7 million before he was arrested and turned government witness. Meantime, some jobless citizen loses his unemployment compensation, his mortgage is foreclosed and he doesn't have money to pay for his kids' school lunches, so he goes out and tries to knock off a gas station, he gets caught with a couple of hundred dollars or less, and the system sends him to the slammer and throws away the key. His spouse and kids are left to their fates of a free enterprise jungle and a grudging welfare state.

6. The average American corporate chief executive officer receives about twice as much in relation to production workers as his German equivalent and 50 percent more than his Japanese equivalent does (Mishel and Simon, *The State of Working America,* p. 18, figure 9).

7. Robert H. Hayes and William J. Abernathy, "Managing Our Way to Economic Decline," *Harvard Business Review* 58, no. 4 (July/August 1980), pp. 67–77.

8. Gregg Easterbrook, "The Myth of Oppressive Corporate Taxes," *Atlantic Monthly* 249 (June 1982), pp. 59–66.

9. Corporate tax data is available from Citizens for Tax Justice in Washington, D. C. Their reports on Reagan's corporate tax giveaway are *Corporate Income Taxes in the Reagan Years* (1984), *Corporate Taxpayers and Corporate Freeloaders* (1985), *130 Reasons Why We Need Tax Reform* (1986), and *The Corporate Tax Comeback: Corporate Income Taxes After Tax Reform* (1988).

10. National Council of Senior Citizens, *Notes on Revenue Raising for FY '87* (Washington, D.C.: 1986).

_____

America in the global economy

There was a time when America was an island unto itself. Our democratic form of government and our belief in liberty and equality set us apart from the decadent European monarchies. We were the New World; they, the Old. We were economically self sufficient, and we had a whole continent to settle. The oceans protected our splendid isolation. Despite occasional flights of rhetoric about international labor solidarity, the American union movement shared this national sense that we were set apart—perhaps even elevated above—the rest of mankind.

That day is past. For better or worse, we are part of a global economy. Any analysis of the economic and social environment in which American trade unions must function today has to include the international setting as well as the domestic one. In economics, the two are interrelated in the global panorama of change, uncertainty and chaos in trade, deficit financing and currency fluctuations.

Ever since conservative governments gained power at the end of the 1960s and terminated the Bretton Woods fixed exchange system by implementing floating rates while simultaneously embarking on an "incomes policy," working people have borne the brunt of disruptions in the international and national economies. The crisis was exacerbated by the OPEC Cartel's move to control and increase the price of oil in 1973/74 and in 1979/80.

The United States, as well as other Western industrialized nations, was plunged into deep recession—the worst in 40 years at the bottom of its trough in 1975, and worse again at the next bottom in 1982—

and mild recovery since then has largely bypassed manufacturing. The result is an economy in the United States which features prevailing high unemployment, a steady erosion of real income and a redistribution of income away from the earned income sector to the unearned sector depicted in the last chapter.

Much of the cause of our domestic economic problems lies in the fact that we have been integrated into a global economy on terms dictated principally by multinational corporations (MNCs) that owe allegiance to no country but only to greed. The development of a global economy is not necessarily bad, but the terms the multinational companies have dictated are awful.

Multinational corporations have done on a global scale what the rise of the conglomerate as a form of corporate organization has done to the domestic economy. The conglomerates' diversification, vertical integration and horizontal acquisitions all have led to the concentration of economic power. That produces administered prices and markets. Anti-trust action, even in those few instances where an effort has been made to implement anti-trust laws, is almost totally frustrated by long, drawn-out legal maneuverings and proceedings. Attempts to regulate and vertically divest the U.S. petroleum giants is a classic example of the failure of anti-trust action and even congressional action. Feeble attempts to control the far-flung enterprises of conglomerates such as ITT are further evidence of the power of the corporate conglomerate and the inability of the government to regulate it in the public interest.

For unions the usefulness of the strike as an economic weapon is diminished by the conglomerate's ability to cover a strike loss in one company with the profits of another or other companies. Trade unions have responded with coordinated bargaining by the several unions that may have contracts with the conglomerate. Even so, coordinated bargaining is made difficult because the real decision maker or power center of the employer is often disguised or far removed from the bargaining table. The result can be long and protracted negotiations. Fortunately, trade unions have been more successful in negotiating common contract termination dates with companies under the same conglomerate umbrella and within highly concentrated industries.

The difficulties posed by conglomerates pale beside those created by the multinational corporations. The rise of the multinational corporation is a relatively new phenomenon with which trade unions and governments the world over must contend.

Seventy percent of the world's multinational corporations are, in theory, American owned. But, multinationals are virtually governments unto themselves. They transcend nation states. Their daily decisions affect the lives of millions of people around the globe.

Multinational corporations' intra-company pricing policies, business transactions, profit-loan swaps, and banking tie-ins mean that orthodox fiscal and monetary adjustments to the national economy do not faze them. Their overseas operations are free from domestic economic restraints. Profits made overseas are not taxable, unless brought back into this country. Taxes paid to foreign countries are treated as tax credits and written off dollar for dollar here at home.

In the case of wholly-owned subsidiaries, multinationals can play two basic games. Through the use of intra-company transfers, each subsidiary can charge the other as it pleases for parts, components and services. Thus, accounting procedures are employed to show profits in countries with low or no taxes, and to show losses in countries with high taxes. Some multinationals avoid paying taxes almost everywhere in the world. Currently, there is no way to prevent these practices, since intra-company transfers are not policed, audited or required to be reported in any objective manner.

A second basic game multinationals play is profit-loan swaps. In this case, where one subsidiary shows a profit or where the parent company at home shows a profit, the multinational escapes taxation by loaning the profit to another subsidiary. The lender can even charge interest on that loan and the borrowing subsidiary deduct it from whatever tax bill it may incur.

Many multinationals have their own financing subsidiaries or hold a favored relationship with one of the multinational banking firms.

The critical question for the U.S. government and other national governments is: How can monetary and tax policies be effective when they do not and cannot reach the world's largest corporations? To be sure, multinationals will take advantage of any tax breaks or tax incentives that may come their way, but they can escape tax increases or loophole closures. Similarly, what do multinationals care if the Federal Reserve Board raises the discount rate, alters the reserve ratio or decreases the money supply? They have their own financial and banking system, which is impervious to current forms of government management of credit.

Since the advent of floating exchange rates and Eurodollars and Asiadollars, the multinationals have, in effect, had their own currency system. The Federal Reserve Board has no control over U.S. dollars deposited in overseas banks and has no fully reliable way of knowing their amount, although various central banks do provide periodic estimates.

In addition to Eurodollars and Asiadollars, multinationals have large deposits of and can manipulate other currencies. Very often they pay off accounts with weak currencies and receive payments in strong currencies. Through their financial and banking arms, they can also indulge in outright speculation to increase their holdings of various currencies, as exchange rates "float" and fluctuate from day to day.

All this gives the multinationals extraordinary economic power. The implications for national economic policy makers are grim. The tools they have used since the war to manage their domestic economies are now antiquated. National monetary policy and fiscal policy as tools for managing the economy work only as long as the boundaries of the nation state have economic meaning. Today they don't. Government policy makers have been outflanked by the multinationals. Few national governments have come to grips with the multinationals so far, and there has been nothing like the international cooperative, coordinated regional or industrial planning necessary to insure orderly international trade and worldwide economic development. Instead we have rampant Economic Darwinism.

THE SOVEREIGN CORPORATION

The behavior and, more and more frequently, the announced goals of the multinational corporation indicate a quest for sovereignty in a global sense. That quest transcends and clashes with orthodox notions of national sovereignty. The drive to control and dominate is a natural phenomenon in Darwin's animal kingdom. Is it surprising, then, that autonomous and self perpetuating corporate oligopolies, which have already united closely with home-based national governments and have become an integral part of the policy making and administrative processes of the national government, look beyond the nation state for new territory to conquer?

Multinational corporate sovereignty overrides and overshadows national sovereignty wherever and whenever it chooses. We see evidence of this global sovereignty in corporate manipulations of international exchange rates, and financial and credit markets, often contrary to national interests and in spite of national central bank policies. Thus, Paul Volcker's tight money and high interest rates ruined small businesses and the housing market, but it did not deter U.S.-based multinationals from getting access to cheaper sources of money and credit. They can go beyond the Federal Reserve's boundaries and meet their needs from huge pools of Asiadollars, Eurodollars, or any number of other currencies where they keep dollars on deposit, or know where dollars are available. The Federal Reserve System does not impede or modify sovereign corporate behavior.

Similarly, such sovereignty permits multinational corporations to circumvent and ignore the home nation's environmental, safety and health and labor standards. They simply transfer capital, technology, management and production to another nation that has lower standards or none at all. Corporate sovereigns can and do export pollution and environmental hazards, as well as the nation's industrial base and jobs.

While minimizing costs and maximizing profits are the conventional rationales for this global sovereignty, those objectives are often secondary to penetrating, securing and dominating resources and markets. Today's multinational corporation acts more like the monarchy of colonialism than the enlightened capitalist of recent modern times.

Like the kings and queens of Ricardo's day, multinational corporations band together in alliances of convenience to achieve resource, marketing and territorial domination. General Motors buys into Isuzu and Toyota. Ford buys into Toyo Kogo. Chrysler buys into Mitsubishi. Toyota and GM produce jointly in California. American Motors sells controlling interest to France's Renault, and then later Renault sells it to Chrysler. International Harvester makes book directly with China to produce there. So does John Deere. NASA approved the use of Chinese rockets to boost Australia's space shuttle. Boeing makes a deal with the Indonesian government to produce the new hydrofoil there, and another deal with China to produce the 737 airliner there. Lockheed and McDonnell Douglas contract with Japanese firms to co-produce military hardware and components, including entire weapons systems, such as the F-15 fighter plane. U.S. shipbuilders build their ships in Korea, and U.S. shipping companies hoist the flag of Liberia, Panama, or some other country, on their vessels to avoid U.S. maritime labor standards.

American corporations have adapted themselves speedily to the new international environment. In their pursuit of the almighty dollar, they quickly jettisoned whatever sense of obligation they had to the national community.

The Chairman of the Board of Kearny Trechor Machine Tool Company, George Marakis, for example, told a 1984 meeting of the Great Lakes Governors' Commission on the Machine Tool Industry in Cincinnati why Kearny Treachor's machine tools are now being built in Japan and his company merely imports them for assembly and resale here in the United States: "Kearny Trechor will remain in the machine tool business, but that doesn't mean we have to build machine tools. All we have to do is make money for our shareholders."

That just about says it all. Machine tool company executives and shareholders get a return through such joint ventures. Only the production workers and their communities lose.

A Phillips Oil Company official put it even more succinctly on behalf of the oil companies during the first OPEC price crunch: "We owe no patriotic duty to any country."

Whenever a U.S.-based multinational transfers capital, technology and production abroad and then ships back components or finished products for sale in the home market, it adds to the red ink trade deficit. Clearly, the U.S. multinational corporation is the foreign competitor, whether it buys into foreign firms or establishes its own foreign operations and subsidiaries. Its interest conflicts with the national interest.

The corporate quest for sovereignty and the ensuing global mobility of capital are at the root of contemporary chaos in the domestic and international economies.

Current monetary and fiscal policies not only aid and abet these corporate sovereigns, they constitute another source of change. American monetary policy tightly controls the supply of money and credit. That makes for high interest rates. Coupled with a fiscal policy that has produced history's largest national deficits, primarily to finance the trillion dollar military buildup, the price of money and credit at home is further inflated. Foreign capitalists, though, find it lucrative to invest in our national debt and to take advantage of our high interest rates. That made the dollar an overvalued currency relative to others in the mid-1980s, but that didn't hinder the corporate sovereigns. Things expensive at home are cheap overseas. That means they can buy more land, labor, and plant and equipment for the dollar overseas than they can at home. And invest overseas is just what they did. It's a neat case of dovetailing the cost-minimizing, profit-maximizing tactic with the market and resource control strategy.

The overvalued dollar further distorted the trade picture. It made exports expensive and imports cheap. Our MNCs were happy to ship us those imports from their overseas plants, increasing the surge of imports that has this nation on a ghostly road toward deindustrialization.

Not all countries take this view. Japan, for instance, isn't about to surrender its sovereignty to U.S. multinational corporations. On the contrary, Japan, Inc. is striving mightily and, in many well publicized cases, successfully to subdue U.S. sovereignty. Japan, Inc. has its own invasion strategy and tactics. Unlike the U. S. corporate strategy, Japan is using an undervalued currency and a tightly protected home industry and market to penetrate and control foreign territory. Wherever Japan, Inc. goes, it flies the Japanese flag.

But wherever America Inc. goes, it flies an ubiquitous flag of convenience.

That makes a difference, and that is at the root of a lot of negative economic and industrial change. It remains to be seen whether corporate sovereignty will win out over national sovereignty in a new international economic order and global political economy.

THE MYTHS OF "FREE" TRADE
AND COMPARATIVE ADVANTAGE

Spurred by the self interest of the multinationals, the world trade scene is a far cry from free trade. The multinational free trade doctrine is based not on comparative advantage or even efficient allocation of resources, but on maximization of profits. There is a basic clash of corporate financial goals and national economic development goals. Multinationals employ labor saving, wage reduction technology as part of a basic corporate strategy that destroys jobs at home and abroad. Licensing agreements, co-production agreements and complete industrial facilities, or turn-key factories enable U.S. multinationals to transfer technology out of the country and often into undemocratic, non-union low wage countries. This is as true today for the capital-intensive aerospace, electrical and mechanical engineering, electronic, machine tool and shipbuilding industries, as it is for the labor-intensive light industries such as apparel, textiles, shoes, leather and plastics.

The result is that, contrary to the free trade doctrine, American MNC's employ few workers abroad and no markets are developed there. At home, the market for goods and products being produced overseas for export back to the United States is undermined by unemployment, underemployment, decreased productivity and depressed incomes.

It is a cruel irony that many nations in the underdeveloped world are rich in raw materials, have a huge labor force and vast potential markets yet are in fact so poor. An extremely small elite and a privileged ruling class live in luxury; a very small middle class of bureaucrats and business overseers live in relative material comfort; and the overwhelming mass of people live in abject poverty. There are absolutely no statistics to indicate the gap between the haves and the have-nots is narrowing in those countries. It seems to be widening instead.

In historical perspective, the so-called "New" International Economic Order began 20 years ago and has developed in four stages.

The first stage occurred in the mid-1950s when light manufacture and labor intensive firms began their exodus to foreign shores. No large machinery or large plants were involved. Capital investment in plant and equipment was relatively small. The decisive cost of production was labor. These firms produced plastics, toys, footwear, apparel, leather products and electronic assembly components. They required work that could be done any place in the world, because skill was not required. In that stage the American worker earning roughly $2.00 to $2.50 an hour was pitted against Korean, Malaysian, Singaporese, Pakistani, Hong Kong, Taiwanese, and Mexican workers making a few cents per hour. The wage scale in America has increased since the 1950s, but those in the developing countries have not increased appreciably. Korean hourly manufacturing compensation, for example, was only $1.69 in 1987, 13 percent of the American rate. International wage parity is a goal yet unrealized, but it is the key to a "level playing field."

The second stage of the New Economic Order came in the mid-1960s, when Japan launched its program to buy U.S. technology in order to cut its own research and development costs, and thereby take a short cut on the route to economic growth. It became heavily engaged in electronics, data processing, sound video systems and cassettes, sewing machines, electrical fixtures and appliances, nuts, bolts and pipe fittings, and sensitive instrumentation and measuring devices.

Other nations picked up the Japanese model and, with the lure of cheap labor, enticed American-based firms into their countries. They demanded that "their" American-owned factories be more than simple assembly operations employing only unskilled and semi-skilled labor. They demanded full-fledged capital intensive operations, requiring skilled labor and sophisticated knowledge. They achieved it through the purchase of technology, co-production arrangements, joint production ventures with U.S. manufacturers, and outright international industrial blackmail through "offset" demands, i.e., those countries would buy U.S. goods and products *only if* they could produce part of them or receive other work in the deal.

In this stage, the export of capital investment began to erode the free trade argument that the American shift out of labor-intensive industry would increase production and employment in the more highly skilled, capital intensive, advanced technology industries. Investment capital, high technology and managerial know-how were shipped, sold, leased or licensed overseas. Air transport, machine tool, ship-building, auto and marine engines and parts, and sophisticated aerospace and communications equipment all became products of foreign countries. Even the Pentagon began making deals to produce military goods and component parts overseas.

Here is just one example of how one country maneuvered into small aircraft production.

About ten years ago, Brazil, once the number-one buyer of U.S.-produced light aircraft, decided to cop the small aircraft market in South America. It had neither the technology nor the capital to begin production. It solved its dilemma with a six-step plan.

First, the Brazilian government barred U.S. aircraft export into Brazil by levying prohibitive taxes on importation of small planes. Second,

Brazil negotiated a co-production agreement with the Piper Aircraft Company for light aircraft on a tariff-exempt basis. Part of the craft was produced in the United States and part was produced in Brazil. Third, Brazil then made new agreements to increase its share of production and marketing. Fourth, Brazil replaced U.S.-made parts and components with Brazilian-made equivalents. Fifth, Brazil then had the means for total production of the Piper Aircraft—parts, components and labor—without the Piper trademark, and the sixth stage saw Brazil take over the market in South America and much of Africa. Recently it has even sold planes to the Federal Express Company here in the United States.

This leaves the Brazilians happy for obvious reasons. Piper is also happy. It gets a share of the profits and royalties for its licenses. Only Piper's American employees were cut out of the deal with loss of jobs, incomes and security. It was not just chance that American aerospace employment dropped from 1.5 million in 1968 to 895,000 in 1978.

There are similar examples involving GTE in Algeria, Fairchild Camera and Instrument Corporation, McDonnell Douglas and others. More recently the General Electric–RCA–Thomson–Snecma (France) combine has resulted in a large transfer of capital, technology and jobs from the United States to Europe.

The third stage in the development of the so-called New International Economic Order came with the OPEC cartel move to use crude oil, a strategic raw material, to apply supply and price levers in international trade. We cannot overlook the fact that U.S. petroleum companies had and still have an interest in the oil cartel. The OPEC cartel's oil price shocks during the 1970s ignited the fires of inflation, impacted negatively on oil-importing nations' trade balances, led industrial managers to engage in a mad scramble for cost-cutting efficiency measures. Other raw commodity and strategic material producing nations quickly followed the OPEC example. Bauxite, copper, chromium, manganese, tin, rubber, coffee, and even tea, became the means to demand U.S. capital, technology, and industrial development.

In the midst of this turmoil, the private banking community, never slow to spot the goose that lays the golden egg, and usually the first to look for the silver lining in the dark cloud, seized opportunity from the clutches of chaos, and, with other people's money, set about to recycle OPEC's petrodollars in the form of extensive loans to impoverished firms and nations that had been pronged on the oil-import hook. Since desperate governments were quite willing to put up their full faith and credit as collateral for loans, and since agencies like the International Monetary Fund and regional development banks could practically guarantee the repayment schedule for those poor countries' loans, then how could the bankers lose?

But, of course, the debt crunch ultimately did hit. The loans turned bad. The banks were threatened. Ultimately both business and government decisionmakers chose consciously to support the overvalued dollar at the expense of U.S. manufacturing and employment. This choice was primarily made to bail out those private U.S. banks with badly overextended loans to Third World nations. The overvalued dollar made imports cheaper, and debtor nations needed to export to earn dollars to repay the banks. It was a short-run ploy to save the banks. But the cost was high: the ruin of our own domestic manufacturing base.

The fourth stage of the development of the "New" International Order began with passage of the 1974 Trade Adjustment Act. Under that Act, Title V provided for a Generalized System of Preferences (GSP), which gave duty free access to U.S. markets to 140 countries for over 2,700 products. At trade union insistence, subsequent legislation has made granting of this duty-free privilege conditional upon those countries meeting certain labor and human rights standards.

Those nations did not reciprocate. They erected their own tariff barriers, import quotas, made industry-to-industry agreements with other countries and implemented other protectionist measures. Japan forbids most competing U.S. imports. So do Australia, Argentina, and Brazil. So do Eastern European nations. And so do the Soviet Union and China.

Cut it any way you like, "free" trade is a one-way street and the consequences are not surprising. When American corporations cannot penetrate foreign markets with their U.S.-produced products, they do the next logical thing. They close down at home and sell, license, or export partial or entire production operations abroad.

The bitter irony is that, in the midst of this flight of capital and jobs and income loss, the business community's pleas for investment funds reverberated through the halls of Congress all the way to the White House, culminating in "supply-side," trickle-down economics. Meanwhile, every dollar that goes overseas means one less dollar for investment here at home.

New York went bankrupt, but Tokyo and Munich did fine.

American corporations' quasi-sovereignty serves only corporate interests. For the past two decades, corporate dominance of the economic decision-making processes has led to the export of capital and technological resources in many industries, with little or no thought given to the consequences here at home.

The result is our declining industrial base.

The U.S. trade deficits mounted to hit an astonishing $171 billion in 1987. Jobs continue to be exported by American corporations investing abroad, and high unemployment remains chronic. Each $1 billion in that trade deficit costs us more than 25,000 jobs. The 1987 trade deficit translates into more than 4 million jobs lost.[1] A balanced trade ledger would damned near cut the official unemployment rate in half, and the tax revenues generated would cut our astronomical federal budget deficit too!

It is little wonder that the average monthly U.S. trade deficit continued to exceed $12 billion in 1988. It is also little wonder that the State, Treasury, and Commerce Departments cannot agree on what to do about our declining trade position. Nor is it surprising that trade negotiations are frustrating, to say the least.[2] Given Corporate America's entanglement in foreign economies, probably no one really knows who represents whom. It is only certain that the national interests of the multinational corporations are obscure to say the least.

The real international scene is a far cry from the free trade notion which is preached by ideological airheads who consider themselves above the real world of work and who are blind to the differences between "free" trade and fair trade.

Free trade is based on the academic theory of *comparative advantage.* That doctrine says that each country produces what it is best suited for and trades it to other nations for the goods they produce most efficiently. Why build greenhouses in Minnesota to grow bananas? There is an intrinsic sense to the theory in agricultural economies and early industrial economies.

But the industrial world is different today. Comparative advantages have to do more with political and economic organization than with climate or natural resources. America's comparative advantages are said to lie in skilled and trained labor, publicly financed research and development, a technology lead, abundant capital and managerial knowhow. I have some doubt about the latter myself.

The main comparative advantages of some other industrialized nations are their closed economic systems and protectionist measures. The main comparative advantages in developing and underdeveloped countries are autocratic governments, an abundance of cheap labor, supplies of a few strategic raw materials and commodities, and lack of environmental and labor protection standards.

A goodly portion of their "comparative advantage" is actually a function of our own distorted tax code. A cluster of foreign investment incentives are stuck in the tax code thicket: the foreign investment tax credit, deferred taxes on foreign income, the Overseas Private Investment Corporation, the Caribbean Basin Initiative, and permissive tax harbor and tax haven dodges are among them.

The truth is that the free trade doctrine is based, not on comparative advantage or even efficient allocation of resources, but on nationalistic interests. Only the U.S. government attempts to play by the rules of free trade dogma, but it is undermined by the flight of U.S.-based multinational corporations overseas and the flight of capital in quest of profit maximization and a quick, easy buck.

In the process, we are told that free trade will result in lower consumer prices here at home. The only study I have seen bearing on this subject indicates that the mark-up on imported products, from manufacture to retail, ranges from 200 percent to 400 percent and more. Importers don't reduce consumer prices but they do increase profits.

At the same time, we look abroad to see if this free trade doctrine is creating jobs or fostering economic growth there. The one characteristic of global corporate strategy is that it destroys jobs at home and abroad. Multinationals employ labor-displacing, wage-reducing technologies. They do not make efficient use of abundant unskilled manpower in the less developed countries, and they abandon skilled manpower in the U.S. Relatively few workers are employed overseas and markets are not developed there for the products produced there. Here at home, the U.S. market is undermined by unemployment, underemployment, decreased productivity and depressed income levels, creating our own underdeveloped economy.

The bottom line is this: someone has to buy that which is produced. Exploited workers in developing countries aren't paid enough to buy the products they are producing. Unemployed workers, part-time workers, low-wage service sector workers, and bankrupt farmers here in America can't buy those products either. The current international trading system is a clear cut case of exploiting foreign and domestic labor markets instead of creating consumer markets through improved labor standards, wages, hours, working conditions, and better standards of living generally.

In short the free trade doctrine doesn't work in the real world.

We see the U.S.-based multinational corporations turning their backs on their country of origin, hauling down the Stars and Stripes to hoist their own nondescript flags of convenience or the skull and crossbones of global profiteering. It is not a pretty sight. It degrades the coin of the realm, debases our American character and destroys our American dream.

When U.S. companies move capital and technology overseas and produce over there, then at that point they are the foreign competitor!

What's good for their balance sheet and income statement is not necessarily good for America's.

THE IMPACT OF CORPORATE PIRACY

This system of unlicensed global piracy by the multinational corporations is not increasing the nation's wealth or the people's prosperity. It is a zero-sum game. Flight of capital, technology and jobs creates unemployment and undermines the domestic market. Exploitation of an already exploited working class in dictatorial or struggling nations creates no market there either. Impoverished workers either at home or abroad cannot consume that which they produce.

The flight of U.S. corporations to exploit cheap and downtrodden labor not only violates international standards of human decency, it has cost U.S. workers 5 million jobs in the 1980s and thrown millions of other once well-paid union members in manufacturing into menial and low-paying service sector servitude. It denies opportunity to millions of first-time entrants into the labor force. Meanwhile, U.S.-based multinational corporations are racking up exorbitant profits, on which they pay little or no taxes to Uncle Sam.

For all this sacrifice, American workers do not see any improvement in the lot of their counterparts in developing and underdeveloped countries. Unemployment there continues to run 25 percent to 40 percent and that does not include underemployment.

The dimensions of global unemployment are truly staggering. Of the 750 million people who will enter the world's labor force between now and the year 2000, 90 percent of them will be in those fragile economies of the developing and undeveloped world. The key resource in the Third World is now, and will continue to be, low wage labor, and that is emerging as *the* decisive competitive force in world trade.

So far, the shakers and movers in U.S. policy circles have opted officially to ignore this wage competition, while at the same time permitting it to erode U.S. labor and living standards. Only we in the trade unions are openly discussing this festering problem with American and other industrialized nations' workers. To add insult to injury, unions are forbidden in such profit centers and export platforms as Singapore, Korea, Malaysia, Hong Kong, and many African and Latin American countries.

How are we supposed to resist protectionism in the face of severe domestic unemployment? What are you supposed to do when you're up against the wall, when your employer has moved or run-out on you, when your plant has shutdown and, you're out of work with little income and no family health insurance protection, and when the unemployment lines are miles long and unemployment compensation expires?

It makes no difference if professors and journalists, government officials and legislators, corporate officers and free market theorists tell you that *in the long run* you will find another job.

"Perhaps it won't require your skill," they tell you. "Perhaps it will require you to pull up community and family roots and move miles away. Perhaps it will pay less. Perhaps you'll have to get reeducated and retrained. But you'll find another job *in the long run*."

No respectable trade union representative is going to tell that to the man or woman who has just been laid-off, because the *long run* doesn't matter.

It is the short run that matters. In the short run, people must eat, pay for shelter, utilities and transportation, send their children to school, and have access to health services.

In the short run people must live.

Let me warn the ideological airheads who can't tell the difference between "free" trade and fair trade that, unless Americans can live decently in the short run, in the long run the rise of protectionism can't be stopped. And quite possibly neither can the rise of militarism, if a military industrial economy is the only game in town.

Protectionism and militarism will roll over us like a tidal wave.

THE BUSINESS OF GOVERNMENT . . . IS BUSINESS

Historically and traditionally, the U.S. government has been in business of promoting capital accumulation and maintaining social harmony.

During the post–World War II boom period—1945 to 1973—the United States achieved rather spectacular economic growth. There was enough economic growth to generate a surplus that enabled the United States to achieve military superiority over the Soviets, pay for its limited welfare state, and lead to rising affluence in the private sector for most, if not all, individuals.

The boom had its contradictions, however. The growth of oligopoly capitalism inside the United States and its expansion from its domestic base to the present-day multinational corporation coupled with the free trade doctrine led to three consequences:

- Intense competition from our allies in the industrialized world;
- The global mobility of capital to wherever profit is greatest, which has compromised essential national interests; and
- That, in turn, brought industrial decline and the rise of protectionism and militarism.

These have characterized the post-1973 period. Our military allies have become our trade enemies. The mobility of capital has drained a number of national economies, including our own. The product is today's low growth economy where the state is aggressively pursuing capital accumulation at the expense of consumption, both private and public. Not only is that true in the United States, it is enshrined in official international economic thinking.

Current economic strategies to cope with the situation are perhaps best exemplified by the orthodoxy emanating from the Organization for Economic Cooperation and Development (OECD). The OECD prescriptions are typical of those coming down from the high reaches of academia, business and government in nearly all industrialized nations. The five OECD nostrums to get out of the mess we're in are:

1. "Restrain growth of real wages in relation to productivity growth and thereby reduce costs and enhance profits." Translated into English, that simply restates old-fashioned cheap labor policy and reasserts the supremacy of capital.
2. "Curb public sector deficits to prevent crowding out private sector investment in a high-interest rate and high-tax environment." That means welfare for the rich and "free" private enterprise for the rest of us.
3. "Legal minimum wages must not be set so high that job opportunities will be denied to the young and inexperienced job seekers." That simply re-enforces the cheap labor policy and guarantees wages will be driven down, not up, the standard-of-living escalator.
4. "Lack of new skills must not hamper the reconstruction of industry." That means full speed ahead with lasers, micro chips, robots and all other labor-displacing technology.
5. "Heavy reliance on imported energy has to be reduced." So we should turn over our natural resources to the Big Oil companies and their banking partners for fast track exploitation.[3]

Even a cursory reading of OECD policies and position papers reveals a strategy of discrediting the European welfare states and of replacing government-managed economies with Corporate America's hyped-up "market system." The OECD wants to Americanize (or, more accurately, Reaganize) the Western European social democracies by tearing up the economic and social contract which exists there and which has permitted those nations to overtake and, in many cases, outperform the dog-eat-dog American market system. The OECD seems to want to lower Western European economic and social standards to U.S. levels. That is bound to exacerbate protectionist conflicts in international trade, as well as to produce labor unrest abroad. It will be tragic if the U.S. government succeeds in exporting its packaged economic mythology which has done such harm to our own economy.

The OECD's nostrums contain a hidden agenda: to preserve the existing order of inequitable income distribution and concentrated control of wealth and resources.

In the United States, in particular, the dialogue pertaining to the hidden agenda is almost never discussed in public forum, media or page. Certainly, it never penetrates political campaign rhetoric.

What is worse, the trade union movement is neither prepared to, nor has the propensity to, challenge it.

If the OECD nostrums contain the hidden agenda of preserving the *status quo*, they also deliver absolution to that agenda's major beneficiaries: Corporate America is absolved from its professional shortcomings, social irresponsibility and perpetuation of class warfare.

THERE ARE BETTER ALTERNATIVES

In order to stop this free trade madness; in order to staunch the red ink-flood of trade deficits and job losses; in order to make United States corporations accountable to workers, their communities and the nation; in order to make Rambo corporate managers better citizens of the world, we must rebuild America's international trade system.

We need congressional action in a number of areas. Here are the most crucial:

1. Control the activity of multinational corporations with respect to licensing, transfer of technology and co-production agreements. We must curb the sovereign behavior of corporations to make them responsive to the national interest.
2. Regulate direct foreign investment by American corporations in the public interest.
3. Repeal tax incentives for U.S. corporations to move production overseas, such as the foreign investment tax credit and deferred payment of taxes on foreign income. These simply encourage the export of jobs and establishment of overseas subsidiaries.
4. Require full multinational disclosure of intracompany transactions, transfer pricing policies, profit-loan swaps and bank tie-ins.
5. Require multinational corporations to give notice and, at local due process hearings, show cause why they must be shut down, move operations from or reduce the workforce in the community where they are doing business. We need to determine the em-

ployment impact at home *before* technology is transferred, direct investment made abroad, or private loans are placed overseas.

6. Demand assurance by recipient nations that employment, wages and work standards will rise to parity with those in similar industries in the United States, when technology is transferred or direct investment and loans are made.

7. Provide fair and just compensation to U. S. workers injured by foreign competition. Apply Trade Adjustment Assistance to secondary and tertiary levels of impact, extend time for filing for Trade Adjustment Assistance, provide relief to "bumped" worker, and continue health insurance to those who lose jobs.

8. Amend Title V of Trade Adjustment Act to withhold GSP designation from those countries who do not, or will not, develop their own domestic markets for goods they are producing for export to the United States.

9. Negotiate quotas with nations to keep their exports to the United States in line with market growth, e.g., if market is expanding in the United States 2 percent per year for nuts and bolts, then limit Hong Kong export of nuts and bolts to the United States to same increase.

10. Get off the flexible exchange rate kick. It just encourages speculation in the dollar and other currencies and disrupts trade and investment.

11. Press for negotiation of international tax policies to eliminate tax havens, and unfair tax advantages in international trade and finance.

12. Review United States trade relations in each major industrial sector on a country-by-country basis and, where unfair trade practices that block or prevent United States exports are discovered, (1) negotiate reciprocal foreign trade agreements or (2) block imports from offending countries or multinational corporations until corrections are made.

Singly and in combination, these measures would turn "free" trade into fair trade.

INTERNATIONAL UNION COOPERATION IS COMMON SENSE

We in the trade union movement must also take steps on our own. It makes little or no sense for the U.S. labor movement to continue to isolate itself or to attempt to go it alone in an international economy, which is tightly controlled by a few gigantic and global corporate organizations. We cannot tolerate our employers' driving a wedge between us and workers around the world, while they make book with other employers and governments, regardless of political persuasion.

We have to recognize that we live in a global economy and that our ability to bargain good contracts and decent living standards in America is related to the success or failure of unions abroad. Strengthening our trade union movement here at home requires promoting economic and social justice for workers around the globe.

It is not the impersonal march of events, or history or technological progress which is battering the American union movement. It is the age-old quest for power and profits and the lust for greed and privilege.

All the western nations, Japan, and particularly the United States incessantly preach the free market dogma. Pick up *The Economist, Le Monde*, the *Manchester Guardian*, or such U.S. publications as *Fortune, Forbes*, and *Business Week*, and you will find constant comment on the need to preserve the market system, preferably free of government intervention, and certainly free of trade union intervention.

The market dogma instills in us the notion that we are a pack of wild dogs, snapping and snarling for the last scrap of meat. The free market mythology pits nation against nation and worker against worker. There is no dignity in that system and there is very little economic and social justice for working people throughout the world, let alone the hundreds of millions of unemployed.

However, as we witness the combinations of capital at the national and international levels, we see less and less of the free market. Instead of a large number of small competing firms, we see the rapid increase in the concentration of economic power. Huge sovereign corporations, which have sales larger than the gross national products of many countries, dominate the international market. The expansion of the multinational corporations in the last twenty years has made a mockery of free market dogma, and has driven the trade unions into an international retreat.

In the trade unions, we've desperately been trying to come up with an effective program to counteract the enormous power of these global entities, but our national differences get in our way. Our members are isolated in our own countries, workplaces, and languages. Most of us don't even know how to make a phone call to another trade union in another country to find out what a common multinational employer may be up to. Scissored and whipsawed by the mobility of multinationals, we take our last ditch stands in the name of nationalism and narrow self-interest. And that is more than ironic, because, by definition, a multinational corporation transcends the authority and power of nation states.

At the national level, all unions need to launch a campaign against what we in the Machinists Union call the Corporate State. The Corporate State is one where a few private corporate entities either own, control or otherwise call the shots for government in the political economy. The Corporate State negates democracy and subverts economic and social justice. In the United States the Corporate State works to freeze wages, while profits and inflation soar; to dismantle federal regulatory agencies in transportation, in occupational safety and health protections and environmental standards; to gain tax breaks and tax concessions for the rich while social funds for the poor, disabled, and retirees are cut.

In the United States, the campaign against the Corporate State means that trade unions must work harder for national economic planning goals and to revitalize union organizing laws and organizing efforts. In concert with progressives and liberals outside labor, trade unions must work to license, regulate and federally charter U.S. multinational corporations. After all, the corporation in the United States is legally a creature of the state. Corporations, in the strict sense of the term, were never private. They were public creations. They have become private corporations only by usage and default of state regulatory authority. Now that their influence crosses not only state lines, but international boundaries as well, only the federal government can effectively regulate their purposes and activities.

Increasingly, American unions must work to make their own government, as well as others, aware that they must accept collective responsibility for management of the evolving integrated world economy. Full employment, income security, social progress and peace must continue to be primary goals.

The Corporate State operates in other countries, too. It wreaks havoc in their domestic economies as well. Labor has been slapped with an incomes policy[4] in country after country, often presented to us in the disguise of a social contract. Ask our British brothers and sisters what they received in return for that bargain in the 1970s.

We see the Corporate State arming nations around the globe in the name of security. The reality is that increased armaments only produce insecurity, through fear, mistrust, tension and the increased probability of war.

It is madness to tell us that arms productions and sales are necessary to address our balance of payments problems, to keep our economies strong or to keep our jobs. That is nothing but job blackmail. Aside from the moral and ethical implications of such nonsense, we know from bitter and frustrating experience that as military budgets escalate, fewer and fewer jobs are created. We get more jobs per billion dollars spent for civilian production than we get in military production.

What we must remember is this: war comes by remote control. Seldom do our provocateurs directly suffer the consequences. It is we, the workers, and our sons and daughters who are inevitably drafted to do the sacrificing, the fighting, and the dying.

The alternative is economic conversion. Economic Conversion means more jobs opportunities at home. It also means a way to avoid the trap of war and armed conflict.

And on a global scale, we see the Corporate State meeting in conclaves in Geneva, in Paris, in Brussels, in Bonn, or in Rome to carve up the globe in quest of cheap labor, union free environments, substandard job safety and health standards, and "stable" governments. When they use the term "stable," they mean the governments that you and I would call dictatorial or anti-democratic.

The Corporate State's transfer of capital to those countries is not intended to develop the economies of underdeveloped and developing nations; that's an afterthought. It is intended to establish export platforms erected on the backs of the downtrodden, the ignorant, the oppressed and the poor. And the product of that abused and misused labor is shipped back to already developed markets where the landscape is increasingly cratered by depressed local economies, by a labor force suffering from loss of real income, and by a demoralized trade union movement.

What it means is that in the Corporate State, only the labor market is "free"—free to be plundered, free to be raped, free to be stripped of dignity.

Meanwhile, those who pilot the Corporate flagships and those in government who minister to their needs, and those who profit from their dividends and coupons, remain undisturbed at the top of the economic pyramid, unmindful of the injustices they are perpetrating and perpetuating.

At the international level, U.S. trade unions must join their overseas counterparts in pressing for internationally agreed standards on exchange rates, capital movements, technology transfer, tax laws and accounting procedures. U.S. trade unions must continue to support freedom of association and union organization; collective bargaining; wage parity; and health, safety and work standards among all nations.

This will be done through our multilateral international organizations, such as the International Labor Organization, the International Metal Workers Federation, the International Transport Workers Federation and others with whom U.S. trade unions affiliate.

Let us not dwell on our national differences, whether legalistic or customary. Let us instead focus on our similarities and mutual needs.

When our governments propose incomes policies, then we should demand programs to increase real incomes, gradually but securely, in annual increments. That's a social contract that makes sense.

When our employers combine capital and technology to maximize profits in one country at the expense of another or others, then we should combine contract termination dates or legislative efforts, or demand joint meetings with governments and employers to rectify the inequities and injustices of such arbitrary and unilateral decisions.

When our governments and employers insist on using the arms trade to divide and conquer us, and when they practice job blackmail, then we should develop our respective Economic Conversion programs, enter them into our respective political campaigns and political dialogues, and even, if we have to, petition the United Nations to address our problem.

And when the Corporate State persists in cruel and inhuman treatment and murderous oppression of trade unionists in other countries and persists in human rights violations, then we should join international organizations such as Amnesty International and other similar human rights organizations to bring those atrocities to light and to swing the weight of public opinion against the offenders.

If multinational corporations can make their own rules of conduct above and beyond national constraints, then we in the trade union movement can move beyond those constraints, too.

Trade union company councils and industrial councils for purposes of coordinated multinational bargaining must be tried and developed. We must do the same thing internationally that we have done among the various American unions that organize different plants of companies like General Electric: agree on our bargaining goals and stick together. Corporations are multinational; unions must respond with a similar international perspective.

The best alternative to protectionism is a system of reciprocal and fair trade rules, written in the form of an economic and social clause in every agreement, treaty and trade contract negotiated among and between nations and corporate entities.

Such an economic and social clause would among other requirements, commit trading partners on all sides to

- economic planning for full employment;
- full development of domestic markets, rather than more exploitation of resources for export;

- redistribution of and social control over concentrated ownership of land and wealth;
- annual real per capita income gains for workers; and
- the full range of human rights, including the absolute right of freedom of association for workers, the right to organize free and independent trade unions for purposes of collective bargaining and determination of wages and compensation, hours, safety and health and other work standards.

The right of workers to use the strike as an economic weapon would be inviolable. The right for workers to participate in the nation's political processes, form political parties and make political alliances and coalitions, and the right of trade unionists to seek public office would be guaranteed in the economic and social clauses of private and public foreign trade and aid contracts.

Only by negotiating for identical goals and the same high standards, whether we negotiate with governments or with corporate entities, can the workers of one country assist the workers of another country in this global economy. That way, we can avoid being pitted against one another in a cruel trade game that eventually reduces us all to the lowest common denominator.

I do not delude myself that all this will be easy. Far from it. But these are not ordinary times. We can ill afford to go on with business as usual. Business as usual has helped put us in our present defensive posture.

The lives, livelihoods and the very survival of people we represent demand much more of our abilities, brains and talents.

We must explore new avenues and frontiers in global labor relations.

We must come to grips with the Corporate State in our respective countries and make it heel to the fact that economic rights, trade union rights and human rights are one and indivisible in the cause of economic and social justice the world over.

NOTES

1. This estimate may be on the conservative side. Faye Duchin and Glenn-Marie Lange argue that the 1987 trade deficit cost 5.1 million job opportunities and that fully 3 million of those were in manufacturing. Their study indicates that the jobs lost were likely to be high-wage jobs and that 2.5 million of the lost jobs would have paid more than $400 per week. ("Trading Away Jobs: The Effects of the U.S. Merchandise Trade Deficit on Employment," *Working Paper* no. 102 [Washington, D.C.: Economic Policy Institute, 1988]).

2. The implicit assumption underlying trade negotiations is that each country bargains from a nationalistic standpoint. U.S. negotiators assume they are bargaining in the national interest, too. A single negotiator or team of negotiating specialists must, therefore, don three hats: those of labor, the government, and the corporations. That would induce schizophrenia were it not for the fact that labor interests are ignored and corporate interests dominate. The major problem with the assumption of nationalism is that multinational corporations have no sense of nationalism. Multinational "patriotism" is determined by the corporate profit and loss statement. Mobility of corporate capital and technology enables multinationals to go anywhere in the world in order to maximize profits, and they do. That mobility of multinational corporations and their utter insensitivity to the national interest undermines labor's confidence in the outcome of trade negotiations.

3. OECD Observer, *Employment Outlook* (Paris: OECD, September 1986).

4. An incomes policy freezes workers' wages while inflation goes up. It means that real incomes are reduced, that unemployment increases, and that those residing at the top of the income and wealth pyramid are left untouched and make no sacrifices to abate inflation or preserve the nation's economic integrity.

beyond the warfare state

The splitting of the atom changed everything, save man's mode of thinking, and thus we drift toward unparalleled catastrophe.
—Albert Einstein

Today there are literally thousands of people in federal government, in the military services, in Corporate America, in dozens of "think tanks" and institutes, in our colleges and universities, preparing and planning for war. War has been a permanent part of our environment.

In my own case, four wars have impacted upon my life: World War I, the aftermath of which was the Depression Era legacy that accompanied my arrival into the world; World War II, which I participated in; the Korean War, which accompanied the birth of my sons and daughters; and the Vietnam War, which in perspective, appears to have launched this nation onto a permanent war-time trajectory. Since the Spanish-American War in 1898, every single generation of Americans has experienced war as its companion.

The constant presence of war and the absence of peace is clearly reflected in our national institutions. The United States has and operates an official War College, but where is the Peace College? Some three million civilians are on the federal payroll to specifically plan and prepare for war—but not one single individual has been hired to plan for peace since 1965. Even then, only a dozen or so people were put to work planning for peace, compared to the millions planning for war. They worked for the Arms Control and Disarmament Agency, which received its charter at precisely the moment of Vietnam. A charter purpose of that agency was to plan for peace, and in a very short time, the few peace planners there produced a remarkable number of studies and proposals, which came to be known as Economic Conversion studies. These studies remain as models for the current outcropping of similar economic impact analyses.

However, the Arms Control and Disarmament Agency has since abandoned its charter purpose to prepare for peace. There are no peace planners there now. Economic Conversion studies and the analyses demonstrating the impact of military spending on the economy are not made by the government. In fact, the Reagan Administration converted the Arms Control and Disarmament Agency into just another Pentagon appendage.

Today, as far as we can detect, not a single individual in the military-industrial complex, or even in the Arms Control and Disarmament Agency, is planning for the possibility of disarmament and peace.

That's pathetic.

The current situation in history is a far cry from the wilderness years of Winston Churchill in England prior to World War II. It is far different from the U.S. position when the winds of war were blowing prior to Pearl Harbor. There are no slumbering giants in the world today. The superpowers are each armed to the teeth, dancing their dirge of death, playing their war games, in an endless celebration of erotic weaponry and the technologies of death and destruction.

This nation needs a strong military defense—one strong enough to protect our continental integrity should some aggressor dare to step across the line, whether that line is in the air, at sea, or on land. Step across those lines and we'll fight to the finish, not surrender or compromise our constitutional democracy.

There is no doubt in my mind that our high-tech, smart weaponry is superior to the Soviets. There is no doubt in my mind that we are out-spending the Soviets—because their GNP is only half of our GNP—and our NATO allies outspend the Warsaw Pact nations by a wide margin. But when each side can blow up the other 20 times over, why continue the arms race madness?

Let's get it straight. Nuclear weapons are not conventional implements of war. Listen to those who had experience with both.

After Hiroshima and Nagasaki, Henry L. Stimson, U.S. Secretary of War during World War II, said: "The Bomb constitutes a first step in a new control by man over the forces of nature too revolutionary and dangerous to fit into old concepts."

General Douglas MacArthur, no dove, urged "The abolition of war is no longer an ethical equation to be pondered by learned philosophers and ecclesiastics, but a hard-core one for the decision of the masses, whose survival is at stake."

In 1959, President Dwight D. Eisenhower declared: "War has become not just tragic but preposterous. There can be no victory with modern weapons for anyone. Controlled, universal disarmament," Eisenhower insisted, "is the imperative of our time. The demand for it by the hundreds of millions whose chief concern is the long future of themselves and their children, will, I hope, become so universal and so insistent, that no man, no government anywhere can withstand it." Then in perhaps his most famous clarion call, Eisenhower said: "I think that people want peace so much that one of these days governments had better get out of their way and let them have it."

Einstein wept when he saw the weapons his genius had made possible. "We are all citizens of a world community sharing a common peril. No one has the right to withdraw," Einstein said, "from the world of action at a time when civilization faces its supreme test. It is in this spirit that we call upon all people to work for and to sacrifice to achieve a settlement which will bring peace."

WINNING THE RACE TO DESTRUCTION

The inevitable first question in the current military madness is "who's ahead in the arms race?"

We might counter with a question of our own: in an age of overkill, what difference does it make? But that is never enough for the nervous nellies who think numbers are all that count, or who frame the issue, not as one concerning survival of the human race, but as one of winning the "big game," as if the subject were merely the World Series or Super Bowl.

So who's ahead? Let the admirals, generals and intelligence experts at the Center for Defense Information in Washington, D.C., tell us. Here are the figures as of 1988.

1. The United States can explode 16,000 nuclear warheads on the Soviet Union; the Soviets can explode almost 11,000 warheads on the U.S.

2. Of the U.S. total, 2,850 are on F-111s, F-4s, A-6s, A-7s, F-16s, and F/A-18s and other tactical aircraft that can fly into the Soviet Union from Europe, Asia or from aircraft carriers. The United States has deployed 99 new B-1B bombers and has developed the new radar-avoiding Stealth bomber. Some 130 Stealths are scheduled to become operational by 1992. Of the Soviet's 11,000, almost 640 are on Backfire bombers that can only hit the United States if they fly at airliner speeds on one-way missions. The Soviets have 60 Bear-H bombers capable of carrying 12 air-launched cruise missiles and have just developed the Blackjack bomber which can carry both cruise missiles and bombs. The Soviets had until recently only 30 aging Bison tankers for air

refueling, but have just made operational the new Midas airtanker. The United States has 600 KC-135 and 55 new KC-10 air refueling tankers.

Of the remaining 12,600 strategic nuclear weapons in the U.S. arsenal, nearly half are on 32 ballistic missile submarines which, hidden beneath the ocean, are practically invulnerable. At least 19 to 20 of these submarines are operational at all times. Of the USSR's 11,000 strategic nuclear weapons, 942 missiles with 3,378 warheads are on 63 ballistic missile submarines. The Soviets have more missile-bearing submarines, but they are equipped with fewer warheads, and most are on liquid-fueled missiles. U.S. subs at sea continually target 3,000 nuclear warheads on more reliable solid-fueled missiles at the Soviet Union. Soviet subs divide their warheads among targets in China and the Pacific, Western Europe, and the United States. Just one U.S. Poseidon submarine carries enough warheads to destroy every large and medium-sized city in the Soviet Union.

The United States has 2,366 warheads on 1,104 land-based intercontinental ballistic missiles (ICBMs). In December 1986, the first 10 U.S. MX missiles became operational. Fifty MXs are deployed now, and another 50 are scheduled for deployment by 1992. The Soviet Union has 6,412 warheads on 1,386 land-based ICBMs. The Soviets have begun to deploy two new, mobile ICBMs: the single-warhead, road-mobile SS-25 and the 10-warhead, rail-mobile SS-24.[1]

Soviet superiority in land-based ICBMs is what our war planners call the "window of vulnerability." That's what the MX misguided expenditure is all about: to close the land-based window of vulnerability. That rationale means that the Soviets have two such windows of vulnerability: one in the air and one at sea, where we have superior numbers and greater mobility at longer range.

So, who's ahead? The United States is "ahead" on the sea and in the air. The Soviets are "ahead" on land.

Quality, though, makes a big difference, we're told. U.S. land-based ICBMs are smaller than the Soviet ones because they have miniaturized, computerized guidance systems, more efficient solid-fuel rocket engines, greater accuracy and more compact hydrogen warheads. This makes "throw weight" a bogus issue.

Perhaps the best way to cut through this numbers game—and I've given you these dreadful statistics because you may need them to hurl back at your detractors in neighborhood or barroom brawls, or in the more restrained atmosphere of seminar debates and community dialogues—is to listen to the warmakers themselves. On May 11, 1982, General John Vessey, Chair of the Joint Chiefs of Staff, told Senator Carl Levin in Senate Armed Services Committee hearings, when the Senator asked him if he would swap the U.S. military capability for the Soviet one, "I would not trade." Just a few days before that, Senator Charles Percy asked then-Defense Secretary Weinberger, in Senate Foreign Relations Committee hearings, which nuclear arsenal the Secretary would rather have, the Soviets' or ours. Said the Secretary of Defense, "I would not for a moment exchange anything, because we have an immense edge in technology."

Think of the current balance of terror in these terms: you and your most-disliked neighbor are standing beside a 100-gallon open drum of gasoline. You have ten matches to strike and your adversarial neighbor has nine matches. What makes the difference if you each are given ten more matches? One lighted match can ignite the gasoline and incinerate you both.

That's exactly what the arms race is doing: giving each side 10 more matches, when one match alone on either side can touch off an all-consuming conflagration.

Since only one or two nuclear warheads, whether of the Soviet or American brand, are required to obliterate a city of one million, then perhaps the Pentagon and Kremlin war planners will forgive us for asking, why spend more for overkill? Cats may have nine lives, but I accept it as a scientific fact that, as ordinary human beings, we die only once.

American political, business—and, yes, most labor leaders—seem to have a view of the world that is at once naive and cynical. We believe that since the United States is protected by two huge oceans on a continent that has never been invaded or subjected to aerial attack, wars are something that always happen "over there"—on the other side of the Atlantic or Pacific. War can't happen on the North American continent. This naive illusion is fed by massive media propaganda and excited by electoral war mongering and missile rattling to the point that crowds cynically shout "Nuke 'em!" without any notion of what that command means.

Imagine, if you will, Dan Rather on tonight's evening news blandly reporting, "A limited nuclear exchange took place today, killing 1,200,000 people in Cleveland and injuring 900,000 others in the area. Names are being withheld pending notification of next of kin."

When we speak of war—*any* war—but certainly nuclear war, limited or unlimited, we aren't talking about the Super Bowl game. In real war, in real nuclear war, we won't wake up the next morning and say, "wait 'til next year."

We won't wake up. There won't be a "next time." Who in their right mind thinks they're going to be around to watch the rubble bounce after even one nuclear exchange? Even those who survive a nuclear blast are likely to die from radiation and radioactive fall-out, far removed from the blast. Life will survive though. Cockroaches and rats are more resistant to radiation than we are.

What do we want the military to do?

The primary task of our strategic forces is to *deter* a Soviet strategic attack on us and our allies. Deterrence has been the underlying principle of our defense posture since the Soviets have had nuclear capability. We called it Mutually Assured Destruction or MAD for short. As long as we each had the capability of destroying the other, fear of annihilation would prevent confrontation.

It was under the MAD umbrella that détente and the Strategic Arms Limitation Treaty (SALT I) took place. SALT II also was inspired by MAD. The 1987 Intermediate Nuclear Forces (INF) Treaty and current Strategic Arms Reduction Talks (START) talks are also a recognition of nuclear MADness.

To put the present scene in perspective, let us go back a bit in time. The Carter Doctrine, in response to the Soviet invasion of Afghanistan, not only dynamited the SALT II Treaty, it committed the U.S. to defend the entire Persian Gulf region. That's why the Rapid Deployment Force was conceived. But the Carter Doctrine took us beyond deterrence. It vaguely called for intervention.

President Reagan, while not publicly committing himself to the Carter Doctrine *per se*, appeared to scrap the MAD umbrella, and to grasp for strategic superiority with first strike capability over the Soviets while developing an interventionist military posture for other areas of the globe.

The Reagan strategy was faulty on several counts.

First, strategic military superiority is impossible. Nuclear warheads can be tossed half way around the globe at close to the speed of light. The Soviets have that capability and so do we. Our missiles may be more accurate than the Soviets', but as soon as we launch a first strike, the Soviets will retaliate anyway. With nuclear bombs, there's no such thing as a near miss. There is only launch, retaliate and world inferno, brought to you in ultra-violet and infrared, deadly radiation color—in 30 minutes or less. In an age of thousands of missiles each tipped with a nuclear holocaust, first-strike capability is a figment of the Mad Scientist's imagination, be he American, Russian or any other nationality.

Apparently, the basic premise of the Reagan military buildup was that one day in the future the United States would achieve a final and certain edge of superiority over all adversaries. But the decades-long arms race demonstrates the shallowness of this superiority premise. We spend more for more and newer weapons. The Soviets do the same to catch up. We spend more to get ahead. The Soviets catch up again. In the world of war gamesmanship, for both U.S. and Soviet defense planners, the future never arrives. The imperative is always to spend more now.

In any case, final superiority would be possible only if the Soviets are technologically or productively inferior. That certainly doesn't square with the Pentagon's annual cry of alarm over the security gap.

Is the Kremlin immune from the same siege mentality and fear psychosis which infects the Pentagon? Given the latter's hysteria at budget time each year, there's no reason to expect the Soviets should be any more calm or cool. It is a case of American Hawks and Soviet Hawks reacting to each other's psychosis—chasing one another in a deadly game of ring-around-the-rosy. As Senator McGovern has said, "The people of each superpower are, in fact, the hostages of the leaders of the other. That doctrine is central to the strategy of both sides."

The whole rationale defies reality. For the reality is, at any given time, we are in a suspenseful state of Mutual Assured Destruction with or without additional and new weapons.

Second, with respect to military intervention in the Persian Gulf and elsewhere, that, too, is folly. Remember the Shah of Iran. All the Chrysler-built tanks, all the Grumman fighters, all the sophisticated radar detection equipment, and all the guns, rifles and ammunition supplied by arms merchants didn't save the Shah. Clubs, slingshots, a war of words and ideas, and his own despotism and repression brought down his regime.

That same thing can happen in any Persian Gulf country—Saudi Arabia, Yemen, Qatar, the Emirates. The natives are restless for a share of power in those countries, as the Russians have learned in Afghanistan. The United States has no business, as a matter of principle, intervening in the domestic affairs, rebellions or civil strife of other nations. It stains our democratic principles, compromises our integrity and blotches our reputation in the world to support autocratic monarchies and military dictatorships.

Consider the argument that we must be prepared to intervene in the Persian Gulf because of our vital oil interests there. The argument is absurd on its face. The quickest way to blow up the oil pipeline is to intervene militarily. General Haig's suggestion that we would resort to limited nuclear war to protect that oil deserved short shrift. Assuming we did "Nuke 'em," what would we gain? Soviet retaliation at worst, and a "hot oil" cargo at best.

Our national interest would have been best served if we had committed the billions of federal dollars that went into the Mideast military quagmire instead to developing job-creating, renewable energy sources here at home instead. Then we could have removed ourselves from the

OPEC oil dependency hook. Rather than doing that, we dumped the money into the military, raised our dependency on imported oil, and set the stage for the next energy crisis.

Or consider our intervention elsewhere. Take Central America for example. What is our national interest in the tragic civil strife in El Salvador and Nicaragua? It ought to be promotion of political democracy and economic security, the right of the people there to free themselves from the yoke of economic despair and political humiliation, forced upon them by a few privileged and powerful families, backed by a brutal and kept military force.

When are our nation's leaders going to learn you don't promote democracy or economic growth of opportunity by propping up right-wing governments and tin-horn military dictators?

What do we want our military to do? We want it to give us the defense posture necessary to deter aggression and attack. We don't want it to call the shots for foreign policy. We don't want it to intervene around the globe, as it sees fit. As the late Senator Richard Russell, of Georgia, when he was Chair of the Senate Armed Services Committee said of a U.S. intervention capability in his time: "If it is easy for us to go anywhere and do anything, we will always be going somewhere and doing something."

And to that we can add, "New weapons are to generals as toys are to children."

PSYCHOPATHOLOGY AND THE WARFARE STATE

What's behind the arms race pyromania?

To paraphrase British historian E. P. Thompson, we are dealing with powerfully entrenched military interests and with government and political leaders who seek to advance their own objectives. It is true in the Soviet Union and it is true in the United States. The military and political leaders in each country are ideological look-alikes. They think in the same terms of "balance" and security through "strength." The nuclear deterrent rationale remains immensely serviceable to them by perpetuating the status quo in their own countries, in Europe, and around the world. Each side uses deterrence to control increasingly disobedient, restless and ungrateful client states. To give up a single missile or warhead is equally painful for the American Joint Chiefs of Staff and for their Soviet military counterparts.

What each knows, but cannot or will not admit, is that the tremendous amounts of money and resources committed to high-tech weaponry, military manpower, and maintenance of garrisons and bases in buffer countries, has made neither side more secure. The billions poured into armaments have only purchased more insecurity.

Meanwhile, military paranoia drives us closer to war.

Paranoia shot down Korean Airlines Flight 007. Paranoia shot down the Iranian Airbus. Paranoia invaded Grenada. Or were there other psychopathologies at work in Grenada?

There is much to be said for the view that the Grenada Affair was concocted to distract us from the Reagan Administration's Beirut blunder that killed our Marines there. It certainly had that effect. Stomping on a postage stamp island like Grenada permitted the President to fulfill his right-wing constituency's pathological desire to prove its "manhood," by sending others to fight and die in a "real" war for "noble" principles, such as open sea lanes, oil deposits, and the safety of rich American students, who were perhaps more concerned about maintaining their leisurely level of living.

This psychological analysis may be disturbing in what it suggests about the lack of rationality behind our military posturing, but it makes more sense than the official claim that a 10,000 foot airstrip, with no parallel runways, and with fuel storage tanks all above ground, built by a British contractor, would make a strategic bomber base for the Soviets. Hell, why go to Grenada for strategic bomber bases? The Soviets have them 90 miles away on Cuba! And the Hollywood blood, guts and glory argument makes more sense than the notion that 670 Cuban airport construction crewmen posed an international communist threat immediately endangering our national security.

Couple Beirut and Grenada with the Reagan's entanglement in Central America, where we find the United States still supporting oppressive right-wing militarists and a few rich landowners in El Salvador and attempting to overthrow the legitimate government of Nicaragua by overt and covert means, and we have the specter of a nation in search of a war. Any war, anywhere. As long as there are enough Marines to go around.

We find Soviet or Cuban plots behind every rebellion or conflict. No doubt the Soviets find American plots behind the same conflicts. But the Center for Defense Information, staffed by Admirals, Generals, Colonels, former Defense Department and intelligence agency experts, tells us the main ideological thread woven through nearly all of those diverse conflicts is nationalism, not communism versus capitalism, or East versus West. Nationalism remains the most powerful force in the international system. The Soviets know it, and they play on it. The conservatives here know it too, and they certainly play on it.

This strong sense of nationalism means that it wouldn't make any difference if Karl Marx had never been born, if the Soviet Union didn't exist, and if there was no such thing as communism. People in undeveloped and developing countries would still be fighting for nationalistic reasons, sometimes coupled with religion as in the Iran-Iraq war. Moreover, as in the cases of El Salvador and Nicaragua, people would fight for human rights, better economic and social conditions, a better life, and the opportunity to govern their own destiny.

Yet the United States and the Soviet Union turn each conflict in the world—and in the 1980s there were some 40 of them, mainly guerrilla wars—into ideological conflicts.

Foreign military sales do not prevent wars. They make war easier. The United States provided some $51 billion in military assistance to all of the nations involved in those wars, over a 10-year period between 1972 and 1981. The Soviet Union was right there with us, matching us ruble for dollar, weapon for weapon. Joining in on the lucrative trade are France, Great Britain, Israel, West Germany, and now Brazil and China. The international arms trade grew from about $6 billion in 1970 to about $36 billion annually in the 1980s. Over the decade, Third World countries have signed arms import deals worth about $250 billion.[2]

The insanity of arms peddling is exceeded only by the "winnable" nuclear war strategy and Star Wars' "impenetrable umbrella" theory. But somehow, we get the feeling those deranged concepts are not the exclusive property of conservatives and right wingers. A hell of a lot of so-called middle-of-the-roaders and moderates harbor those Strangelove fantasies, too.

Until Gorbachev, it was apparent to all but the principal actors in the play that twin psychological demons of paranoia and distrust dominated the script.

Those twin demons still hover over each side. The extent to which they afflict the psyche of U.S. foreign policy makers is no small obstacle to overcome as we attempt to discuss rationally disarmament and detente with the Soviets.

Veteran Washington correspondent Tristram Coffin points out that a "gallant ally" of World War II, has been systematically transformed into an evil monster, the singular source of the world's troubles, and an overwhelming threat to Western Civilization. That once-gallant ally, of course, is the Soviet Union.

This fear ignores the fact that the Soviets have been thrown out of almost as many countries as they've come to dominate over the years. And we might ask just how reliable would Warsaw Pact nations be as Soviet allies, if hostilities broke out in Europe? The Soviets should depend on the Poles? And they no longer can include China in their sphere. In fact, when we look at the geopolitical position of the USSR, it may well be, as journalist I. F. Stone once noted, that the Soviet Union is the only country in the world surrounded by hostile communist neighbors!

Look at the Russian perspective. In the Soviet mind's eye, they look east and see big, potentially belligerent China; they look South and find themselves stalemated in Afghanistan and see fierce Moslem resistance to domination by any foreign power; they look West and see NATO; and to the North there's only the polar cap. Russia's defense perimeter faces three directions at once, against three distinct and potential rivals, none of them in close alliance with each other.

A number of distinguished Americans are concerned about demonology inhibiting better East-West relations. Former Ambassador to the Soviet Union, George Kennan, examined the demonology phenomenon in a speech in 1982. Here's what he said: "I find the view of the Soviet Union that prevails today in our governmental and journalistic establishments so extreme, so subjective, so far removed from what any sober scrutiny of external reality would reveal, that it is not only ineffective but dangerous as a guide to political action . . . these, believe me, are not the marks of the maturity and realism one expects of the diplomacy of a great power; they are the marks of an intellectual primitivism and naivete, unpardonable in a great government."

The Ambassador concluded that "We must learn to see the behavior of the leadership of that [Soviet] people as partly a reflection of our own treatment of it. Because, if we insist on demonizing these Soviet leaders—insist on viewing them as total and incorrigible enemies, consumed only with their fear and hatred of the United States, and dedicated to nothing other than our destruction—that, in the end, is the way we shall assuredly have them—if for no other reason than that our view of them allows for nothing else—either for us or them."

McGeorge Bundy, National Security Advisor to Presidents Kennedy and Johnson, raises the same question when he asks, "For 65 years now, Americans have been having a hard time with the dark side of the Soviet system. Are they such cheats and liars and murderers that we cannot do business with them? Are they merely ordinary despots with the ordinary habits of the breed? Or are they more sinned-against than sinning, so the real enemies of Soviet-American harmony must be sought in our own ranks?"

As President George Washington warned in his Farewell Address, "The nation that indulges towards another an habitual hatred, or an habitual fondness, is in some degree a slave. It is a slave to its animosity or to its affection, either of which is sufficient to lead it astray from its duty and interest."

Ordinary citizens the world over, including Soviet and Warsaw Pact citizens, recognize the links between excessive militarism and economic decline and deprivation and violation of human rights. War, poverty and oppression too long have been the results of a polarized world. Mikhail Gorbachev apparently realizes that as well as the economic and social costs to the USSR. It remains to be seen whether George Bush does.

We are all citizens of the world. But in an age of nuclear overkill, we are all prisoners of war. The time is overdue for ordinary citizens to begin to liberate themselves and humanity from the bondage of technological terrorism and the threat of thermonuclear homicide. Along with it, the time has come for us to demand that our political leaders quit conducting our foreign policy on old nuclear superiority concepts.

By thinking globally, acting locally and behaving rationally, we can put this great country on a true course toward peace and prosperity.

THE DOMESTIC COST OF MILITARY MADNESS

When he was President, Dwight D. Eisenhower said, "Every gun that is made, every warship launched, every rocket fired signifies, in the final sense, a theft from those who hunger and are not fed, those who are cold and are not clothed. This world in arms is not spending money alone. It is spending the sweat of its laborers, the genius of its scientists, the hopes of its children."

Recent federal budgets have given us a gigantic wrong-way transfer amendment. It takes from the poor and the middle class and gives to the war planners and those who profit from investment in the Warfare State.

Military spending is the most harmful of all government spending. It creates no useful product for consumers to use. Weapons are an end product in and of themselves. In fact, according to the Pentagon, the purpose for producing bombs and such is *not* to use them.

The Pentagon is a perpetual inflation machine. It drives up prices by pumping dollars, but not goods or services, into the economy. It siphons off resources that could be used to create goods and services, and creates a whole industry based on waste, cost over-runs, and downright graft. Witness the wave of Pentagon contract scandals exposed in 1988. The government has to borrow the money to pay for it all. It competes for funds that otherwise would be available in the private money market, and drives up interest rates, which in turn drives up the cost of servicing the federal debt. It drains scientific, engineering and skilled trades talent away from the civilian sector, which is in a state of decline due to that brain drain.

Since Adam Smith, economists have warned that if resources such as capital and labor are used for production of guns, fewer will be available to produce butter. Opportunities to create and strengthen civilian industries are sacrificed when resources are diverted to the military. This traditional economic logic has statistical support. Our study[3] found that, when comparing the economic performance of thirteen major industrial nations over the past two decades, those countries that spent a smaller share of economic output on the military generally experienced faster growth, greater investment and higher productivity increases. Those, like the United States, that carried a heavier military burden had poorer economic performance.

When we compared the United States economy with those other industrial democracies, the results were startling.

Among fourteen western industrialized nations and Japan, the United States ranks first in military R & D, first in military spending, but fifth in civilian R & D, tenth in civilian spending, eleventh in economic growth, thirteenth in annual real wage increases, and tenth in wage levels. We are however, damned near first in unemployment—only Canada had a higher unemployment average over previous twenty years. Those figures suggest the damaging effects of the military budget.

In fact, then as now, the United States no longer has the highest standard of living in the world. We are in about tenth place and still on the decline.

The link between the arms race and America's deindustrialization and economic decline is clear. A dollar spent on dead-end military production simply cannot be spent anywhere else. The United States pours hundreds of billions—and it has been over *$30 million an hour* during the Reagan/Bush Administration's buildup—into weaponry and high-tech, capital intensive, military production systems, and military contractors increasingly export military production through co-production and licensing agreements, joint ventures, offsets, and memoranda of understanding (MOUs). That simply means that those huge sums are not available to refurbish, rehabilitate, and rejuvenate our civilian industry. In the United States, for every $100 available for domestic capital formation, $46 is spent on the military, compared to $14 for West Germany and $3.70 for Japan. No wonder, then, the United States now trails those two nations in the international trade sweepstakes.

Current calls in the Congress for greater burdensharing of defense by our NATO allies aren't being well received in Europe. In the first place, NATO nations are already providing for well over half the defense forces and expenditures in Western Europe. Second, our NATO allies have a more realistic view and scaled-down vision of what it might take to "defend" Western Europe from a possible Soviet and Warsaw

Pact attack. They don't share U.S. policy makers' phobia about the Soviet Union.

As will be seen later, greater burdensharing is certainly not what the Japanese would like to see. Japan is milking the Pentagon cow for cash and technology in a very self-serving and rewarding way.

My experience as a twenty-year participant in the International Metalworkers Federation (IMF), 10 years of which have been as Chair of the World Aerospace Conference, tells me that the NATO nations and Japan will gladly accept production contracts and subcontracts for U.S. military weapons systems. They not only gain business and jobs by doing so, they benefit from the research, the development, and the technology transfers inherent in producing for the U.S. military machine. They then apply that technology to their respective civilian industrial bases.

But even should the NATO nations and Japan accept the full burden of their own defense, that would mean a further decline and reduction of our U.S. industrial base. And history warns us that we should not lightly discount the specter of a Europe or a Japan rearmed the way they were before World War II, should full military burdensharing ever come about. Hopefully, unification in the European Economic Community, scheduled in 1992, will preclude that seemingly remote possibility there. This digression aside, my point is that burdensharing and similar calls for greater international cooperation through a global production system for weapons present Catch-22 propositions for the U.S. and our allies.

The Empty Pork Barrel

But doesn't military spending create jobs?

One of the great myths about military spending is that it is an immense pork barrel of jobs. That simply isn't true. Military spending is so highly capital-intensive and automated, it creates far fewer jobs per billion dollars spent than if that money were spent elsewhere in the civilian sector of the economy.

Of course military spending does create some jobs. And in the current economic environment, military Keynesian policies have probably put a floor under employment levels. But virtually every study we've seen over the past decade, including those conducted by the Department of Labor, as well as by a number of private and not-for-profit organizations, conclude that one billion dollars spent in the civilian sectors of the economy would generate more job opportunities than spending the same billion in the military sector. In the jargon of professional economists, those job impact analyses are called *opportu-*

nity costs. Choosing to spend on the military forces us to give up other opportunities. A preponderance of available evidence produced by those studies shows that current excessive military spending, while sustaining employment levels in the military contracting business, is costing more job opportunities elsewhere in our economy.

The most recent job impact study we've seen was conducted by Employment Research Associates of Lansing, Michigan. Here are the conclusions of that study:

"Between 1981 and 1985, the largest peacetime military build-up in the history of the United States took place. The Pentagon's budget rose from $147 billion in 1981 to $239 billion in 1985. The four-year total expenditures were $823 billion.

"Some of this increase was for inflation. But far more was due to political decisions made at the White House and the Pentagon and ratified by Congress to make large real increases in the military budget.

"These increases cost the American public over 1,146,000 jobs during the period 1981–1985. This was a *net* loss of jobs. It took into consideration all of the additional jobs generated through military spending on contracts and salaries, as well as for increased numbers of military personnel. This was compared with the number of jobs which would have been generated if the money had gone for normal civilian economic activities: investment, consumption, state and local government and (civilian) federal government.

"The total amount spent on the military build-up was $190 billion between 1981–1985. This was the expenditure made in excess of the amount needed to cover inflation. If this sum had been spent on normal economic activities within the fifty states, it would have generated 8,370,000 jobs. Spent on military procurement and personnel, it generated 7,224,000 jobs. This is 1,146,000 fewer jobs than if the money had gone for normal economic activity. There was a net loss of over 6,000 jobs for every $1 billion that went for the build-up."[4]

This negative impact of military spending is not difficult to understand. A dollar spent on military goods and services cannot be spent on civilian priorities. Had those federal dollars not gone to the Pentagon, they instead could have been used by consumers to buy goods and services or to save the people programs Reagan was cutting from the budget. Or they could have been invested in the nation's civilian capital goods stock. The employment results would have been dramatically different.

We get more job bang per billion bucks in civilian production than in military production. A billion dollar investment in guided missile production will create 20,700 direct and indirect jobs. That same $1 billion invested in iron and steel production would create 34,700 jobs.

Or if we put that $1 billion into public services instead, we would create 71,550 jobs in education, 54,260 jobs in health and hospital services, and 39,500 jobs in local transit and intercity transit systems.

Besides, there is sound historical reason to be alarmed when the argument is made that we need the arms race to provide jobs. Three other times in recent world history, industrialized nations have sold their people on the idea that a military buildup was the way to full employment. Those nations were Hitler's Nazi Germany, Mussolini's fascist Italy, and Tojo's imperialistic Japan.

The Erosion of the Military-Industrial Base

For years after the end of World War II, the American economy appeared capable of sustaining high arms budgets. In the last decade, however, the accumulated effects of heavy military spending—particularly from the Vietnam War onward—has helped to slow economic growth, pushed inflation higher and has stranded many unemployed.

Projections into the future, even at current excessive levels, show military spending will produce little or no gains in national employment, income or growth, due primarily to the introduction of labor displacing technologies on a fairly massive scale in military production. The "workerless factory," (see Chapter 5) after all, is an official U.S. Air Force objective, programmed in 1977. These new production technologies have wiped-out platoons of workers on the assembly lines and have hit hard at the skilled trades in metal cutting and metal shaping operations.

Offshore procurement, through licensing, co-production agreements, and similar deals, also diminishes military spending as a job provider, and production of U.S. military goods overseas is an accelerating trend. The General Accounting Office released a report in March 1982, conducted for the Subcommittee on Trade of the House Ways and Means Committee, which listed over 100 military co-production agreements U.S. military contractors and the Pentagon had made with Japan at that time. The list of military products covered everything from landing gears to gyroscope systems, from complete fire control systems and missile guidance systems to giving Japan full production capability for the F-15 fighter (McDonnell Douglas/Mitsubishi) and the P-3C aircraft (Lockheed/Kawasaki). The title of that GAO report says it all: *U.S. Military Co-Production Programs Assist Japan in Developing Its Civil Aircraft Industry.*

The assembly line for many of our weapons systems is globe girdling. Some weapons systems are produced in foreign countries under co-production and licensing agreements. Besides the McDonnell-Douglas

F-15 fighters, Mitsubishi in Japan is building Raytheon's Hawk and Sparrow missiles, Westinghouse fire control systems for the F-4 Phantom, and Hughes Aircraft's fire control system for the F-15. Nippon Electric has licenses with 15 U.S. companies and produces pieces of the F-15 and an anti-submarine patrol plane. If any enemy, whoever the enemy may be, should shoot down one plane load or sink a boat load of fire control systems for fighters assembled in St. Louis, then those fighters may never get off the assembly line.

As we know today, Japan has used its industrial policy and managed economy to turn those co-production programs into full-fledged competition. The *Wall Street Journal* (August 19, 1987) reported that a group of Japanese industries—all Pentagon contractor licensees—are now lobbying to build a new fighter-bomber, with U.S. companies getting only a partial role in its production. Japan has long had a dual industrial policy that emphasizes civilian and military development and the dual use of technologies. When the Japanese Ministry of International Trade and Industry (MITI) isn't calling the shots, the Japanese Defense Agency is now calling them. By 1990, Japan could be the fourth largest military goods producer in the world. Not bad for a country whose national budget limits military expenditures to one percent of gross national product (GNP).

How does Japan do it? By producing for the U.S. military and using U.S. taxpayer dollars!

Military co-production agreements with Japan aren't the only factors leading to erosion of our industrial base, however. In a recent solicitation of bids for avionics on six E-3 AWACs for the British Royal Air Force, Boeing pledged to provide offsets worth 130 percent of the $1.3 billion acquisition cost, if U.K. officials chose it over other competitors. In other words, Boeing would gain a $1.3 billion contract, but to get it, would give away $1.6 billion worth of other business to the United Kingdom.

With deals like those, no wonder we're losing the trade war! No wonder $9 billion worth of military contracts went overseas in 1987 and the amount is growing! Twenty U.S. allies are now demanding offsets as a condition of weapons purchases. Offsets mean the export of jobs whether from the military sector or some other sector. Thus the arms trade and foreign military sales are often contributors to our international trade deficit, rather than a bulwark against it.

What's happening in aerospace is happening in the machine tool industry, too. It's common knowledge a solid and technologically sophisticated machine tool industry is the foundation of a viable industrial base. Yet the National Machine Tool Builders' Association tells us the Department of Defense and the Services are increasingly turning to foreign sources for machine tools. Navy purchases of foreign machine tools quadrupled between 1982 and 1985, while purchases by all three Services doubled during those same years.

Shipbuilding, of course, has long since been conceded to foreign yards. The Merchant Marine Act of 1936 makes shipbuilding and the U.S. merchant marine essential to our national defense. But since less than four percent of our international trade cargoes are carried on U.S. ship bottoms plying the seas of international trade, then there aren't merchant ships being built in U.S. shipyards. In fact, commercial shipbuilding has dried up. Currently there are no orders for merchant vessels on U.S. shipbuilders' books. Only the fading 600-ship Navy goal keeps our few remaining shipyards active.

The best estimates are that U.S. military production overseas in 1987 totaled between $20 and $30 billion, at a cost of 500,000 to 700,000 American jobs.[5] It all points up the little known fact that the arms trade and foreign military sales are often contributors to our international trade deficit, rather than a bulwark against it. Despite a strong foreign military sales export program in the 1980s, sales abroad were more than offset by the costs of military bases and overseas production deals. By 1986, the trade deficit on those transactions was running at $4 billion a year.[6] The arms trade isn't helping us win the international trade war.

In domestic military production, we are heavily dependent on foreign sources for critical minerals. The United States is more than 50 percent dependent on foreign sources for more than 20 minerals essential to military production. Many of these minerals come from just two parts of the world: Siberia and South Africa. According to a recent House Committee on Armed Services report, the United States relies on the Soviets for 12 percent of the chromium, 22 percent of the platinum group metals, 17 percent of the gold and 6 percent of the vanadium consumed in our industrial processes.

I find this an astounding revelation!

If the Soviet bear is poised at our jugular, why is it exporting critical minerals to be used in production of our own war machine? Or, looked at from another angle, how in the hell have our war planners hooked us on the presumed enemy as our supply line for raw materials?

The danger is these idiots might get us into a high-tech war, then not be able to deliver the weapons to fight it. So if you want to know why I'm a belligerent advocate of disarmament and peace, there's one good reason why.

War doesn't make sense when we're trading with the enemy. And I say trade, not war! It's that simple. And it's a lot healthier and far less costly proposition.

Ending Job Blackmail

Each time the military budget or a weapon system such as the MX missile, B1 bomber or Star Wars comes before the Congress, the Secretary of Defense, military contractors, local elected officials and affected members of Congress are all certain to argue that we must spend the money and build the weapon, because it means jobs, jobs, jobs.

In the Machinists Union, we call that job blackmail. No other segment of the labor force is subjected to such brutal economic determinism. Job blackmail into military production robs us of our dignity and degrades the dignity of work. It insults our intelligence and denies us freedom of expression and thought. Job blackmail does not give us credit for being rational, intelligent, free-spirited, thinking and principled citizens. Job blackmail treats us as if we are the lumpen proletariat, interested only in our own economic belly button, and quite incapable of discerning the issues in guns vs. butter. Job blackmail makes us slaves to remote war lords, and forbids us to contribute to the essential public dialogue about disarmament, reversing the arms race and negotiating for peace.

Be that as it may, the fact is in too many local communities and a half-dozen or more states, military production may be the only economic game in town. When that's the case, it's damned difficult to tell the people in those captive political economies that the particular weapon system they are working on ought to be curtailed or scrapped.

Former President of the United Auto Workers Union, Walter Reuther, framed the issue best: "It is a terrible thing for a human being to feel that his security and well being of his family hinge upon a continuation of the insanity of the arms race. We have to give these people greater economic security in terms of the rewarding purpose of peace."

When defense contracts are canceled, weapons become obsolete or procurement shifted overseas, the contractors never lose. They receive indemnity payments in lieu of profits. Only workers lose. In the defense industry, we have socialism for the contractors and corporations but "free enterprise" for the workers—another case of national hypocrisy and upside-down priorities, which must be changed.

Defense workers face a moral dilemma every day of their lives. In a system that deliberately plans for chronic and excessive unemployment, how can the defense worker support the noble causes of disarmament and peace and still keep bread on the table for his or her family?

How can the Machinists Union, which has a large number of members making their living by producing the hardware and weapons in military production, oppose escalating military budgets and expenditures, oppose Star Wars and support defense cutbacks and ending the arms race?

The answer is simple. Military production workers are no different than other production workers. They can see the futility of the arms race, too.

In the context of war or peace and life or death, what the hell does an individual's job mean? There'll be no paychecks in a Nuclear Winter. There'll be no life in Vonnegut's "Ice-Nine" environment. Not even undertakers will have work if rocket and nuclear technology combine to destroy the universe as we know it.

But our experience is that nothing angers our members more than when some well intentioned, but naively romantic group, whose members don't have to depend on a weekly pay check to survive, blithely ignores the vulnerability of our members, *who do*!

We have to answer the question: How do we support military budget cuts and disarmament and keep bread on the table, too?

ECONOMIC CONVERSION

Economic Conversion is the answer.

If the federal government is going to draft or lure workers into military production in the name of providing for the national security, then when they are no longer needed for that purpose, the government owes those workers alternative means to make a living and contribute to the net national product, with no loss in income or injury to their dignity. And that economic alternative should not be viewed simply as support for directly impacted workers, it must also be seen as lifeline support to the dependent community.

Whenever military production goes into a community, or a military base is located in a community, then those local communities and school districts receive some special federal assistance to help pay for additional public services caused by the military production.

On the other hand, when military activity ceases or is taken out of that community, then the workers and the community are left to their fate of unemployment and the "free" labor market. The Pentagon does have an Office of Economic Adjustment, but its solution to the problem historically has been to hire Booz-Allen Consulting Company to make a survey, give the Mayor and city council a plaque for dedicated public service, then recommend that the shut down facility and abandoned land be turned into an amusement park or nonunion industrial park. The trouble is that, after Booz-Allen gets its fee, there's no money to follow up on even those silly recommendations.

Reductions in the military budget and military spending are bound to occur in the near future. Those reductions and cutbacks mean a good many workers are going to lose their jobs. Their communities are going to become economic casualties, too. The time to prepare for these contingencies is before—not after—they occur.

The logical and rational way to meet this need is to direct federal monies from the military into civilian business and industry through planned Economic Conversion. For the past decade, the IAM has been teaching the concept of beating swords into plowshares—by converting skills, plant, and equipment engaged in military production into socially useful civilian production. This alternative is our answer to those who insist on asking us: what are you going to do for a living if peace breaks out and the arms race is halted?

Economic Conversion is both practical and idealistic: practical because it provides job security for workers and their communities in the broadest sense; idealistic because it permits workers and local citizens to support the causes of disarmament and peace on their merits, without fear of sacrificing their bread and butter and without submitting to job blackmail.

The core concept in Economic Conversion is that whenever, wherever and for whatever reason military production ceases or is transferred from one locale to another, then a plan for alternative civilian production will automatically be implemented in the impacted facility and community to replace the lost economic activity with socially useful production.

Simply put, Economic Conversion means planning now to avoid unemployment in the future for those workers affected when a defense plant or program is cut back or terminated. It means converting idle defense and military plant and equipment to civilian and socially useful production. It means the possibility of building railroads, mass transit systems, houses, and solar energy systems, rather than redundant missiles, bombs and nuclear warheads. It would provide real employment rather than unemployment, when defense work stops.

In practice economic conversion requires that advance notice of an impending cutback, transfer of production, or shutdown of operations or closing of a military base be given to the community and workers who, after all, were "drafted" into producing for the national interest and security. That notice should trigger an immediate economic action plan which would provide money grants to the local community to plan for alternative use of skills, equipment and plant that military-industrial complex is abandoning. The conversion plan itself should provide displaced and laid-off workers income maintenance, health benefit protection, education, job training and retraining assistance and/

or the means to transfer to another firm or another community to work, if that is necessary.

The logical time to authorize and enact an Economic Conversion program is while the military buildup is on the upswing. Then there will be a program already in place to avoid the adjustments and hardships that communities and workers inevitably suffer when the defense boom goes bust. And the current defense boom *is* going bust!

We've long urged the Congress to enact an Economic Conversion Program that would provide money for education, training and retraining programs for displaced military workers whenever and for whatever reason military production ceases. Education and training should be coupled with alternative production planning and programs to keep impacted workers and their local communities economically viable and whole, in the event they lose their military contract work. Displaced workers should be given income maintenance, health benefit protection, and job training and retraining assistance. And the local community should be given grants to plan for alternative and socially useful civilian production opportunities.

We have urged that Congress require, when future military contracts are awarded, that contractors design and have ready to put in place a contingency economic program, to be funded by a small fractional surtax on contractor profits. As military investment winds down, those released resources and funds can be transferred to locally impacted communities to rebuild the enterprise and to restore the civilian economy. An Economic Conversion Program would surely be more satisfying to the American taxpayer than the current trend toward export of tax dollars, technology, capital and jobs overseas for national security purposes.

Economic Conversion can be used not only to deal with shutdowns of individual military production programs or ends of individual production contracts. It can be used more generally to convert from a warfare economy to a peaceful economy. What would a peaceful economy look like? Even just a little more peaceful economy?

The IAM asked Marion Anderson, of Employment Research Associates, that question a decade ago. The report with which she answered contained the following information.

If we cut the 1978 military budget by a mere $7.7 billion and invested that money in building the nation's badly deteriorated railroads, we'd put nearly half a million people—474,000—to work in the plants and factories making rail equipment.

If we cut an almost infinitesimal $3.1 billion from military spending, and put that money into mass transit and subway systems, we'd provide jobs for about 200,000 people—192,000 to be exact.

If we shaved just a $1.4 billion sliver off the Pentagon budget and put it into building resource recovery systems, we could add 40,000 people to the payrolls.

Finally, a $2.1 billion cut in the arms budget, if invested in solar energy systems and solar equipment would give socially useful employment to some 71,000 Americans—and help get us off the Persian Gulf oil hook, too.

Put it altogether, and a mere $14.3 billion military budget cut—just 7 percent of the $200 billion budget buster Reagan gave us in 1982—would put over three-quarters of a million workers back to work in those four industrial areas alone. As the ripple effect of that new economic activity spread through the economy, peace and prosperity might just have a chance to prevail in this country. And we could meet the international competitive challenge, too.[7]

Since military production is the nearest approximation to a socialized industry we have, Economic Conversion permits us to play with fundamental concepts, such as economic planning, at national, regional or local and plant levels. Economic Conversion lets us theorize about social accountability in the production process. It enables us to manipulate human and capital resources in a context other than profit maximization. It gives us the methodology to canvass unmet national needs and to design a system that will marry loose or inefficiently employed resources to fulfillment of those needs. Economic Conversion affords us an opportunity to exercise our pragmatic skills in the redesign of obsolete and unneeded tools, equipment and workplaces, while it employs our imaginative talents in the creation of socially useful products.

If Economic Conversion legislation is enacted, a federal precedent would be established which logically could lead to similar legislation pertaining to the private civilian sectors of industry and commerce, whenever and for whatever reasons production ceases and economic catastrophes and dislocations occur.

On an international scale, the task of Economic Conversion is immense, but the opportunities are readily available.

Consider these facts:

- Around the world, the average expenditure per soldier was $19,300, while the average expenditure per school-age child was only $380.
- The money required to provide adequate food, water, education, health and housing for everyone in the world who needs those necessities has been estimated to cost $18.5 billion. The world spends that much and more on arms every two weeks.

- Third World countries now annually contract for more than $30 billion worth of arms from industrialized countries—principally the Soviet Union and the United States. That's ten times more than those poor and undeveloped countries spend on health, education and welfare combined.
- The world's military budget equals the annual income of 1.8 billion people in the 36 poorest nations.
- In 2 days, the world spends on arms the equivalent of a year's budget for the United Nations and all its specialized agencies.
- The developed nations spend 20 times more for their military programs than for economic assistance to the poorer countries.
- The cost of one Trident submarine equals the cost of a year's schooling for 16 million children in developing countries.
- The cost of the *existing* stockpile of weapons in the world is estimated at more than twice the value of the capital stock of all manufacturing industry in the United States.[8]

Those are mindboggling costs—the cold, hard, cash cost of the arms race versus the human race.

The human race is losing. More than half a billion persons suffer serious malnutrition or starvation. One half the world's people have substandard or no housing and have little or no health care. Here in the United States, a half a century ago, Franklin D. Roosevelt found one-third of the nation ill-fed, ill-housed, and ill-clothed. Today nearly one-third of the nation's families are still ill-fed, ill-housed, lacking decent health care and living in poverty or on the marginal edge of poverty.

Since the end of World War II, the United States has spent almost $4 *trillion* on the military. Since taxpayers pay for it, we have a right to ask, what has it bought us?

It has bought us the ability to blow up every Russian city of 100,000 people or more 38 times. Russia can blow up each of our cities of similar size 19 times. Existing nuclear weapons in the world contain enough explosive to blow up—obliterate—each man, woman and child on earth, many times over.

It has also created the possibility of that the world's fate could hinge on the chance of a computer or some other equipment malfunction in the various electronic defense networks. Doomsday rests on the probability of human error resulting from either an innocent level of technical incompetence or a high and cynical level of political madness.

The whole scene is so pathetic, so tragic in its consequences, that we really need some comic relief from it. Several years ago, Senator

William Roth, a Republican from Delaware, erected what he called "the world's most expensive Christmas tree."

He decorated it with overpriced military hardware. Hanging from its branches were a 12-cent allen wrench like the one the Pentagon paid $9,606 for; a 17-cent plastic stool cap that the military was charged $1,118; and antenna motor pin worth 2.4 cents that cost $7,417, etc. Senator Roth bought all the trimmings on his tree for exactly $110.25. But the Pentagon paid $101,119.00 for the same items.

The military budget has become a colossal welfare scheme for much of Corporate America and overseas contractors. Profits for military contractors average some 56 percent higher than profits for businesses serving the civilian sector. Big banks and institutional investors make huge profits when the federal government borrows a billion dollars every other day at current high interest rates to pay for the military buildup.

Between 1980 and 1986, the average American household was forced to spend $10,000 on the military and defense. All we have to show for that good money is a more dangerous and tense world, more people living in poverty, infrastructures crumbling in our cities and towns, our agricultural system bankrupt and incapable of delivering its surpluses to a starving world. For $10,000 per family, we have conquered that mighty fortress Grenada, engaged in acts of terrorism in Nicaragua and El Salvador, and taunted Qaddafi into more terrorism.

LET'S PUT AN END TO THIS MADNESS

I am not a technical expert in the madness of modern weaponry; nor am I a strategic or tactical analyst in the conduct of nuclear warfare. The National Security Council doesn't brief me each morning on the latest movements of that International Chess Game, formerly called the Cold War, which we may now call the Pointless War. I do not profess to be a student of Kremlinology or Soviet attitudes and behavior. I can't even understand my own government's behavior, let alone that of another country.

I only know that I am one of 160 million Americans who, according to the national opinion polls, want an end to the arms race, a halt to brinkmanship and macho diplomacy, and a permanent moratorium on nuclear madness.[9] I am convinced that it was this pressure of public opinion galvanized by the church and peace groups of the country that sent the Reagan Administration first to Iceland and then to Geneva and Moscow to negotiate the INF Treaty and to get the START talks on conventional weapons underway.

I've never met a worker making weapons to kill and overkill who wouldn't rather be making plowshares for peace, instead of implements of death and destruction.

We would be remiss in our obligation to our sons and daughters if we did not discuss their futures within the war and peace context. *They* are the ones who will have to decide whether to fight any future wars. If the Warfare State wants the military draft, then let it draft the robots and give our kids real jobs. They'll need jobs to pay for the Warfare State's colossal mountain of debt in any case.

To say this does not make us weak, gutless or spineless. Promoting the cause of peace and world disarmament—as opposed to unilateral disarmament—certainly doesn't make us un-American. Working to prevent the world from being blown up and poisoned by radioactive fallout isn't un-American.

At a time when millions of citizens are enduring the ravages of inflation, unemployment, unfair tax system, and general economic distress, when federal programs to help the poor, the homeless, the disabled, senior citizens and minorities are being hacked to death by budgetary neanderthals, when the United States is losing the global trade game, and when federal programs to protect people from the callous indifference of Corporate America's power in the marketplace are being dismantled, then our work to cut fat, waste and fraudulent expenditures from a privileged military budget is as American as apple pie.

In each superpower, the military controls and dominates the political economy. In the United States a corporate sovereignty, alien to democratic principles and ideals, helps direct and link the military establishment to the rest of the world through geopolitical designs on countries large and small. There is nothing democratic in either structure or function of military and corporate entities. Working in tandem as they do, they constitute an economic threat as grave as the political peril they pose to our constitutional democracy. Therefore, advanced technology—hatched from the fantasies of these Warfare State creatures—will not enhance or preserve our democratic values and institutions, for the simple reason there is little or nothing democratic about those institutions that design, control and implement it.

THE SKY IS FOR STARS, NOT WARS

The Space Defense Initiative—an oxymoron if ever there was one—presents the world with the ultimate terror in economic and technological tyranny.

The Star Wars scheme not only threatens to increase our military expenditures by anywhere from $24 billion to $40 billion a year, it also threatens to destabilize the whole trip-wire national and global security system. Since there's not a reputable scientist or engineer in the world who supports this hair-brained scheme—every reputable scientist from Hans Bethe to Jerome Weisner discredits it—it is being sold as a big public works program here in the United States, and overseas, a big Marshall Plan in the sky. It isn't purchasing us more security; it is increasing our insecurity on more borrowed money.

Our NATO allies, with the possible exception of Chancellor Kohl of West Germany, don't want any part of Star Wars as a credible defense system. Even Maggie Thatcher is squirming against this one. But Administration salesmen are trying to buy West Europeans with fat offers to participate in Star Wars research and production contracts. Japan already has its space agency cranked up to get a big piece of Star Wars cash and technology.

For those who may be counting on Star Wars for their personal economic security in the future, and who may believe that is the way to launch this nation onto a new growth path toward peace and prosperity, we say nix. Conservative estimates make it a $100 billion program. But most engineers and scientists who are in the business say Star Wars is an open-ended scheme, since no one knows *whether* it can be made to work, let alone *when* it might be made to work.

Where are we going to get the dough? Wring it out of military production workers' compensation? Lay some more cuts in people programs onto the unemployed, the poor, the elderly, minorities, women and single parent children? If the current $300 billion a year military budget gives us six to seven percent unemployment, what makes anyone think another $100 billion, let alone $26 billion, will get us to anything approaching full employment? Star Wars may well increase unemployment, at home and around the globe.

The truth is, if we, the people, don't have economic security, and our government and major corporations don't have industrial and financial integrity in this country, then there is no way we can purchase national security with Star Wars or chemical wars or biological wars or conventional wars or dirty little Central American Wars or all of the above.

Uncontrolled arms spending, a staggering national debt no longer controlled by U.S. national interests, and our international trade deficit are now inextricably intertwined. They feed on each other to undermine our economic security and, hence, our national security.

As Thomas Jefferson, one Founding Father who conservatives almost never quote, put it, "The care of human life and happiness, and not their destruction, is the first and only legitimate object of good government."

Let us rebuild America on the principles of real peace and prosperity, rather than war and poverty.

NOTES

1. The U.S. and Soviet statistics come from the Center for Defense Information, *The Defense Monitor* 17, no. 5 (1988).

2. Statistics on the number of wars and international arms sales come from Ruth Sivard, *World Military and Social Expenditures 1987–88* (Washington, D.C.: World Priorities, 1987).

3. *The Costs and Consequences of Reagan's Military Buildup.* This study, commissioned by the IAM and the Coalition for a New Foreign and Military Policy, was conducted by the Council on Economic Priorities and released in 1982.

4. Michael Dee Oden, *A Military Dollar Really Is Different: The Economic Impacts of Military Spending Reconsidered* (Lansing, Mich.: Employment Research Associates, 1988), pp. 14–19. In this report, "jobs" are full-time, full-year employment. One job equals one person-year of work.

5. IAM Research Department and the National Council for Industrial Defense, September 1988.

6. Ruth Sivard, *World Military and Social Expenditures 1987-88* (Washington, D.C.: World Priorities, 1987), chart 23, p. 39.

7. Marion Anderson, *The Impact of Military Spending on the Machinists Union* (Lansing, Mich.: Employment Research Associates, 1978), pp. 10–11.

8. Ruth Sivard, *World Military and Social Expenditures* (annual) (Washington, D.C.: World Priorities, 1976, 1979, 1980).

9. See *Americans Talk Security: A Series of Surveys of American Voters: Attitudes Concerning American Security Issues,* no. 6 (Boston: Marttila and Kiley, 1988).

science, technology, and the corporate state

If there is technological advance without social advance, there is almost automatically an increase in human misery.

—**Michael Harrington**

Thorstein Veblen predicted that the rise of scientists and engineers into corporate management positions would lead to conflicts between the manager's quest for profits and the scientists' devotion to technical efficiency and conservation (doing more with less). Veblen felt that these conflicts would have beneficial results that would transform the social power structure.

He appears to have been wrong. Instead, for the most part, scientists and engineers have either wittingly or unwittingly, willingly or unwillingly, placed their expertise at the service of the Corporate State, a productive system efficient in details, but supremely wasteful and irrational in its general tendencies.

This failure is not an indictment of scientists, but an observation that the notion of technological determinism, of technology shaping society is a myth. Far from revolutionizing society, technological changes merely reinforce the existing distribution of power and privilege.

Max Weber was closer to the mark when he observed that modern technology at the service of the Corporate State would weave a paralyzing web of instrumentality that would enslave us. The Corporate State has come to assume the guise of modern technology; the management experts lend to the power of capital the sanction of science. Not only the actual machinery of production, but the entire bureaucratic operation of corporate enterprise has taken on the look of an efficient, well-oiled mechanism—the very embodiment of technical reason—against which opposition could not but appear irrational.

There are three important observations to be made in this regard:

1. Scientific knowledge is not ever apolitical (i.e., neutral) in its application. For example, when new machines are designed using a particular new technology, there are design paths that can be followed that would strengthen the power of the workers, and there are design paths that weaken the power of the workers and their unions. Since the technology is in the hands of the corporation, you can imagine which design paths are followed.
2. Scientific knowledge at the service of the Corporate State assumes the purpose of the Corporate State.
3. When competition is reduced through concentration of economic power, the role of innovation through the application of scientific knowledge diminishes, just as do all other costly or risky devices for enhancing efficiency. The resulting slowdown of technological advancement is just another manifestation of the general stagnation that results from economic concentration.

Nobel Memorial Prize winner in Economics, Robert M. Solow, of Massachusetts Institute of Technology, argues that "it's not only how much wealth a country has, but how well it uses that wealth to increase the level of technology that matters."

Obviously in the United States those who control capital and make investment decisions have misused much of the nation's wealth. The Wall Street stock market debacle in 1987, the foreign trade deficit, the federal debt crisis, the merger mania, leveraged buyouts, and takeovers by corporate raiders, and the transfer of wealth from low and middle income people to high rollers at the top of the pyramid are all indicators of misused national wealth.

There is an anomaly in Mr. Solow's analysis, however. In spite of widespread misuse of the nation's wealth, investment in a host of new technologies has been increasing at an accelerating rate. The level of technology in the United States is very high indeed; second only to Japan, if we are to believe Japanophiles. Why doesn't it produce the beneficial results we've been led to expect?

The answer is that not all technology represents progress. We know that nuclear power generation doesn't. Three Mile Island and Chernobyl have proven that. Neither does advanced war technology. The notion that we can more efficiently kill off humankind and destroy the planet, with an ever-growing inventory of high-tech weapons, remains a primitive Stone Age idea. It doesn't square with sane notions of progress.

Outside the war technologists' Frankenstein laboratories and Strangelovian think tanks, civil technologists and technology pundits almost always assume technology is neutral in its impact—an assumption that flows from their dogmatic belief in the free enterprise/free market mythology.

But they are wrong. Technology is never neutral in its impact. Its creation and implementation is going to affect someone, somewhere, for good or ill. The rivers of technology do not flow from or through unpeopled lands. Technology can never be considered in the abstract. People create it. People live or die by it. People give it its essence and purpose.

While technology's emergence and implementation are probably inevitable, its goodness and trustworthiness are not innate. There are good technologies and bad technologies. We determine the goodness or badness of technology not alone by its design, use or efficiency, but also by its consequences upon humankind: its impact upon those who use it, work with it, and consume its products and services. With the exception of nuclear technologies and their radioactive poisons, and some chemical and perhaps biotechnologies, bad technology can be altered, modified or made good. It is our challenge to begin making value judgments about the new technologies coming into our workplaces and into our lives outside the workplace.

The promises of technology are vast:

- more jobs and better job opportunities for everyone;
- more leisure time with higher living standards;
- improved quality of worklife;
- improved quality of goods and services at lower cost;
- winning the international trade sweepstakes; and
- securing a more peaceful world.

But as we look around us, real unemployment is stuck at recession and depression levels. Six out of ten new jobs created pay a poverty wage or a wage on the marginal edge of poverty. Four out of ten new jobs are temporary ones, with no overtime pay or life-support benefits like dental, health and medical care plans; or no pension and retirement programs. Poverty in the United States has been increasing over the past decade, not decreasing. The movement of people out of middle class ranks into lower ones overwhelms the few who find their way into the higher ranks.

What the hell good is leisure time, if we don't have means and money to enjoy it? There's a surplus of leisure time in the Army of the Unemployed.

Improved quality of worklife? That may be true for engineers, researchers, writers, consultants and managers. It may be true even for skilled machinists and technicians. But how about machine operators and clerical and office word processor operators? Chained to monitored machines, the resulting drudgery, monotony and stress hardly contribute to improved quality of worklife. Carcinogenic and hazardous substances in the workplace—they, too, are technologies—reduce the quality of worklife. Polygraph tests and undisclosed personnel information storage and retrieval systems violate privacy in the workplace. There's a technological big brother on the job who is no champion of improved worklife quality!

Improved quality of goods and services at lower cost and lower prices? Not if we judge by health care costs, auto prices, or insurance costs, all produced by industries undergoing rapid technological advancement. Even that paragon of technological "progress" the Pentagon produces no evidence that costs and prices can be moderated through technological advancement. On the contrary, the military budget and weapons costs have accelerated three-fold during the 1980s.

New and advanced technologies promise to make us winners in the global trade game? A staggering international trade deficit says no. The transformation of the United States from the world's greatest creditor nation to the history's biggest debtor nation in the 1980s belies that promise.

When sovereign global corporations transfer technology around the world and interface it with the cheapest labor available to make products that will be imported back into the United States, that transferred technology serves only a private corporate interest, not a national interest. Such technology transfers undermine the home market and fail to create a new market in the exploited one where it is deployed. Technology transfer is central to the whole international trade puzzle. It must be controlled and so must those who control it.

The last unfulfilled promise of technology is self-evident. The escalating arms race with all its super weaponry has not given us a more secure and peaceful world. Star Wars will only increase the insecurity. For those who may believe Star Wars technology will have important civilian applications, it is interesting to note the French Ministry of Defense has completed a study that concludes otherwise. Star Wars technologies are too narrowly dedicated and expensive to be useful for civilian commercial purposes, say the French.

The way we as a nation design, implement, and control the current invasion of new technology into our lives is absolutely critical to our future good and welfare. Yet, as in so many things, we find ourselves at the mercy of self-serving corporate sovereigns, who are restructuring the international and national economies, our workplaces, our lives and livelihoods.

In short, while technology holds out the promise of human liberation—shorter working hours, higher pay and safer working conditions at home and abroad—that promise will not automatically be realized. Achieving it demands economic analysis and political will. It demands that we assert public rights and the common good over selfish corporate interests and private greed.

THE BRAVE NEW WORLD
OF WORKPLACE TECHNOLOGY

The relationship of worker and machine is being radically transformed. Heretofore, machines by and large replaced muscle in the world of work. Human labor remained the principal factor of production in the creation of wealth, although it has never been adequately recognized or rewarded as such.

But there are signs the new technology currently being put in place will relegate labor *as a factor of production* to secondary status. When robots build robots that cut, shape, weld, paint, assemble and load and unload autos and appliances, then we're talking about the primacy of capital, because the labor input into production has been drastically reduced or eliminated on the shop floor. Academics will begin talking about the productivity of *capital*, not labor.

The new technology not only replaces human muscle, it is replacing human brainpower and the human nervous system. Artificial intelligence has long plagued management, but it is no laughing matter to learn that *real* artificial intelligence is being produced in university and corporate laboratory machines.

A number of new base technologies, primarily related to the silicon chip, microcircuitry, and computer technology, coupled with speed-of-light telecommunications systems, are being used to reshape the production of goods and services on a global scale. Some instant historians call it "the third industrial revolution."

The gamut of "new" technologies is not limited to the chip, computers, miniaturization, microwave and comsat. It includes fiber optics, gene technology and genetic engineering, chemical compounds, and an amazing number of materials substitutions and metal composites, all of which have a bearing on the content and organization of work in labs, fields, factories and offices. Taken together, these new base technologies are blurring the distinctions between goods and services; altering the inputs and ratios of the factors of production in production, and, therefore, recreating, remaking and revising arts, crafts, commerce, mathematics, and science. They even affect the language that universalizes and transmits all this knowledge and permits us to communicate about it and do something with it.

War technology and the nuclear era have brought us under the tyranny of technological terrorism. The military conceives, controls, consumes, and deploys the lion's share of new technology. War and the threat of war control and dominate our national psyche and behavior. Those twin demons dictate our politics, our economics, our educational orientation, our industrial base, and our research and development priorities.

Advanced technology is first researched, developed and tested by and for the military. Later some of it is licensed for civilian use. Even that which is licensed for civilian use is subject to tyranny and terrorism. A conceptually flawed, purely privately owned, but taxpayer developed, nuclear power industry has demonstrated that at Three Mile Island and a score or more other sites. Nuclear power has proven to be a dumb, dangerous and expensive way to boil water to produce steam and turn a turbine and generate electricity. And the technology from which nuclear power is derived, the nuclear bomb, is a dumb, dangerous, expensive and futile way to attempt to settle international conflict.

Nuclear power is a depressing example of the offspring of the marriage between technology and the Corporate State. It's no secret that the Machinist Union is on record opposing continued construction of nuclear plants. We represent about 25,000 workers directly exposed to radioactive materials and substances in the manufacture and processing of nuclear reactors, nuclear weapons and other radioactive hardware. Another 50,000 of our members are indirectly exposed to low-level radiation in the transportation and storage of radioactive materials. The incidence of cancer and leukemia among exposed workers is 2 to 2.5 times greater than the incidence of cancer in the population at large. Make no mistake about it: those little magic pellets of radioactivity are a cancer connection in our workplaces. There is no "safe" level of radiation.

It would be an absolute dereliction of duty if the Machinists Union failed to consider the health and safety of its members working with radioactive substances and materials. We oppose nuclear power because it's deadly. As medical physicist John Gofman, who worked on the Manhattan Project that developed the atomic bomb, has testified, "Licensing a nuclear power plant is, in my view, licensing random premeditated murder."

The conceptual flaw in nuclear power is that we cannot control or contain radiation. Radiation is deadly. We can't see it, smell it, or hear it. But it contaminates everything it touches. It's there in large concentrations around nuclear power plants. It is in cess pools of radioactive wastes that can't be disposed of safely. We just pile it up for our kids. We've piled up millions of gallons of high level nuclear wastes that will still be deadly tens of thousands of years from now. By the year 2000, we'll have 1 billion cubic feet of low level radioactive wastes—enough to cover a four-lane highway from coast to coast with poisonous radioactive garbage one foot deep. And we have only begun to dismantle nuclear power plants.

We are told we need nuclear power because building nuclear plants means jobs. Of course it means jobs! So do dope, prostitution and pornography. Airline crashes and auto collisions mean jobs too. But the IAM doesn't go around the country promoting *those* disasters.

We're not buying the job blackmail argument any more. Nuclear power is the most expensive power on the market. It makes our basic industry less competitive. It gouges consumers. Moreover, there are ample safe energy alternatives to nuclear power that promote greater economic growth, create more jobs, employ more people and provide much cheaper energy. A $6 billion dollar investment (in 1982 dollars) in alternative energy, including solar, garbage, alcohol fuels and conservation would create about 475,000 jobs over five years; the same $6 billion invested in nuclear power would create only about 40,000 jobs over the same period.

Three Mile Island still stands as a monument to mad scientists working in the employment of greedy, selfish interests. So do some 20 other sites where accidents, partial meltdowns, and power failures have cause community-wide alarm and anguish. Maybe we should just leave Three Mile Island as a national historical monument to the consequences of greed and technological tyranny.

There is nothing democratic in the way technology is introduced or managed by the military or the privatized corporate entity. There is nothing democratic in the principle, structure or function of the military. (That's why in theory, at least, the Department of Defense is put under civilian authority.) Nor is there anything democratic in the corporation's structure and function.

Therefore, new technology will not enhance the prospects of preserving our democratic and humanistic values, for the simple reason there is nothing democratic about those institutions that control it. We, as citizens, must challenge the policy assumptions, or lack of them, which underlie the current wave of technological mania. And we must challenge those who control it.

Over twenty years ago, Robert Heilbroner, in a remarkable book that discussed the future as history, raised a number of questions about technology, and drew the following conclusion:

The main control we exercise over technology is economic. . . . we have narrowed our control over the incursion of scientific technology into our lives, to the main and single criterion of its profitability . . . as long as control rests primarily on economic calculation, man is not likely to be master of his machines. . . . we must bring technology under deliberate social control.[1]

The arguments we hear today from technology's ardent advocates in the civilian industrial sector are all economic, whether they are couched in terms of "efficiency," "productivity" or "profitability." (Efficiency and productivity are, after all, coefficients of profit; they are also euphemisms used to disguise harmful effects on people and society.)

The introduction, implementation and use of much of today's new technology directly threatens to eliminate labor as a factor of production. In a society devoted to the work ethic, however hypocritical that devotion may be in a system of planned unemployment, elimination of labor as a factor of production is bound to fracture some minds, and lead to some behavioral excesses. For example, the Chairman of General Motors bragged to the *New York Times* in 1982 that for every $1 per hour increase in labor costs, he could install 1000 robots.

Remember the elementary economic fact of life: technology cannot consume that which it produces. Robots do not buy what they build. Nor do they pay taxes. Technology that leaves us unemployed ruptures the elementary economic loop. Even now, this nation's ability to produce outstrips its ability to consume. That helped lead to the Great Depression and to World War II.

THE INVASION OF ROBOTS

Now, let's be more specific and less philosophical.

In the corporate and military hierarchies, systems designers and systems analysts are the new fair-haired heroes. They are the "invisible hand" in today's mystical marketplace. In the workplaces, workers don't stand a chance to communicate with them. Institutional structure, conflicting values, class bias, and the neo-scientific language of software are all barriers to communications.

As the collective bargaining representative for many of America's most highly skilled craft workers and semiskilled and unskilled workers, we in the Machinists Union are experiencing technology's impact across a broad section of industrial sectors and job definitions. As long as Machinists displaced by robots could move upstream and find work in the manufacture of robots, then we had only to worry about retraining for those upstream jobs. Robots, I used to say, cannot reproduce themselves.

That was in the 1970s.

In the 1980s, robots *have* been reproducing themselves. They're doing it in those factories in Japan that we hear so much about. There an unskilled machine loader and an unskilled operator twist a knob, turn a dial, and throw a switch on a few robots and computer-programmed machines, turn out the lights and go home, while all through the night those robots and computer-controlled machines manufacture more robots.

That's productivity. Only it's not the productivity of labor, it's the productivity of capital.

Like rabbits, robots are beginning to multiply geometrically. In 1969, sales of industrial robots totaled $1.5 million. Ten years later, in 1979, robot sales totaled $60 million. Sales are projected to reach $2 billion by 1990 in constant dollars.

Corporate officials at General Dynamics in Fort Worth tell us that robots not only have more endurance and accuracy than human workers, but give management "more flexibility." What they really mean is that robots don't take coffee breaks, don't need lunch periods, can't negotiate for wages, hours, and working conditions, don't demand vacations, holidays or sick leave, and don't file grievances with their union steward.

Robots, though, aren't the only form of new technology displacing human beings in our workplaces. Other advanced technologies including new materials, metal composites and alloys, computer-aided design and manufacturing equipment and "unmanned" flexible manufacturing systems combine with robots to create what the Air Force calls the "workerless factory." Surely "peopleless wars" would be better than workerless factories. I've always said we should draft robots for the military, and give their jobs to people.

THE AIR FORCE ICAM PROGRAM

Most of the robotic technology originated in the military industrial sector. A project begun in 1977 at Wright-Patterson Air Force Base, Dayton, Ohio, is called ICAM (pronounced Eye-cam) for Integrated, Computer-Aided Manufacturing. It is linked to a Computer-Aided Design (CAD) system. ICAM's charter was to develop computerized manufacturing methods, processes, tools, machines and assembly systems in the military aircraft industry. Today we know it as Computer-Integrated Manufacturing (CIM).

Among the Air Force's announced goals in 1977 was to raise the U.S. ranking for computer-aided manufacturing (CAM) from nineteenth in the world to number one. (That may be tougher than it sounds, because U.S. military aircraft makers have been transferring a lot of the aerospace technology overseas. Boeing, for instance, has sold some sophisticated new technology to Japan along with a co-production agreement for the 767 airliner.) It's interesting that the military undertook this industrial policy task, rather than one of the several civilian agencies that dealt with economic and industrial development at that time.

The second announced goal was to increase military contractors' return on investment to 25 percent. It can be reliably reported that the 10 largest contractors achieved that goal in 1984. By contrast, the average profit for all manufacturing corporations was 12.8 percent in that year, according to the *New York Times*.

The third announced goal called for ICAM to develop a completely automated sheet metal factory center. Using robots, that center automatically retrieves raw sheet metal or other alloys from warehousing floors, runs it through metal forming, shaping, cutting, grinding and polishing processes, welds, rivets and chemically coats it, inspects it and sends a completed fighter fuselage out the back door—untouched by human hands!

That's what the Air Force dubbed the "workerless factory."

A single sheet metal center displaces some 62 workers. Some, like welders and quality control inspectors, lose their jobs. Most skilled machinists get new jobs monitoring or doing maintenance work on the new computerized machines. Some become operators of the machines, but they suffer the boredom of deskilled work because ICAM takes discretionary judgment and decision-making—and hence the pride—out of their control and puts it in the hands of a remote, centralized control room, where management runs the programmable automation and calls the shots.

Each aircraft manufacturing plant is capable of installing several such centers, and the Air Force is installing totally automated flexible manufacturing systems in most of its fighter plane production companies. The development of that technology was paid for by the taxpayers but has been made available to the aircraft industry at no charge.

McDonnell Douglas, the nation's second largest military contractor, installed in 1982 a pick-and-place robot that uses a two-step vision system that picks up parts, aligns, and then feeds them into an automated riveting machine. In Fort Worth, Texas, General Dynamics, the nation's largest military contractor, has installed laser technology that permits robots to see and feel in sheet metal drilling and routing in the manufacture of fuselage panels for F-16 fighter planes.

When the Air Force began the ICAM program in 1977, one-third to one-fourth of the IAM membership was engaged in military production. By 1983, military production occupied only one-fifth to one-fourth of our membership. The decline in membership has occurred as the overall military budget, new weapons systems, procurement outlays and the value of our employers' prime military contracts have all increased two, three, or four fold. Productivity on the shop floor has already increased tremendously. However, those remaining production workers' increased productivity hasn't decreased the manufacturing and acquisition costs of military aircraft, in spite of its vaunted productivity gains.

What the "workerless factory" *has* decreased is the number of production jobs. To take a single example, its development cost some 6,000 IAM members their jobs between the late 1970s and 1983 at United Technologies' Pratt and Whitney division. We can be fairly certain of the number of technologically unemployed people at UT, because that corporation was not affected by the general economic depression. On the contrary, UT's military contracts increased to make it the third largest military contractor in the country by 1982.

What's happened to those displaced machinists? The sad truth is, we don't know. No one knows. They answered the call and probably traveled half-way across the country or all the way across country to fill a billet in a skill-short military production job, but when the production crisis was over, or the contract completed, or the work subcontracted out, or systems design and engineering did away with the job, then those machinists moved on, and depending upon their skill or fortune, may or may not have found work in another metal-working, electronics, or military production firm. We're reasonably certain, though, from one-eighth to one-tenth of our membership has been permanently displaced from military production over the past decade.

Forget about that nice, clean, pink and white collar work we're supposed to get when technology drives us from the production floor or skilled machine shops, because the new technology is already emptying people out of whole office buildings. Apply for a job there, and you'll get a short spin through the revolving door by an exodus already underway.

At the beginning of each year, the military services and corporate chief executive officers meet in Washington and go over agenda addressing the goals and problems related to improvement of our military industry. Included on that agenda, invariably, is a section dealing with manpower and productivity. To my knowledge, neither the IAM nor any other trade union representing military production workers has ever been asked to take part in those deliberations, or asked to comment upon the decisions made and courses of action explored there. Our input in planning is never solicited, but our output on the production floor is taken for granted.

We should be there. It is in those executive working sessions where we can get an answer to questions like: What happens to those 62 machinists that are going to be displaced by an ICAM sheet metal center? Or to the 6,000 machinists displaced at Pratt and Whitney? Or the 100,000 displaced in military production?

It's legitimate for us to be there too when we compare the millions of dollars spent developing this technology with the pennies spent identifying and implementing retraining programs for workers who will be displaced.

THE SPREAD OF THE WORKERLESS FACTORY

Having created "workerless factories" in military production at taxpayer expense and given the technology away for free to private defense contractors, the Pentagon is intent on doing the same for civilian industry. A close relative of the Pentagon's ICAM system is the CAM-I (pronounced Cam-Eye) system being developed in Arlington, Texas, by the Air Force. It will do the same things ICAM will do, but it is for methods, processes and tools that have general purpose application in industry at large. It is non-profit, too, and will be given away to the automotive, civil aircraft, farm implement and machine tool industries. The Navy is doing likewise in the shipbuilding industry.

By coupling computerized equipment and machine tools with robotics, CAM-I is slated to eliminate manufacturing and assembly personnel in those industries. The spread of such systems in civilian production plays a major role in Department of Labor projections that show precipitous declines in employment for molders, machine tool operators, machine set-up workers, tool and die makers, boiler tenders, and production painters.

As early as 1983, Allis Chalmers, AVCO, Boeing, Caterpillar, John Deere, General Electric, Hughes Aircraft, and Ingersoll Rand had all installed complete flexible manufacturing systems somewhere in their far-flung corporate operations. These flexible manufacturing systems consist of three primary elements: miniaturized computer-programmed machine tools, made possible by the silicon chip; automatic part transfer machines (robots); and an overall computer-controlled system that integrates the three elements. Thus, the system puts the machine shop and assembly line functions together on a single line. The typical flexible manufacturing system reduces the number of people normally required to perform all the jobs in manufacture and assembly of durable goods to two loaders, three operators, one quality control specialist (although X rays and television are now replacing that job, too) and three supervisory personnel.

This new technology is a reality in industrial America. Its sociological impact, however, is unknown and rarely discussed. Previous new technologies were introduced to do work that was either difficult for human beings to perform, or that could not be performed by humans. The main frame computers and duplicating machines, for example, substituted for human labor admirably, and in the process, created an expansion in job opportunities by providing for the manufacture of new products and additional services. But the sole justification of the new technology, particularly robots, is to eliminate workers. We're talking about whole systems of production being programmed to displace people, not simply a few dirty jobs or heavy-lifting jobs, or, in the office, nit-picking tedious jobs.

What are the costs in employment? If the estimate that each robot costs four jobs somewhere in the economy is accurate, then the 250,000 projected to be in place in 1990 will have cost a million jobs.

The invasion by robots and high technology has found the metalworking industries particularly vulnerable. Carnegie-Mellon Professor Robert Ayres predicts that robots could replace 13.6 percent of the metalworking manufacturing workforce and 16 percent of its machine tools. In addition, Ayres says that those robots with vision or tactile abilities could replace up to nearly 40 percent of the jobs in metalworking where those abilities are required. He also warns that the robotic impact will be heaviest in those regionally concentrated industries that currently have decently paid semi-skilled workers. The impact will be particularly acute in states like Michigan, Ohio, Indiana, Illinois and Wisconsin.

And that's only jobs lost to robots, only one of many forms of new technology. Computerized numerical control (CNC) machines, microcircuitry and robots are only the visible signs and symbols of labor displacement. The job displacing technology invading the blue collar work force today is more than hardware and more than the software that programs the hardware. It is found in new metal composites, new ceramic and plastic substitutes for metals and new fabricating processes. New materials and processes are changing the organization of work, the nature of work and in the process displacing large numbers of skills and workers.

For example, pieces and bars of raw steel and steel alloys have long been cut, ground, deburred, and polished to arrive at their final shape as either a miniscule or major component part of an aircraft engine. Platoons of skilled machinists are required to perform each of these operations in large aircraft engine factories. Today, however, powderized metals are poured from bags like ready-mix cement into heated and pressurized molds, and the parts are produced at near net or final shape. The cutting, grinding, and deburring operations are eliminated. So are the skilled machinists who performed those tasks. Where powderized metals aren't used, lightweight heat and wear resistant ceramics and plastics are apt to be substituted for metal. Where that substitution occurs, precision-made parts are produced from casts, molds, and even stampings. That eliminates more machinists.

A typical aircraft engine requires hundreds of small metal air foils, each with fifty or more tiny pinpoint perforations. Four or five years ago, those foils were individually cut, shaped and machined. Their perforations were bored with semi-automatic boring machines. Today, the foils are cast to net shape from powderized metal and the perforations are made all at once at the speed of light by a laser gun.

At one General Electric aircraft engine plant, more skilled and semiskilled machinists have been displaced by these material substitutions and new production processes than have been displaced by computerized numerical control machines. More skilled and semiskilled work was displaced by them than unskilled work was displaced by robots.

According to Harley Shaiken, MIT scholar and expert, who is probably the nation's leading authority on technology in the manufacturing workplace—he not only knows the theory and operation of the new stuff, but he also has had several years of real shop floor experience as a journeyman machinist: "If productivity rises by 5 percent in an industry or a firm over a ten-year period, then, all other things being equal, 39 percent fewer workers are needed to produce a given product."

So the rule of thumb is: an annual 5 percent productivity increase means 39 percent fewer workers over a ten-year period. And Shaiken says that's a very conservative estimate.

When you go to work tomorrow, count the first nine co-workers and colleagues you see. Then tell yourself in a few short years at least four of you—yourself included, perhaps—are going to be put out of work by new technology.

In the current climate, the stuff is worshipped like a religion. Call it technological idolatry. Pundits think more of robots and machines than they do working men and women. Those are the cold-hearted facts.

The global impact is somewhat more speculative, but a report by the International Metalworkers Federation at Geneva, Switzerland a couple of years ago came to an astounding conclusion. Within thirty years, only 2 percent to 10 percent of the world's current industrialized labor force will be needed to produce all the goods necessary for total demand. Melvin Klerer, Professor of Computer Science at Polytechnic Institute of New York, Brooklyn, recently confirmed the Metalworkers' finding in a paper he delivered to a University of Kentucky Conference on Harmonizing Technology With Society. Professor Klerer states that, within the next few decades, less than 5 percent of the full-time employable population will be necessary for the direct production of basic utilitarian goods. And he defines full-time as a thirty-five-hour week.

Pretraining and retraining programs for displaced workers are practically nonexistent, unless we in the trade unions have bargained some training and retraining language into our contracts. But according to the Bureau of National Affairs, only about 17 percent of collective bargaining contracts include that language.

The Congressional Office of Technology Assessment tells us what little training employers do provide is given to professional engineers and data processing personnel.

Perhaps the job outlook picture was best summarized in *USA Today* in 1983 (March 23, 1983, p. 1). That corporate tout sheet reported that twenty years from now the nation will need only 200,000 new computer analysts, but some 600,000 janitors; we'll need only 150,000 computer programmers, but 800,000 fast food workers. Jobs requiring the least skills will proliferate and far outstrip high-tech jobs. We are talking about becoming a nation of fast food workers, emptiers of bedpans, cashiers, clerks and secretaries. Altogether, only 7 percent of all new jobs during the next 20 years will be in high-tech industry.

That, of course, assumes high-tech firms will all stay here in the United States and produce, and not pull an Atari and flee to Hong Kong and Taiwan. And, as the evidence in Chapter 3 on the global mobility of new technology suggests, that's not a safe assumption.

The Reagan Administration's corporate tax giveaway in the early 1980s paid, dollar for dollar, for practically every word processor, video data terminal, microprocessor, computer and computer-driven piece of equipment installed in our workplaces. The employer received not a tax deduction, but a tax credit, and he wrote off the whole cost from his taxes, over a five-year period. Virtually all computerized new technology and new process machinery and equipment, such as lasers and pressurized heat treatment apparatus, is paid for by tax subsidies. Thus, we have corporate management installing new technology for the purpose of tax reductions, without any thought given to economics or social accountability. Vaunted efficiency is often secondary to tax considerations.

In the civilian sector, that's called the Accelerated Cost Recovery System. In the military industrial sector, the stuff is paid for by the Pentagon. That's called the Defense Budget. In both cases, workers not only lose their jobs, they wind up paying for the machines that put them in the unemployment line.

Such a tax policy is extremely shortsighted. The fact is that nearly 90 percent of all tax revenues in this country are derived from taxes on labor. Displace labor, and the primary source of tax revenues for all levels of government is laid waste, too.

Inside the workplace, new technology can raise havoc with our collective agreements. Work rules, job definitions and job classifications, bumping, seniority rights, and unit jurisdictional disputes all fester and come to a head.

In event of a strike, employers can use new technology to get around striking workers. A new computerized "Flow Control" system enabled 9,000 strikebreakers and military personnel to replace over 12,000 Air Traffic Controllers in 1981. New technology enabled the *Washington Post* and other newspapers to break printing trades strikes. New technology enabled Blue Cross-Blue Shield in San Francisco to withstand a 133-day strike by the Office Workers Union in 1980. When that dispute was resolved, the Blues got rid of 448 workers, who were made redundant under the new telecommunications system installed during the strike.

The list of technology's negative impacts on workers, their communities and the nation is enough to fill several Congressional hearing volumes. But so far, the Congress hasn't asked to hear about it.

THE TECHNOLOGY BILL OF RIGHTS

So what do we do about it?

We do what Robert Heilbroner suggested. We bring the rate of introduction and the implementation of new technology under socially accountable control.

Today it is the sovereign corporations which are combining chip technology, microcircuitry, and computer technology with speed-of-light telecommunications to reshape production on a global scale. In the process, they are manipulating and redefining the value of labor as a factor of production. They are not only telling us how we will be used and when and where we will be used, but whether we will be of use!

Technology is not neutral. It gives our employers and corporate sovereigns enormous flexibility and autocratic, centralized, totalitarian power both on the job and outside in the national economy and global economy. What we as trade unionists must wrestle with is the fact that technology, in and of itself, cannot and will not equalize the social consequences of its deployment and use; nor will technology democratize the political processes and realities in which it is deployed and used. It is up to us to make certain that technology serves the mass of humanity and our noblest ideals. It all begins by getting a grip on it in our own communities and workplaces.

In the Machinists Union, we've developed a technology control program, which we call a Technology Bill of Rights. We borrowed and adapted it from the Norwegian Metalworkers Union.

When technology deprives workers of employment or employment opportunity and deprives them of income, then in no sense of the word can that be called progress. Article I in our Technology Bill of Rights states, "New technology shall be used in a way that creates jobs and promotes community-wide and national full employment."

How do we do that? We catalog the unmet needs of people for public goods and services in their communities and link them to similar unmet national needs. That requires something other than the divine direction of free market forces. It requires a Domestic Investment and Production Plan to coordinate local, state, regional and national economic development efforts, and integrate those with international trade and national security requirements. The IAM has constructed and defined such a plan in our *Let's Rebuild America* proposal.

Computer and information technologies have made economic modeling and economic forecasting a fine art. There is no logical reason why that modeling cannot be used to give us the full employment program that would utilize other new technologies and put the nation to work in fulfilling the promises of America.

A second pragmatic question concerns increased productivity and lower unit labor costs. On both counts, all official statistics report that U.S. production workers are more than competitive with those nations beating our socks off in the trade game. Article II in our Technology Bill of Rights, says unit labor cost savings and labor productivity gains resulting from the use of new technology shall be shared with workers at the local enterprise level and shall not be permitted to accrue excessively or exclusively for the gain of capital, management or shareholders. Computerized research and computerized contract proposals can help us determine what our fair share of labor cost savings and productivity gains ought to be when we get to the bargaining table.

The community and the nation should share in those profits, too. States should adopt a robot tax to replace tax revenues lost by the displacement of tax paying workers. We must not permit technology to reward the wealthy few and the working few, while lower living standards and welfare dependency are forced on a permanent standing Army of Unemployed.

Article II also states that reduced work hours and increased leisure time made possible by new technology shall result in no loss of real income or decline of living standards for workers affected at the local enterprise level. That's another way of saying that workers won't be sacrificed on the alter of "flexible" work schedules and work rules, which often accompany technology's introduction. Article II also invites negotiation for a reduced workweek.

If we're going to compensate leisure time made possible by technology, and if we're going to share the limited work available in the nation, then we have to reduce worktime and the workweek. We have to redistribute the limited work as well as the increased wealth brought about by the new technology.

Collective bargaining is a practical way to begin reducing the workweek from the 40-hour standard established half a century ago. To prevent whipsawing, though, we need to enact a new national workweek standard. Most West European nations have recently reduced their workweek through national legislation. In light of the new technological wave, the U.S. trade union movement needs to commence its campaign for a thirty-hour workweek with no overtime and no loss in pay. We ought to coordinate that with our trade union counterparts throughout the industrialized world. For those corporations that would then flee to exploitable lands, we should tell them to get the hell out. Go ahead and flee. And when they're gone, we should shut the home market door on them so they can't re-import finished products and components for unskilled final assembly. We'll build back anew right behind them and produce for ourselves. If they want to sell that which they produce, if they want their technology to pay off, then they'll have to create a market where they make it and that means raising living standards, rather than exploiting depressed ones.

A third question we should ask about technology in the workplace concerns reorganization of the workplace. "Flexible work rules" is the term management prefers to use. Article IV in the Technology Bill of Rights confronts that issue. It reads, "New technology shall enhance and expand opportunities for knowledge, skills and compensation of workers. Displaced workers shall be entitled to training, retraining and subsequent job placement or re-employment."

That's self-explanatory. Many of us already have education and training provisions in our contracts. The Omnibus Trade Bill, enacted by the 100th Congress, contains extensive provisions for technological education and training programs. That bill also established a National Institute of Technology at the National Bureau of Standards' Automated

Manufacturing and Research Center, located at Gaithersburg, Maryland. There's a window in that proposed Institute for labor education and training, but if there are any trade union members enrolled in education and training programs there, it is not apparent or advertised.

On the other hand, there are some 50 U.S. corporations and the Navy Department already ensconced there, ramming full speed ahead with Computer Integrated Manufacturing systems and substitute materials. It's called the "Factory of the Future," and closely parallels the Air Force "workerless factory" concept.

Since the federal government is building and paying for model manufacturing technology programs, we would like to propose that the federal government, in cooperation with its contractors and the trade unions involved, jointly develop the corollary job and skill training and retraining model necessary to minimize job displacement, and ease the transition along the path toward the completely automated factory.

Workplace safety and health have long been a major concern for most of us. Article VI in the Bill of Rights requires new technology to be evaluated in terms of worker safety and health impacts. It states that new technology shall not be destructive of the workplace environment, nor shall it be used at the expense of the community's natural environment. We adopted this Article from the Norwegian Metal Workers and the Norwegian Workplace Environment law. Other West European nations have similar protections from bad technologies. We have to prevent disasters like Union Carbide's Bhopal catastrophe and those at Chernobyl and Three Mile Island. We have to take action against the epidemic of job-related diseases associated with new materials and chemical compounds introduced almost daily into the workplace. Hazardous substance disclosure laws are the best way to prevent disease and disasters in the workplace and in the environment generally.

Article VII in the Technology Bill of Rights tackles reorganizing workplaces around new technology. It reads, "Workers, through their trade unions and bargaining units, shall have an absolute right to participate in all phases of management deliberations and decisions that lead or could lead to the introduction of new technology, or the changing of the workplace system design, work processes and procedures for doing work, including the shutdown or transfer of work, capital, plant and equipment." When workplaces are reorganized around new technologies, and employee skill requirements are changed or downgraded, or cross skilling pits worker against worker, and job classifications are changed or eliminated, then the individual worker and the union have problems. This consultation and participation clause can help head off those problems and resulting grievances and economic injury.

One of the characteristics of the "Brave New Workplace," as socio-technologist Robert Howard calls it, is the use of surveillance and monitoring systems. In traditional workplaces, foremen and supervisors used the naked eye to police the place. In the "Brave New Workplace," hidden feedback in computerized equipment, and hidden and closed circuit TV camera and monitors, and even electronically-bugged ID badges are used to police workers. It's Big Brother using new technology to watch you and control you.

We need to control Big Brother in the workplace. Article VIII in the Technology Bill of Rights addresses the new forms of surveillance: "Workers shall have the right to monitor control room centers and control stations and the new technology shall not be used to monitor, measure or otherwise control the work practices and work standards of individual workers, at the point of work." If we can't get management to agree with this language, we can seek federal legislation. Limitations on the use of polygraph testing by private employers marked a breakthrough by the Congress in 1988. That set the precedent, but much more needs to be done on the workplace privacy issue.

Article IX of the IAM's Technology Bill of Rights limits employer dossiers on employees and gives individual workers the right to inspect his or her personal data file. Secret files are inimical to democratic rights, all the more so if they can be used to deprive a person of his or her livelihood.

Finally, the Technology Bill of Rights' Article X gets at the military technology issue. It reads, "When new technology is employed in the production of military goods and services, workers, through their trade union and bargaining agent, shall have a right to bargain with management for establishment of Alternative Production Committees, which shall design ways to adopt that technology to social useful production and products in the civilian sector of the economy."

We call this the Economic Conversion Article. Military production workers are typically on a contractor roller coaster. They usually endure boom and bust cycles of work. An economic conversion article negotiated into their bargaining agreements would help prepare them for the day they lose their military contract work, for whatever reason. It is really contingency planning for lay-off and shutdown. Article X would also prod managers and technologists to adapt military technology to civilian production, something that rarely happens in the current military industrial complex.

THE LAG IN BASIC RESEARCH

Innovation has an enormous impact on our life-style and standards. Edward Denison of the Brookings Institute has estimated that advances in knowledge were the biggest single sources of national economic growth from 1929 to 1969. Data Resources, Inc., a respected economic consulting firm, has found that companies that invest heavily in research and development increase employee productivity 75 percent faster than all manufacturers. They also create jobs 120 percent faster, while raising prices only one fifth as fast.

Yet corporate America, while anxious to use robots, and the like to eliminate skilled, well-paid jobs, displays little enthusiasm for basic scientific research or for developing any new technologies that improve the quality of life without enhancing corporate power. They try to smother those technologies in their infancy.

American industries' technical resources are being moved away from long-term basic research toward short-term projects to improve existing products. The amount of total basic research performed by industry dropped to just 14 percent in 1988 from 38 percent three decades earlier. This decline has allowed other nations to chip away at America's technological leadership. It has been estimated that as much as two-thirds of worldwide research and development is now conducted in foreign laboratories. The nation's trade surplus in research and development intensive goods has been eroding steadily.

American corporations have adopted the philosophy that growth through acquisition is preferable to growth through innovation. Large corporations capable of generating cash tend to hold it or use it to acquire other firms. As a result of increasing numbers of mergers and acquisitions beginning after World War II, corporate power has been concentrated into fewer and fewer hands. A handful of large corporations, as described in Chapter 2, dominate the American economy.

Oligopoly has the same unsatisfactory result on competition for innovation that it does on price competition. This is why the majority of significant product and technology advancements have arrived on our shores from abroad in recent years.

Of major importance among many decisions left in corporate hands are decisions about research and development—how much to spend, the appropriate allocation between research and development, the appropriate rate of introduction of new products or improvements. When the threat of competition has been removed, there is a shift of emphasis away from pure research and development of new products into enhancement of already existing products, and even into marketing research or psychological inducement through advertising.

Our monopolistic multinational firms receive a majority of the government funds for research and development. Between 60 and 70 percent of research in the United States is performed in laboratories of private companies. Most federal laboratories are operated by major companies under service contracts. Industrial research today is dominated by a small number of very large corporations. The top 10 percent of those firms in 1976 performed almost 70 percent of the total U.S. research and development effort. The top ten firms accounted for more than 36 percent of all R & D expenditures that year and for 38 percent in 1987. There are strong indications that these firms merely use government funds for research and development to displace corporate funds rather than to increase the total research and development effort. Small firms get less than 4 percent of government outlays for research and development.

Yet an unpublished study by the Office of Management and Budget (OMB) credited firms having less than 1,000 employees with almost half of the industrial innovations between 1953 and 1973. These are the firms the conglomerates are gobbling up to get the new technologies they need, but cannot create themselves despite spending all the government's research and development money. One Commerce Department official associated with the Carter Administration's Domestic Policy Review on Industrial Innovation, when asked if the government intended to continue to reserve a portion of its research and development dollars for small business, replied affirmatively, stating that acquisition of these firms seemed to be the only way of getting new technology into the larger firms!

No one has a measure of the amount of scientific knowledge that is being withheld from development by the Corporate State, but it is knowledgeably reported to be substantial. Market statistics suggest that technology is way ahead of American industry's willingness to absorb it. And I am further convinced that such withholding is consistent with their prime objective.

We have on every hand evidence of industry's resistance to alternate technologies which might endanger their control. Technologically orientated companies are bought up not only to exploit new technology, but often to suppress or to delay it. We see evidence in the automobile industry's reluctance to develop more fuel efficient smaller cars, or to pursue vigorously alternatives to the gasoline-driven piston engine, or to meet pollution standards that at least one foreign competitor has met with ease through the development of the stratified charge engine.

Consider the energy issue for a moment to see the impact of the Corporate State. Currently, corporate income tax deductions, mineral depletion allowances, investment tax credits, accelerated depreciation schedules, and federal ownership and subsidization of uranium enrichment facilities provide energy companies and utility generation, transmission and distribution systems with a negative or zero income tax for new investment in conventional or nuclear energy sources. In fact, over the last few decades, the federal government has provided well over $100 billion worth of incentives to these energy suppliers in order to stimulate production of their nonrenewable, dwindling, sources.

Solar Energy

Think of what could be done for the development of solar energy technologies if solar developers had received the same tax subsidies, the same federal promotion and the same federal incentives. If we were serious about achieving energy independence and utilizing a national energy policy to achieve full employment, that's what we would do. More than a decade ago, a 1976 study by the Energy Research and Development Administration showed that solar systems were economically competitive with residential electric heating in most regions of the country. In twelve of thirteen cities chosen for variations in climate and fuel costs, positive savings were possible from solar power within five years or less. A 1978 study by the Council on Environmental Quality suggested that solar energy could provide 25 percent of the national energy needs by the year 2000 at rates competitive with some fossil fuels and with nuclear power, given a proper federal commitment.

A permanent national strategic commitment to a solar development policy was first recommended to President Truman in 1952 by the Paley Commission. Would that we had opted for solar then instead of pouring billions of dollars into nuclear power which is extraordinarily costly in economic terms and will prove a 100,000-year curse on the earth!

Enhancing the solar prospect is the photovoltaic cell, the principal power source of space satellites. Photovoltaic cells generate electricity directly when sunlight falls on them. They have no moving parts, consume no fuel, produce no pollution, operate at environmental temperatures, have long lifetimes, and can be fashioned from silicon, the second most abundant element in the earth's crust. Solar expert Dennis Hayes forcefully argued more than a decade ago that a total investment of $1 billion, which was then one-thirteenth of the total Department of Energy budget, in photovoltaic capacity would make solar power cost-competitive with nuclear power and other high cost energy sources. Hayes compared the feasibility of the photovoltaic process with the development and use of transistorized semi-conductors. Early appliances and equipment using transistors were expensive, but through federal promotion of their use in defense and space production, they rapidly became inexpensive. The classic example, of course, is the transistorized voice recorder. Early models sold at $100 to $200 each. Today it is not uncommon to find the same or improved recorders selling for as little as $10 or $20.

Yet despite the promise of solar energy, we have not seen a major national commitment to its development. Instead there has been a serious effort to delay the development of solar energy technologies. The reason is simple enough. The oil companies, which already owned huge coal reserves and virtually controlled the uranium industry, obtained in the 1970s a substantial interest in the copper industry— copper is critical for installing and operating solar systems—and in solar technology companies. They bought up nearly all photovoltaic cell manufacturers while, at the same time, they conducted a major campaign to discredit solar as a viable alternative energy source.

One would like to think that their motivation was simply not to be left out should their assessment prove erroneous (i.e., that they were hedging their bets). However, the result is that they gain the means of controlling the development and the rate of introduction of these technologies. With such control, they can sit on this technology until they have exhausted the potential of their investments in more conventional energy sources and technologies. You need not be convinced, as I am, that this is happening to see that something is very wrong when this behavior is possible. Under existing law, there is little that we can do to stop it. However, it is interesting that of all industry groups whose expenditures for research and development are reported, companies in the category of fuels spent the least.

The eight largest energy companies have a lock on petroleum from the wellhead to the gas pump. They own 60 percent of all coal reserves and 40 percent of all uranium reserves. They have joint ownership and control agreements with most natural gas producers and pipelines, and are interlocked with each other, big banks, and most investor-owned utilities (IOUs).

Through their interlocking directorships and interlocking equity ownership with local and regional utilities, they will allocate and distribute solar energy, when they finally bring it on stream, the same way they have been allocating and distributing conventional energy for the past 100 years. That is true despite the fact that solar energy by its nature lends itself to *decentralized* development. How unlike nuclear power. And how unlike the existing oligopolistic structure of the energy industry. No wonder the energy companies want to delay solar power until they can figure out how to hang a meter on the sun.

Moreover, the banks and other financial capital sources are all tied to the existing energy companies. When we examined this question in 1978, it was easy to demonstrate the ties between all the big names. Fourteen banks were tied to eighteen of the largest oil companies through interlocking directorates: Exxon and Morgan Guaranty; Exxon and Chase Manhattan; Exxon and Bank of America; Gulf and Mellon National; Mobil and Chemical Bank; Mobil and First National; Texaco and Continental Illinois; Texaco and Chemical; Atlantic Richfield and Chase; Atlantic Richfield and First Chicago; and there are dozens more. Insurance companies, investment companies and other energy companies were all tied in too. For example, Continental Oil (Conoco) then had primary interlocks with Bankers Trust, Morgan Guaranty, and Continental Illinois. All of these banks, in turn, had interlocks with insurance, investment and other energy companies. The Conoco-Morgan Guaranty tie alone brought secondary interlocks with four of the nation's largest insurance companies (John Hancock, Aetna, Metropolitan and Penn Mutual), two coal companies, three other major oil companies, two large utilities, and a gas pipeline company. A diagram showing the lines running from oil companies to banks and back looks like a piece of string art.

Imagine a solar energy entrepreneur approaching Morgan Guaranty or any of these other major banks and asking "How about a loan for a new nonpolluting renewable energy source system that makes oil obsolete?" He'd get better odds at the track betting on the daily double.

Corporate America's failure to develop the promise of new solar technology not only increases pollution and puts our grandchildren unto the 100th generation at risk from the radioactive wastes of nuclear plants, it also misses the opportunity for job creation. Study after study has demonstrated that solar energy produces more jobs than the alternatives. James Benson, who directed the jobs study for the Council on Economic Priorities, for example, compared the impact of constructing a nuclear plant with a solar/conservation package. He found that the solar/conservation package would produce 270 percent more employment than would the construction of the nuclear plant. Dovetailing the development of alternative energy sources, including solar, co-generation, biomass, small hydroelectric and wind with a national manpower policy and full employment program is a tremendous opportunity. Development of the new energy technologies and their widespread use would create several million jobs directly with the ripple effect adding a great many more.

In an age when the economic gurus proclaim we have "full employment" when 10 million Americans are out of work, it ill behooves the Congress and the President to ignore the employment potential of solar energy and other alternative energy technologies that the energy cartel wants to suppress in order to maintain its bloated profits.

Space Exploration

The answers to some of our problems of protecting and enhancing life on this planet lie in the area of developing the potentials of space exploration and use. These potentials range from environmental protection through eventual removal of polluting industrial processes from the earth's atmosphere through space manufacturing to eventual cheap raw materials sources to totally new manufacturing processes and products that could be developed in zero gravity to unlimited cheap power through an array of solar power satellites. If perfected and made ecologically sound, a solar power satellite system offers a virtually unlimited, renewable and safe energy source. Most of the basic research and a good deal of the design work has already been accomplished. Yet, it has not been possible to convince NASA or Congress to proceed at anything other than a financially starved snail's pace with respect to exploiting these potentials. I think we can see the hand of corporate America in this decision, from the power companies and the oil industry, to the companies which make up the traditional military industrial complex and the conventional aerospace industry. They all feel threatened by the potential transformation that could result. These are powerful opponents of scientific and technological developments.

Innovation means disruption and inconvenience. As companies become larger, richer, more insulated from the necessity to adjust prices to demand fluctuations, they start to trade innovation for convenience and efficiency for stability. Apparently without the spur of competition, industry, with a few notable exceptions, will not continue to invest in genuine innovation.

In recent years, our recognition that we live in a finite world with finite resources has been growing. This is good in that it represents the truth, even if we misperceive where the boundaries are. It encourages an appropriate concern and respect for the appropriate use of all of our resources. But it can be bad when it is used to frighten us into acceptance of limits of freedom and potentials of development, fostering the notion that solutions should not be sought because there are not any.

Scientists, researchers and designers are the true conservationists. The whole history of the advancement of science and technology can be capsulized as "learning how to do more with less." I do not believe that the limits of this advancement have been reached. But I do believe that the Corporate State has managed to tighten its grip on research and development so that they now, more than ever, serve to advance the interest of the corporations. And these interests are not compatible with what is needed to strengthen our economy and our society.

We are at present in the midst of a *capital strike.*

With their monopolistic positions, corporations' and banks' investment decisions are not made just to maintain market position. Without effective competition that position is already pretty secure. Therefore, investment decisions can be designed to consolidate further their economic and political power, weakening their enemies, or just keeping workers, governments and the population at large in a dependent position of insecurity and uncertainty. With no competition, an assured market and control over prices, corporations can withhold investment in more efficient plant and equipment. That puts pressure on the economy and, therefore, on the government to obtain favorable regulatory, legislative and financial allocation decisions. The result is that corporate America will not take investment risks on new plant and equipment or on the development of new products or on the furtherance of scientific research because they don't need to do so and because they have concluded that the return on such investments is not high enough with respect to the risks involved. And further, they have learned that there are power leverage advantages with respect to the allocation of their investments. So they chose high return, short-term investments instead.

Ever wonder why the Japanese and Europeans are winning the trade wars? Corporate America's *capital strike* is a major reason. A national capital strike is as serious economically as a national labor strike would be. What it amounts to is an escalation of class warfare.

If we have, in fact, entered a new period in the history of life on this planet where scarcity of resources is a prominent feature, then we must become more prudent in the use of all of our resources. Not just the natural resources, but also the knowledge that results from scientific research. Decisions about the support of scientific research and particularly the development of possible technologies and products can no longer be left strictly in the hands of private conglomerates any more than we can permit them to keep a complete lock on production, prices, plant location and investment.

We often think of corporations as being somehow sacrosanct quasi-autonomous entities, allowing ourselves and them to forget that they are creations of the state. However, if in their actions they fail to make a positive contribution to the common good of the state, their charters to do business could be pulled by the state.

Corporations do have an obligation to do more than simply maximize the return to shareholders. Through laws and regulations, the state continually redefines the exact nature of how the corporation must operate to serve the common good. Somewhere along the way, we have allowed the notion to creep in that there are definite limits to how far the state can go without infringing on some God-given rights of the corporation. Well, there really are no limits on the requirements the state can place on corporations to remind them of their obligation to serve the interests of the state's citizens, even where those obligations may override stockholder interests. And I, for one, believe it is time there was a little more reminding done.

Unless we move quickly to establish stronger mechanisms for public control over investment decisions and credit allocation, power will continue to become even more concentrated in the hands of a few and corporate priorities will continue to overwhelm all human considerations. We see this both in the kind of technological changes implemented by American corporations and in those they suppress.

HARVESTING THE FRUITS OF NEW TECHNOLOGY

We have to come to grips with technology's accelerating and uncontrolled impacts on the human factor of production in both the domestic and global economies as well as in our workplaces, if the promises of technology are going to be fulfilled for the many as well as for the few. Our objective is not to block the introduction of new technology. If that were possible, and it is not, it would not be desirable.

We believe that corporations owe it to the public to produce the best and cheapest product possible with the most advanced technology they have available. We criticize them for their failure to develop promising new products and technologies, especially when they have been developed in part or wholly with taxpayer monies. Corporations that do so should lose their exclusive rights to any patents involved.

A corporation should not have the power to delay or withhold the fruits of research and development. It seems to me that a procedure whereby petitions by interested parties for the setting aside of patent restrictions or forced licensing should be instituted in instances where compelling evidence indicates that the patent owner has not made a reasonable attempt to develop all promising applications.

The issue is not whether we should have new technology or not. We should. The real issue is under what circumstances it is introduced and to what ends. Should it benefit only the few and impoverish the many? Should we permit it to be imposed on the premises of corporate America, stripping production workers of decent jobs and throwing them into the Standing Army of the Unemployed and Underemployed?

Here the answer is no. That is suicidal for both the labor movement and the United States.

We have to control the rate and the manner of the introduction of new technology and we have to control the way that it is used in order that it be adapted to our needs. Technology should serve people, rather than our being servile to it. It can go either way. Right now, in the hands of our corporate sovereigns, it is headed the wrong way.

What we have to do is to find a way to distribute the benefits of new technology to everyone, not just the wealthy few. Now is the time for a shorter work week without loss of real pay. Otherwise, some of us are going to have leisure time we never dreamed of—but, just like those millions out of work now, that leisure time is not going to be compensated.

As one commentator has already put it, "we'll be starving in Paradise."

NOTES

1. Robert Heilbroner, *The Future as History* (New York: Harper, 1960).

SIX _____

labor relations today: cooperation or a new class war?

Show me a country without strikes and I will show you a country without liberty.

—Samuel Gompers

The election of Ronald Reagan in 1980 marked the end of a forty-five year compromise between labor and capital in this country. In that compromise which was reached during the New Deal, trade unions gave up pursuit of socialism and independent political action in return for certain economic rights, such as minimum wages, hours, work standards and limited protections for workers wishing to organize unions for purposes of collective bargaining.

Today, both government and employers have reneged on that deal. In that pitifully small portion of the labor force represented by trade unions, employers are demanding their workers take wage freezes or cuts, give up cost-of-living adjustments, reduce health care coverage, cut back pension and retirement benefits, and give back break periods and washup times. Employers are demanding absolute power to discipline employees without union representation. They refuse to act upon grievances filed by workers, or they force those grievances they do act on to go all the way through arbitration, thereby delaying justice on the job and draining local union treasury funds.

God knows what's happening where workers have no union or collective bargaining rights.

To get an idea, we can look back at our experience when industrialization was beginning in places like Lowell, Massachusetts, some 150 years ago. Young farm girls, age ten to fifteen, were recruited to work in "this wonderful city of spindles and looms," as one observer described it at the time. For awhile, it may have been wonderful, but as factory ownership passed from paternalists to absentee owners, the "marriage of morality and manufacturing" abruptly became decadent. Under absentee owners, Lowell's paternalism became a cover for outright tyranny in the workplaces and the community. Labor recruiters, called "slavers," lured young women into the factories and mills with all sorts of deceptions. But those country girls were not long deceived, and turnover at the mills was extraordinarily high. To keep this city of spindles and looms humming, employers began hiring platoons of Irish immigrants. And when the Irish rebelled, German immigrants were readily available to take their places.

In that fashion, the cost of labor was always bid down, the dignity of labor was degraded, and the rights of women violated. We can observe this same corrupt "slaver" system today in exploited Asian Rim countries and in the Mexican maquiladora system. It should not be surprising, therefore, that we now find cottage employment and sweatshops in the electronic assembly and needle trades industries invading the depressed rural economies of states like Iowa. It is *déjà vu* economics. And the least common denominator becomes the norm in a savage global, rather than national or local, competition.

THE DEVELOPMENT OF LABOR LAW

The current concession-bargaining era is reminiscent of the 1920s, when free trade union rights were widely held in contempt and union after union was smashed. Then, as now, a wave of labor-saving technology was invading the workplaces in the form of mechanization and workplace reorganization. Then, as now, the bulls on Wall Street were rioting in paper-profit splendor. Then, as now, stock exchange euphoria was fed by the endemic corporate disease of mergermania. Unfriendly takeovers, leveraged buyouts, labor-displacing technology, and corporate executives' illusion of power in the White House were also hallmarks of the "Roaring Twenties." So was adulation of the rich and super rich. Then, as now, government withdrew from the regulation of business while business took over the government.

During the Roaring Twenties, with the Farm Depression already underway and rural to urban migration swelling the ranks of unemployed in cities, the employers in National Association of Manufacturers (NAM), National Machine Tool Association, and Railway Executives Association were determined to break the toehold that unions had gained during World War I. Their so-called "American Plan" was a deliberate campaign to establish the Open Shop and company unionism.

Harding and Coolidge used the federal government to give free rein to the American Plan offensive, under guise of a "return to normalcy." One of the most amazing acts was the sweeping injunction obtained by Harding's Attorney General, Harry Daughtery, that literally banned free speech, freedom of association, and trade unionism during the 1922 Great Railroad Strike.

Extreme right-wing groups rose to new heights on this wave of "Americanism." By 1926, there were more Ku Klux Klan members in the United States than there were union members. Mussolini had come to power in Italy and installed his Corporate State, a system much discussed and admired by many American businessmen.

In grappling with the situation, the IAM's 1928 Organizing Report listed four major barriers to organizing new members: (1) unemployment and fear of unemployment; (2) technological change; (3) illegal management conduct; and (4) the pervasive anti-social sentiments and behavior which included euphoria over movies, radio, music and religious revivalism and bathtub gin. Business and government championed the one and drank the other.

Aside from the bathtub gin, that all sounds awfully familiar.

Much was made of "new prosperity" in 1920s. But it was phoney. Nearly 50 percent of the population lived in poverty. As the "American Plan" continued to put screws to working people through union busting and wage cuts, consumption declined. Business economists didn't worry, because they subscribed to Say's Law that supply creates its own demand—the basis of today's supply-side economics. The real problem, however, was underconsumption: the lack of purchasing power by working people. It was lack of demand, not lack of supply, that caused the tailspin of the Great Depression.

Labor law of that day provided few protections. If your grandfather had been a machinist, he might have been covered by the Railway Labor Act, which in 1926 gave railway workers right to organize and created procedures to settle disputes. But if he was in a shop or factory, he had no rights except those his skill might afford him. Highly skilled tool and die makers and machinists might easily strike and close down the shop, but in Cincinnati and other machining centers, employers used government and police to break strikes by force, and then they blacklisted strikers and union leaders. Injunction judges summarily supported employers.

If Grandfather was an unskilled or semiskilled worker, all he had going for him was guts, because he could be replaced easily by someone unemployed.

Prior to about 1930, the struggle of trade unions in this country was a continuing saga of civil disobedience. During the first part of the last century, trade unions were legally and extra-legally viewed as conspiracies in restraint of trade. When that legal theorem itself was restrained in the Hunt case (1842), the substitute legalism became the "factor of production" theory in which property rights were asserted over human rights. We haven't moved very far since then in our legal thinking as the current despotic "Law and Economics" school of legal thought demonstrates. In the latter part of the nineteenth century, government troops were regularly used to break strikes and to assert the primacy of property rights.

There was a brief moment when the Clayton Anti-trust Act (1914) stated that labor, as the human factor of production, should not be treated as just another article of commerce. However, that prescriptive legality wasn't hard for capital and its compliant government to circumvent. All they had to do was make Eugene Debs and Joe Hill and Big Bill Haywood, among others, political undesirables, rather than "articles of commerce." The government looked the other way when employer thugs murdered radical union organizers. Government authorities clapped hundreds of labor leaders and socialists in jail, including Debs who ran for President from his prison cell, and they did their share of killing too, gunning down strikers and framing radical leaders, like Joe Hill who was executed in Utah in 1915. The Palmer raids, named after Woodrow Wilson's attorney general, led to the arrests, trials and deportations of many foreign-born radicals in 1920.

As we read history and view trade union politics even today, it is obvious that the fear and threat of being labeled a "political undesirable," or a "radical," or a "socialist," or a "communist" remains the most powerful intimidating force to make workers and trade unionists conform to conservative values and right-of-center economic and political ideals.

Historically, trade union leaders have been less militant than rank-and-file members and have been more concerned about appearing "responsible" with respect to management and in the eyes of the public. Similarly, they have refrained from and restrained their members from participating in "Labor Parties" or other left-of-center movements. Occasionally, though, membership rank-and-file pressure can build forcefully enough to move leadership in a direction it would not choose on its own. Such was the case in the trade union flirtation with LaFollette's Progressive Party in 1924. And such was the case in John L. Lewis' much eulogized walkout from the AFL Convention in 1935. However much Lewis has become the darling of the left for that maneuver—or was it for punching Bill Hutcheson in the mouth?—it is worthwhile to note that he never made a move toward radicalism or broke from his Republican Party affiliation during the persecution of the IWW and Debs' Socialists. Nor was he to be found in the Progressive Party thrust, after Debs and the "Wobblies" were jailed, exiled, or shot.

The Coming of the Wagner Act

Most labor historians choose to ignore what was probably the real impetus to form the CIO and to pass the New Deal's labor protections: the formation of Unemployment Committees and councils in practically every major city in the United States during the late 1920s and early 1930s. Spearheading those local drives to organize the unemployed into self-help and mutual support groups, and hence educate them toward egalitarianism and socialism, were local Communist Party organizers, inspired by the success of the Bolshevik revolution in Russia, and other radicals.

Many of them were intellectual activists. Others were just street-smart and mule-tough veterans of union organizing drives who had survived the Lawrence and Lynn strikes of 1912–13, the 1919 Steel Strike, the Palmer Raids and red scare campaign of the 1920s. Nor had they been entrapped by the American Plan.

Whoever galvanized unemployed citizens and bitterly disillusioned trade unionists into forming those Unemployment Councils, it was they, much more than John L. Lewis or any of the AFL hierarchy, that moved Franklin D. Roosevelt to put a labor agenda at the top of his early priorities. Wherever FDR visited in his 1932 campaign, he was confronted by large crowds of organized unemployed people. And those Unemployment Councils were challenging established AFL city central trade union bodies around the country. William Green and his conservative building trades cronies clearly were not in command of the situation. By 1935, both John L. Lewis and FDR had gotten that message.

In late 1920s and early 1930s, the LaFollette Committee hearings provided eloquent testimony to the rampant employer abuses of workers. The hearings became a full scale expose in 1931–32 and led to the Norris-LaGuardia anti-injunction Act (1932). That act gave new life to union organizing efforts. Trade union city central body actions and the growing wave of local general strikes increased nearly fourfold after enactment of Norris-LaGuardia. General strikes put pressure on the AFL, politicians, and employers alike. The usual "red scare" tactics were employed, but didn't have the effect they had had in the days of the Palmer raids a decade earlier.

Finding some relief and remedies in political action outside the scope of trade unionism wasn't seriously considered, not even in the

1932 campaign, when both major parties looked alike and sounded alike. Franklin Roosevelt ran on a promise to balance the budget, but he did sound some selective populist themes in strike-torn cities.

Once in office, however, Roosevelt had to grapple with the problems of the Depression. His legislation included basic workers' rights. First there was the National Industrial Recovery Act (1933) and its Industrial Codes that sought to compel labor-management cooperation through the right of workers to form associations and organize. It was a boon to trade union organizing efforts in basic industries and skilled trades, but not in the service sector (for example, auto repair). General Hugh Johnson enforced those codes by permitting company unions, rather than free trade unions. General Johnson's brand of "official company unionism" was modeled, some scholars are convinced, after Mussolini's system of labor relations in vogue in Italy at the time, which was subsequently aped in Hitler's Germany, Franco's Spain, and Salazar's Portugal.

So, if father was joining a union during the first five months of 1935, he might well have been joining or forming a company union under the National Recovery Administration (NRA).

But in May 1935, the U.S. Supreme Court declared NRA unconstitutional.

Two months later, on July 5, 1935, the National Labor Relations Act (the Wagner Act) was passed by Congress. It was a marked improvement on the NRA. It prohibited financial support for company unions, and declared collective bargaining to be the national labor policy. It prohibited certain unfair labor practices on the part of employers: discrimination against union workers, interference and coercion against workers seeking to organize, firing workers for union activities or for testifying under the Act. It also made the employers' refusal to bargain in good faith an unfair labor practice. Disputes settlement machinery was provided through the National Labor Relations Board (NLRB).

The Wagner Act gave great impetus to a wave of organizing in mass production industries, especially after the CIO was formed expressly for that purpose. So after July 1935, father had a good chance of organizing a union and getting improvements in wages, hours and working conditions. He probably had to strike for recognition because employers, who were convinced the "nine old men" sitting on the Supreme Court would declare it unconstitutional, openly flouted the law. The law stood, however, and provided the legal framework within which mass production—autos, rubber, steel, and the like—was organized in 1936–38.

It was out of this experience that the New Deal compromise that guaranteed labor's basic rights emerged. That's the compromise that Reagan and his Rambo corporate managers tore up.

After the Wagner Act

The Wagner Act was the high tide of American labor legislation. The history of labor law in the post–World War II period has been one of retreat from positions of the Wagner Act. After unions had faithfully and fully cooperated in the war production effort and had gained some footholds in scaling the Mount of Economic Democracy, they were kicked in the teeth after the war by employers who wanted a second "return to normalcy" and the open shop. And a reactionary Congress complied with the employers' demands by enacting the Taft-Hartley Act in 1947.

The original intent of the Wagner Act was to establish government neutrality in labor-management relations. Some academic observers will claim that the intent of Taft-Hartley was to provide balance in labor-management relations, since the balance of power had shifted, they say, to unions under the Wagner Act. That is an indefensible position, however. The relationship between employer and employee is inherently unbalanced, because the employer has hiring and firing power, because the employer has the jobs, because the employer has all the economic power he needs to deal with employees, even with the Wagner Act before Taft-Hartley. The power of one man to deny bread to another says it all.

Taft-Hartley rolled back union rights. The Taft-Hartley, on secondary boycotts was not just a matter of "restoring the balance of power," it was a matter of preventing general strikes of the kind that erupted in cities across the nation in 1932. If workers can't conduct general strikes, then they obviously can't put effective pressure on the Corporate State, nor can they bring the kind of pressure to bear on employers, government and the public that produced the Wagner Act in the first instance. For the individual company, banning the secondary boycott means a struck employer has virtually all the power he had in pre-Wagner Act days, because if he has access to his suppliers and distributors, he has unimpeded marketing. And in a high unemployment economy and highly automated workplace, and with a cadre of supervisory personnel who, by law, cannot belong to a union, he has all the production capability he needs to circumvent the strikers and break the strike.

Beyond restricting union rights, Taft-Hartley encouraged employers to attack unions directly. It established the right of management to interfere in workers' right to organize freely. Employers can wage anti-union campaigns inside the workplace, just as they could before the Wagner Act. Many employers, who have never accepted the legitimacy of free trade unionism, did exactly that. The outrageously misnamed "right-to-work" section of the law—which, of course, gives no one the right to a job—encourages employers to pack up their equipment and move to an anti-union environment. Here the old open shop drive reared its ugly head under the guise of "states' rights." Under Section 14(b), 19 states have told us they don't believe in free trade unions. Other sections of the law that impede free trade unionism include the exclusion of certain employees from bargaining units and trade unions; the reimposition of injunctions; and the strike notice requirements. Even under Union Shop conditions, trade unions can't protect themselves from infiltrators, criminals, or company agents, because they can't dismiss anyone from their unit except for nonpayment of union dues.

Taft-Hartley, of course, was followed by Landrum-Griffin Act in 1959. Clearly this law was designed to shift the balance of power further from workers and their unions to the employer. Ironically, this law was enacted in the name of promoting democracy and freedom in unions. It was, of course, promoted by those who consistently have tried to destroy unions in America. Hypocrisy has always been their strong suit.

Kennedy's New Frontier and Johnson's Great Society gave us the crucial civil rights acts, important social measures like Medicaid and Medicare, and other major reforms. But despite the pledge in the Democratic Party's platform to repeal the Taft-Hartley Act's Section 14(b), the right-to-work-for-less provision, the vital labor law reform did not occur.

Legislative hearings, however, did produce the evidence for why reform was needed.

On February 2, 1960, the panel of labor law experts chaired by Archibald Cox filed its report with the Senate Committee on Labor and Public Welfare. The report concluded that "A major weakness in labor-management relations law is the long delay in contested NLRB proceedings. In labor-management relations, justice delayed is often justice denied."

In 1961, the House Subcommittee on Labor Relations, chaired by Representative Pucinski, held fifteen days of hearings on labor law reform. Among other things, the Pucinski Committee found, "Labor Board orders constitute in many situations no more than 'a slap on the wrist.' They are both too little and too late. They constitute . . . a license fee for union busting. The Subcommittee recommends that the Labor Board reconsider the problem of remedies with an eye to taking the profit out of unfair labor practices."

More hearings were held in 1965, and in 1967 the Special Subcommittee on Labor issued a report entitled "National Labor Relations Act Remedies: The Unfulfilled Promise." The Subcommittee recommended, among other things, that "Congress expedite the processing of unfair labor practice discharge cases by (a) delegate to Administrative Law Judge greater finality of decision making process . . . (b) make decisions of the Labor Board self enforcing and (c) require immediate reinstatement of discharged employee upon finding that discharge was unlawful."

In 1971, the Special Subcommittee on Labor held 8 days of hearings on expediting elections and other processes and strengthening remedies against abuses of the law. A total of 19 days hearings were held in 1975 and 1976, which summarized findings and conclusions of all previous committees. After those hearings, the Subcommittee on Labor-Management Relations concluded, "There is no effective penalty for disobedience of the National Labor Relations Act . . . there are rogues who must be curbed by law for the benefit and protection of all others. . . . The inability to curb and remedy such egregious conduct turns what purports to be a protective law into an entrapment to disaster. . . . This goes unremedied because of the twin problems of delay and inadequate remedies . . . for violations."

Finally under Jimmy Carter during the 1977–78 legislative season, the entire trade union movement reached a rare degree of consensus, put its collective shoulder to the Congressional millstone, and launched a drive to achieve some sorely needed national labor law reforms.

Those proposed reforms were certainly not revolutionary. We weren't even asking for repeal of the nefarious right-to-work-for-less law. All we wanted were some half-dozen legalistic changes that would (1) remove some choke points in torturously long NLRB proceedings, (2) close some loopholes that employers had gouged out to defy the letter and spirit of the national labor law, and (3) restore a measure of balance to labor-management relations, particularly with respect to the declared right of every employee in this land to form and join a trade union, for purposes of collective bargaining over the terms and conditions of his or her employment.

The importance of obtaining that balance is suggested by a 1982 *Washington Post/Newsweek* public opinion poll which found that well over half of non-union workers polled said they would join a union *if they could*. Removing some of the barriers to their free choice was the point of labor law reform.

All seven living former Secretaries of Labor supported the Labor Law Reform bill. Employers, however, from those in the supereconomy's

Business Roundtable, to those in the county seat Chambers of Commerce, right down to the Mom and Pop store on rural America's gravel main street, rose in mean-spirited wrath against the very idea of free trade unionism. Some elements of the opposition to labor law reform have a long history and record of being anti-union, anti-labor, anti-Jewish, anti-black, anti-chicano and anti-government. Neither democracy nor economic fair play nor human decency and human rights are among their values. Absolutely incomprehensible, however, was the alignment of some of the nation's foremost corporations and employers with those outlaw elements. The shroud of silence that enveloped others was no less disturbing. Employers with whom the Machinists had had years of good positive collective bargaining and community relations turned on us.

Those and others joined hands with every right-wing nut and fright peddler in the country to "put us in our place." Damned few of our friends in academia stepped forward to argue in our behalf. Most chose to remain aloof and neutral, when such a posture, given the intensity and nature of the conflict, clearly constituted passive support for those opposed to trade unions. The frenetic scene was punctuated with a multimedia campaign costing millions. Whole squadrons of executive jets ferried anti-union forces into Washington from all over the country.

In the end, we were defeated not by democratic majority rule—which any trade union member has to abide by—but by the minority rule of a Senate filibuster.

Lessons of Labor History

You don't have to be a Marxist to observe the conflict between capital and labor is as old as the history of the world. Each one's behavior has been remarkably consistent throughout history. Labor always seeks to preserve and improve its material lot, to gain a greater share of the wealth it produces, and to achieve a greater degree of economic and political freedom. Capital is remarkably consistent in its resistance to labor's quest. Corporate management has always relied on absolute power, authority and control—the ultimate and most ancient order of political supremacy—to achieve its goals of cost minimization, market domination and profit maximization.

It reminds me of an anecdote told about oil baron John D. Rockefeller, founder of the Standard Oil Company empire at the turn of the century. "How much is enough?" someone is reputed to have asked him, reflecting on his enormous wealth. "Just a little bit more," Rockefeller is said to have replied.

When labor is militant, history tells us, trade union goals are advanced. Workers in the United States do have a high threshold of pain, but when they draw the line, management crosses it at its peril. The history of free trade unionism is a saga of oppressed workers daring to challenge capital and management's unilateral and often dictatorial authority in the workplace and in the political economy at large.

THE NEW CLASS WAR

In the last decade, class war has been declared not by trade unions or working people on their employers, but by our employers and, recently, by our government on us.

That was the message sent to us by the Business Roundtable when it joined forces with the radical right to kill Labor Law Reform in the Senate in 1978. That was the message when corporate personnel officers bragged in business magazines that "take-away drives" or "take backs" would be a permanent feature of contract negotiations. That was the message when R. Heath Larry, the supposed great architect and intellect of labor-management partnerships, announced formation of a "Union Free Environment Committee." That is the message that continues to be broadcast across every bargaining table. And that is the message conveyed by virtually every corporate political action committee in choosing candidates for financial support in the past decade.

A declaration of class war was the message in the 1970s when the Carter Administration intervened in the Mineworkers strike, in the Rubber Workers strike, in the Oil and Chemical Workers negotiations and in the Rock Island Rail strike. Class warfare was the message when Corporate America, with the Carter Administration's acquiescence, launched a full-scale assault to dismantle federal regulatory agencies, such as the Occupational Safety and Health Administration, the Environmental Protection Agency, the Civil Aeronautics Board, the Interstate Commerce Commission, and the Federal Trade Commission. These agencies were created to protect people from the overweening power and unbridled profit-motivated behavior of insensitive corporate management.

Class war was intensified with the Reagan Administration's policies. Reagan started his administration with the Professional Air Traffic Controllers dispute. He threw the full weight of government against those 13,000 federal workers, put their leaders in jail, used the military to replace them in the control towers, and broke their union. Ironically at the same time he vehemently condemned the Polish Communist government for using the same tactics to put down the Polish Solidarity movement. Curiously, while the Air Traffic Controllers were striking over a safety and health issue, the Polish workers were seeking a role in enterprise management, their own political identity and guaranteed access to the public media—none of which U.S. workers have. Polish workers wanted self-determination and self-management in the workplaces as well as political processes. Did Reagan really know what he was championing over there?

Reagan's appointments to the National Labor Relations Board were signals that free trade unions have no claim to legitimacy in his labor relations policy. The decisions rendered by Reagan's NLRB confirmed that view.

In the private sector, employers by the thousands took Reagan's cue. His business and corporate constituency tore up the collective bargaining system. It was hell-bent on establishing a "union-free environment." The unwitting ally in this drive was the 15 to 20 million member Standing Army of Unemployed during Reagan's managed recession in the early 1980s. The conniving ally was a billion dollar union-busting consulting industry. Put it altogether, and it made a mockery of the nation's labor relations laws. It made a mockery of our notion of democracy, too.

Give Backs, Take Aways, and Union Busters

Beginning in 1977, employers began bragging they were going to launch "take-back" drives at the bargaining table. Here's how Wayne Horvitz, of the Federal Mediation and Conciliation Service, described it to the *Wall Street Journal* (January 1, 1978):

> Management is testing the relationship to see what it will bear. The employers believe that for many years they have given away more than they should across the table, and that perhaps this is a good time to get some of it back.

Both 1977 and 1978 were record-smashing, profit-laden years for our employers. It wasn't hard times that put them on the concessions track. It was an unadulterated, mean-spirited, anti-trade union animus. The 1982-83 depression made continuation of their "take-back" drive easier. And that is what concession bargaining was and is all about.

Concession bargaining is a take-it or leave-it proposition. Workers and trade unions confront it whether the employer is making a profit or not. Most employers backup their concession demands by threatening to shut down—with generous federal tax write offs—move away, and open up shop—with more generous tax incentives—where trade unions are nonexistent. That "union-free environment" could be in right-to-work-for-less states that are notoriously anti-union, or it could be in some poverty stricken, cheap labor, dictatorial developing or undeveloped country that has no respect for human and trade union rights like Indonesia, Malaysia, Singapore, South Korea, or Taiwan.

"Take a wage freeze or we'll shut down—with generous tax write offs—and open up shop where unions are weak or non-existent," they say. "Take a wage roll back, give up your cost-of-living adjustment, pay for your own health insurance, forget about a pension or retirement program or we'll strand you on the shores of despair and set up business in some cheap wage, dictatorial developing or underdeveloped country that respects neither human rights nor trade unions rights."

"Give up your union, tear up your collective bargaining contract, or we'll spend millions to bust your strike, break your union and hire replacements to take your job from the ranks of the army of the unemployed."

Obviously free trade unions have to reject this management stance. Underlying the obvious objections is a more fundamental one that trade unionists must come to grips with ethically and morally: what right do contemporary trade union leaders and members have to give back gains, benefits and standards that have been won by the blood, sweat, tears and ingenuity of trade unionists in the past? If concessions will truly save an enterprise and jobs in the short run, that is one thing. But if concessions mean submitting to job blackmail or choosing the path of least resistance, it is quite another matter. We in positions of trade union leadership and trust today do not have the right to give away gains and rights won by our predecessors yesterday. They are not ours to give away. They are our heritage and belong to our progeny.

When workers refuse to budge on concessions and invoke their weapon of last resort—the right to strike—the employer is apt to hire professional union-busting consulting firms and replace striking workers with desperate and wretched souls from the ranks of the Army of Unemployed.

Indeed, the perversion of the New Deal's labor law protections has reached the point where employers use "surface bargaining" techniques to bring about a bargaining impasse that will provoke an economic strike. And then employers will rely upon further perversion of the law to permanently replace strikers with scabs. The absurdity is that, according to the law, workers on an economic strike can't be fired, but they can be permanently replaced. A year later, after the strike has been broken, and all the strikers "permanently replaced," the scabs then file for a petition to decertify the union. Of course, after a year's time has passed, only the scabs get to vote. This legal veneer makes a mockery of worker rights and labor union protections.

The new breed of union busters aren't toting guns or blackjacks or hiring Pinkerton detectives to infiltrate our ranks as *agents provocateurs*. They wear well-cut, three-decker suits, tote slim-line brief cases, use slick direct mail missiles and psychologists to coerce, intimidate, divide and conquer us. Their ranks include lawyers, psychologists, and academic lecturers.

Management consultants work behind the scenes to undercut the authority and power of every decent personnel and industrial relations executive in this country. For $500 or $1000 a day per head, they counsel and help orchestrate abuse and evasion of the law, spying and harassment of workers, violations of human and legal rights on and off the jobs, and incitement of mistrust and fear between sexes, races, ethnic groups. Unorganized workers, who may attempt to organize to do something about their defenselessness, may never get the chance, due to the professional union-busting industry running amuck in our democracy and twisting labor law into employer tyranny. Underwriting this kind of activity with loose corporate change is no way to build a stable, progressive, democratic society.

If these mutants of the legal profession and the psychological profession have their way, this nation will be on a fast track to totalitarianism. If they have their way, there won't be collective bargaining contracts for industrial relations personnel to administer or interpret or rule upon or argue over with union stewards and shop foremen. There will only be pseudo police, snoop artists and informers to keep workers in line and subjugated on the job.

That repressive system of labor-management relations didn't last in Poland and it won't last in the United States. In the long run, it won't work because trade union rights are human rights. The innate desire to be free pervades the workplace environment as well as the political economy outside.

In the meantime, employers are wasting millions of dollars and unquanitifiable amounts of energy, talent and time to destroy and vilify the trade union movement. It isn't contributing to economic growth or the nation's wealth; nor is it putting people to work in productive and socially useful jobs. It is a nonproductive, anti-democratic and antisocial behavior, and it belies all we like to think our country stands for.

Take-away demands, concession bargaining, plant shutdowns and the licentious global mobility of capital are all directed and engineered by a self-appointed corps of Rambo managers. They are producing a deindustrialized America, destroying the living standards of millions of Americans, polarizing our society, and creating huge trade deficits and foreign indebtedness. Corporate America's apologists call it "meeting the competition" with a "free" labor market.

We call it what it really is: a direct road to national economic suicide.

Reagan's NLRB Rewrites the Law

Backing up these Rambo managers is the full weight of the federal executive branch of government and a National Labor Relations Board that is hell-bent on reviving class warfare. When Mr. Reagan's appointees became the majority on the NLRB, they sought to transform labor law, not in the halls of Congress but through their backdoor decisions. Their chairman was Donald Dotson, a political hack who previously worked for the National Right-to-Work(-for-Less) Committee and who said, shortly before he took the NLRB job, that "collective bargaining means destruction of individual freedom." What he meant was that he preferred individual begging over collective bargaining, and his board decisions repeat that Neanderthal philosophy.

In the NLRB's decisions on key cases, we see three distinct—and disturbing—trends:

(1) If a case presents a conflict between the employer's freedom to manage its business and the union's right to bargain about matters affecting its members' lives and livelihoods, such as plant closings, relocations, and subcontracting, then management prevails even if that means voiding a contract covering the point.
(2) If a conflict is between employer rights to control the workplace, and the rights of individual employees, such as electronic monitoring and Big Brother in the workplace, then employer rights are paramount.
(3) If a conflict is between the rights of a union or its members to act collectively and the rights of individual employees to refrain from union activity or persist in anti-union activity, then individual rights become paramount.

Historically, the NLRB and federal courts have respected neutrality in conflict resolution between unions and employers. As previously noted, we have experienced a slow erosion of that neutrality after the Taft-Hartley amendments in 1947 and the Landrum-Griffin reporting and disclosure amendments in 1959. That erosion has accelerated since the defeat of the Labor Law Reform bill in 1978. The Reagan Labor Board's conduct became so onerous that we and other unions abandoned it as an enforcer of worker rights, collective bargaining contracts and cooperative labor-management relations. We have almost reached the point where no law may be better than the law we have.

The "Law and Economics" Movement

Justifying the legal assault on the rights of labor to organize freely is a new right-wing movement called "Law and Economics" which has invaded the federal judiciary and is spreading into state and local jurisdictions. (For a description of this movement and its advocates, see the *Wall Street Journal*, August 4, 1986, pages 1 and 16.) The Law and Economics movement applies strict cost-benefit analysis to all conflicts and problems—whether they be economic, human, legal, political or social. In the eyes of Law and Economics judges, all legal doctrine is swept into free market jargon and ideology. This movement's ideology threatens not just collective bargaining and trade unions but virtually all our democratic ideals and institutions.

The Law and Economics group's chief disciple is Richard A. Posner, a Reagan appointee to the Seventh Circuit U.S. Court of Appeals in Chicago. Posner carries the free market economists' ideology to a legal extreme. For example, according to the *Wall Street Journal* article, Posner wants to legalize baby sales and take adoptions out of the hands of adoption agencies. His reasoning goes something like this: people's willingness to pay for something shows how much they value it, and parents who value a child the most will pay a top price for it and give it the best care. Posner not only wants to sell babies on the auction block, he once opposed free counsel to a prisoner, because if a prisoner can't retain a lawyer, he was quoted in the article, "the natural inference to draw is that he doesn't have a good case."

That is a restatement of the old "wealth is a sign of salvation" doctrine, which we believed was buried along with Warren G. Harding or Calvin Coolidge.

The law, according to Posner, should provide incentives for efficient competitive behavior. Efficiency, which can be translated as "productivity," outweighs intangible democratic values such as equality, fairness, individual and human rights. Indeed, Posner is quoted as saying that words like fairness and justice "have no content."

The "intellectual"—if that term can be applied to this deification of avarice—centers of this legal school are the University of Chicago, where Milton Friedman is entrenched, and the Law and Economics Center at George Mason University in Arlington, Virginia. Some 260 federal judges, most of them Reagan appointees, have received training in Law and Economics there. Reagan's Attorney General Edwin Meese sponsored Law and Economics "tutorials" for another 100 judges. And Reagan Supreme Court appointee Antonin Scalia has a record of writings and opinions as a lower court judge that sounds like he's been trained by the Law and Economics group.

The Law and Economics movement has infiltrated the federal judiciary at all levels. Those federal judges are backing up Labor Board decisions that are turning the nation's labor law into legalized anarchy. Its dogma provides the rationale for the National Labor Relations Board's abrupt reversal of labor law in a dozen areas. It directly threatens free trade unions and collective bargaining as a means to conflict resolution in the workplace.

Yet neither Rambo management's breast beating nor the Law and Economics crowd's efforts to cast trade unions into legal limbo has delivered the goods or jobs that they promise. The "free" labor market that they claim to admire so much is far from free. It reflects the distribution of advantages and power within society, not the real value of the work or relative worth of the individual. They idolize the market because it serves those who hold power and authority. This effort to turn the clock back to the 1920s—or the 1840s—and that "lean 'n mean" Rambo management bunch, rewarding its members with six figure salaries, stock options, and bonuses, parading across the covers of *Business Week, Forbes,* and *Fortune,* full dress with golden parachutes, sure as hell isn't winning the international trade war. Instead, they are shipping capital, technology and production overseas to add to our trade deficit and then rewarding themselves with astronomical bonuses for eliminating our jobs.

That's bad law and bad economics.

LABOR-MANAGEMENT COOPERATION— BUT ON WHOSE TERMS?

For the last two decades, the study of blue collar work has been an obsession for many behavioral psychologists, economists, personnel experts and sociologists. We should not confuse these academic professionals with a new breed of anti-union hucksters, who sell their services under the euphemistic title of "management consultant." The former are, in all probability, unwittingly anti-union. The latter are conscious union busters—mercenaries for hire. Yet both employ the pseudo-scientific methods and techniques of behavioral scientists to study— and manipulate—American workers.

Why single out blue collar workers? At a time when corporate management in America is hell bent on a binge of anti-unionism, it is obvious that management alienation a more fertile field for these social lab technicians than the "blue collar blues." There is enough social hostility in management's mental madness to provide full employment for behavioralists for the next half century. Indeed, Corporate America's social hostility has always been around to observe, as any trade union steward or business representative can testify. Studies of this phenomenon are few, however.

All discussions of job enrichment, improving the quality of worklife (QWL), and humanizing the workplace inevitably relate to increasing productivity and, hence, employer profits. Since employers' investment decisions, made behind closed boardroom doors, have far greater impact on the workplace and productivity than anything workers or their unions can do, it is fair to ask behavioralists why they don't put corporate management under their social lab microscopes.

Blue collar workers, though, won't hold their breath waiting for such a shift in focus. Besides, it cannot be overlooked that the image of blue collar work in America is not a product of how workers regard their work, but rather how the media, intellectuals and professional educators portray it. They gain work by studying work. It matters little that they cannot have *their* productivity measured and, in all likelihood, they have never worked for a living on a shop floor or participated in trade unionism and collective bargaining, except perhaps "during summer vacation while I was going to college."

The resentment is intended. My message to these "people peepers" is this: don't tell me what's wrong with me or my job, or what's good for me, unless you've worked with me day after day, year after year. Don't tell me what's wrong with me unless you have walked in my shoes.

The crucial oversight of the behavioralists is that they seldom talk about pay and income. Hell, yes, in these economic straits there is bound to be widespread worker dissatisfaction. The wonder is there isn't open rebellion. But for the harsh discipline of high unemployment, there unquestionably would be. No job enrichment program is likely to reduce worker dissatisfaction with pay and income. How does one teach a garbage collector there is dignity in work? The answer doesn't require an advanced degree in sociology: you pay enough to provide a decent standard of living.

Quality of Worklife

Over the years American unions, including the IAM, have shown flexibility and willingness to cooperate with management in productivity and quality of working life programs. In the workplace, we have implicitly, if not expressly, looked on our bargaining agreements as essential to a partnership in promoting the aims and goals of the enterprise. Profits, productivity and industrial peace we've always considered to be in our members' best interests.

Managing the job, rather than managing the enterprise, has been our concern. The average IAM member has always been less interested in selecting the Chairman of the Board for the enterprise than in his own job standards, rights of transfer, promotion, and pay. The key to making the system work has been our firm insistence that the contract, once agreed upon, should without exception be faithfully enforced.

Bargaining and contract administration are essentially adversarial in nature. Even so, the IAM has found it beneficial to expand the scope of bargaining and enter joint agreements, some provided in the contract and others not. Whether contractual or not, at the heart of these agreements has been a concern for productivity and the quality of working life.

We are not against job satisfaction or improving the quality of working life. Far from it. That's exactly what unions have been trying to achieve for generations. We have tried to enrich the jobs of our members by increasing their safety, seniority rights, grievance procedures and compensation on the job. But when management begins to talk to our members about job satisfaction and job enrichment, we know this is not what they have in mind. Their intention is to get more production with less labor. In the old days they called it time and motion study and they did it with stop watches. Today they call it job enrichment and do it with questionnaires. But the objective is identical. As Thomas Brooks, the noted labor historian and author, pointed out some time ago in the *American Federationist*, "Substituting the sociologists' questionnaire for the stop watch is likely to be no gain for the workers. While workers have a stake in productivity, it is not always identical with that of management. Job enrichment programs have cut jobs just as effectively as automation and stop watches. And the rewards of productivity are not always equitably shared."

Nor are we against improving productivity. As noted in Chapter 2, improved productivity growth is vital to raising American workers' living standards. But when we read the behavioralists' productivity studies, we become concerned. Consider the problems which the Work in America Institute, for example, addresses in its productivity series: absenteeism, tardiness, turnover, alcoholism and drug abuse, strikes, shutdowns, grievances and accidents. Movement toward solving any one or all of these problems, unquestionably would improve productivity, but it may or may not improve the quality of working life. Improving the quality of working life is not so much a function of an individual worker's or a trade union's attitude and philosophy as it is a function of management's attitude and philosophy.

The list of problems surveyed by the Institute in its productivity studies is incomplete. Conspicuously absent, for example, is the question of occupational diseases and health hazards in the workplace. This is not a minor problem as it relates to productivity or quality of working life. Every worker knows that at the source of every pollutant dumped into the atmosphere or waters or onto the market place as edible and nonedible and industrial products, there are working men and women who are exposed to industrial strength doses of that pollutant.

Some 400,000 job-related cases of disease are discovered each year. Workers in metals, stone, clay and glass production, for instance, suffer abnormally high incidences of silicosis, emphysema and other respiratory diseases. Coke oven workers at steel mills are ten times more apt to develop cancer than average citizens. Petroleum refinery, chemical manufacturing and nuclear materials workers have extremely high rates of cancer. Recent revelations of asbestosis tell us that disease is about to explode into 5 to 8 *million* cases of cancer. And the official maximum dose of radiation is *one thousand times higher* for workers in nuclear power plants and processing facilities than for the general public. There are 15,000 toxic chemical agents used by industry and 3,000 new chemical compounds or combinations are introduced each year. Yet, few legal exposure standards exist to protect the workers who handle these toxics and chemical compounds. They are treated as guinea pigs.

Every year 100,000 workers die from job-related causes.

How can you talk about "quality of working life" without mentioning such basic issues as workers' health? The fear—and fact—of cancer is bound to induce anxiety. The fear—and fact—of lung diseases, chemical poisoning, hearing loss, and back problems induce anxiety. According to the AFL-CIO's Industrial Union Department's researchers, every year at least 100,000 American workers die and another 340,000 are disabled by these chemical agents and toxic substances.[1] An additional 32 men and women are killed on the job *every day*, and more than 5,500 suffer on-the-job injuries. Here are *real* sources of alienation, absenteeism, and excessive turnovers. As nearly as can be determined, about one out of seven workers faces certain occupational disease or death in America's workplaces. Yet employers stubbornly resist compliance and enforcement of the Occupational Safety and Health Act.

Neither academic experts nor management can afford to ignore or deny the impact occupational diseases and health hazards have on productivity and the quality of working life. Management can't have it both ways. It can't plead for increased productivity while one-seventh of its workforce is dying of its jobs. Academics can't discuss the quality of worklife without considering the effects of occupational disease and health hazards.

Regrettably *real* quality of work life isn't on management's agenda. "Quality of work life" programs—with a couple of honorable exceptions—are much less concerned with the quality of working life than with the quantity of profits.

Labor-management Cooperation

Those university professors who are naively unaware of the political battle being waged in the halls of government and the political economy at large regularly admonish trade unions to become involved in cooperative and participatory management schemes. However, as we examine the American scene today, we don't see many signs of a management desire for cooperation. What we *do* see is a management offensive that makes union busting and union concessions on wages, hours, and working conditions the thrust of labor-management relations. We see the human carnage and misery in the social economy, the corporate corruption of government, and the myopia and greed of macho managers trussing themselves with golden parachutes while shirking their patriotic duty to help pay for the government that harbors and protects them. As we observe the value system of those who are inviting us to a love-in on the shop floor, the new cry for greater labor-management cooperation rings hollow.

Poor, shortsighted, greedy management—not the trade unions—is responsible for the economic mess we're in. Management, not workers, makes the key investment decisions. Management has the ear of government under any administration—not workers. Management controls and reads the markets—not workers. Management designs and engineers our industrial processes and products—not workers. Blaming production and maintenance workers for poor product quality is a bum rap. Workers don't design products, don't engineer products, don't determine what materials, tools and methods of production to use. Those are all managerial prerogatives by law.

Corporate management has gotten everything it wants: control of government, a high unemployment economy, an unprecedented peacetime military build up, a reduced tax liability, the elimination of the economic and social safety net for people, the virtual repeal of the anti-trust laws, and freedom from economic and social responsibility. And now when management and its government find themselves in an economic mess, the cry goes out for labor-management cooperation.

When we step away from the everyday pursuit of making a living in the workplace and at the bargaining table, we in the trade unions have to ask ourselves what's really "new" about these recent pleas for greater labor-management cooperation. There is nothing new about a labor-management relations system that builds on the old system's flaws and inequities. None of our suitors in academia, business or government are talking about changing any of the rigid principles of management prerogatives, the sovereignty of capital, the expendability of labor, and the autocratic alliance between employers and government that continue to characterize contemporary labor-management relations.

When these flaws are ignored or glossed over by a new intellectual fad which titillates a cadre of bright but bored academics and which is being promoted by professional management *apparatchiks* for their own self-serving ends, then trade unionists have to be skeptical.

We watch what employers do, not what they say. We watch their hands, not their lips.

We remember too well their union busting, their support of Reaganomics, and their campaign against Labor Law Reform. The names of the principal players from management and Corporate America in those witless exercises are the same today. Now we hear them pleading for "labor-management cooperation." Colleges and universities all around the country have taken up the topic. Maybe it is because the Federal Mediation and Conciliation Service has been dispensing a million dollars worth of grants to researchers and writers on the subject. Or maybe its just another academic fad, like "worker alienation" was a decade ago.

This scam today comes with many code words and in many disguises. There are vague tripartite "industrial policy" schemes designed, on closer inspection, to hustle the largest pool of money in the world: worker pension funds. We all know pension funds belong to workers, but ignore the fact that workers have precious little control over their investment and use. Another vogue is "participatory management" where trade unions are offered token representation on corporate committees. These involve no real power sharing; just ego stroking and window dressing.

Most popular with academics and management are productivity circles, quality of worklife and quality control circles. On the surface, these appear to permit workers to participate in enterprise and shop floor decisions. In their early moments, they are apt to be enthusiastically accepted by workers. But as time tolls, reality sets in. They're gimmicks, designed to meet the same old objectives: cut costs, produce more, open the way for labor-displacing technology, and circumvent the collective bargaining contract and process. They also weaken local trade union influence and control of safeguards in the work environment and at the point of work.

This brings to mind an incident that took place when a quality circle was being established by an employer who shall remain nameless. The corporate labor relations manager and the CEO were approached by a labor relations consultant who said to the labor relations manager,

"I have found a way of getting workers to increase production, take less pay, spy on their fellow workers, and think it is for their own good." "How do you do it?" asked the astounded labor relations manager. "I get them to form a quality circle," says he.

That pretty well summarizes the reality behind many "quality of worklife" programs.

There is nothing that a QWL program can do that can't also be done through the bargaining contract, except one thing—and that is to weaken or destroy collective bargaining and trade unions. In the Machinists Union, we've never yet seen the existence of QWL prevent an employer from closing down and moving out on us when the grass looked greener somewhere else.

Besides QWL, there are gain-sharing, bonuses, profit-sharing and all those other schemes which are not designed to reward individual skills or labor's value-added to the product, but are devices to lure employees into assuming some managerial functions without receiving management pay or perks. There are also "pay-for-knowledge" schemes designed to lure workers across craft lines and skill lines—to do another worker's job—to do more work for less pay.

To join any of those schemes outside the bargaining contract and process, is, in and of itself, a major trade union concession. The trade union leader that agrees to such concessions is destined to lose credibility in the eyes of his own membership. Moreover, he loses credibility for the trade union movement in the eyes of those potential and future trade unionists in the large unorganized sectors of commerce and industry.

Still, we hear the cry for greater labor-management cooperation. It comes from academia. It comes from a suspect government and from traditional political enemies. It comes from some Democratic Party trade union friends and allies. The plea for cooperation comes, even, from some trade union leaders themselves.

We ask: Has the corporate leopard changed its spots?

If our employers and their government have gotten rid of their anti-union spots, then why do they not uphold the nation's labor laws? Why did they invent and continue to support a multi-billion dollar industry of vicious union-busting, psychological manipulators and legal tormentors, called management consultants? Why do they oppose decent and affordable health care for all Americans? Why do they oppose strict and strong safety and health laws and regulations in our workplaces? Why do they not seek an economic alternative to massive and permanent unemployment? Why do they shirk their duty to carry a fair share of the nation's staggering military budget load—even as some of our military contractor employers bilk and milk billions of taxpayer dollars from the military production system. Why do we find our multinational employers, virtually without exception, coaching, egging-on, and financially bankrolling conservative and right-wing zealots at home and abroad?

If our employers desire our cooperation in the workplace, in the office or on the shop floor, then why do they plot our demise in the secluded corporate boardrooms, or in annual midwinter management retreats in the Bahamas or some other sunny paradise?

If our employers have suddenly found a soft spot in their hearts for our economic and social welfare, then why do they wage their flinty-eyed capital strike against us by investing money in money, by practicing corporate cannibalism, by exporting capital and technology overseas, by investing millions in politicians who openly vow their hatred and contempt for us?

If our employers have found a place in their hearts for our dignity, comfort and welfare in the workplace, then why don't they exhibit the same tenderness and concern outside in the political economy?

Management cannot kick workers in the teeth with takeaway drives and job blackmail and expect productive cooperation inside the work-place. Management cannot hire million dollar union-busting consulting firms, replete with behavioral psychologists and Ivy League lawyers, to deny workers their constitutional rights to organize and bargain collec-tively and expect union members to believe that management wants workers to participate in any meaningful way. Nor can management outside the plant gate and office, in complicity with its right-wing government, practice economic and social genocide on workers and their families and communities, and expect an era of cooperation and good will to ensue.

Government and employers ought to understand they can't plead for workers and trade unions to cooperate on the shop floor, while at the same time they are knifing them and trying to put them out of business outside in the political economy at large. That's not cooperation. That's playing workers for fools. And there's nothing new about it. Phoney cooperative work schemes were all part of the 1920s package.

We've been tokens on too many boards and committees, turkeys in too many tripartite arrangements, to subject our unions and our self respect to those forms of chicanery again. We've cooperated with management too many times in the workplaces, carried water for them and packed their mail too many times on Capitol Hill, only to be mugged, raped, or stabbed in the back outside the plant gate and away from the legislative fray, by decisions adversely affecting our lives, our livelihoods and our trade unions. We don't intend to fall sucker for the same old ploys again.

Of course the leopard hasn't changed its spots. What all this hype about labor-management cooperation really means is Corporate America and its accomplices in government want workers and trade unions to take the blame for economic collapse, and shoulder the sacrifices that they think will save their asses. But we did not make the decisions that have led us into this current economic swamp. We refuse to be held responsible for the greed, incompetence, myopia and power lust of decision makers, over whom we have no influence, let alone control. There's a whole body of legal precedents in this land that says making the decisions is management's prerogative. Management's right to mismanage is legalized, and management jealously guards that prerogative.

If we're expected to make the decisions, then we may as well own the business.

Models for Workplace Cooperation

One symptom of what American employers mean when they talk about cooperation is the enthusiasm that they and their shills in the media and universities have for imposing a Japanese version of labor-management relations on us. (A good research project for some of those bored academics who waste their time studying why workers are dissatisfied would be to examine what's behind American managers' love affair with the Japanese model.) The truth is that the best examples of labor-management cooperation are found not in Japan but among the democracies of West Europe. The West European model is much less autocratic and dictatorial, and more democratic and worker oriented, than the hierarchical Japanese system.

For dynamic, young, educated, affluent and ambitious workers, the West European model provides more challenge, exacts more skill and more individual ingenuity, and provides more autonomy and opportunity for genuine input into enterprise decision-making processes than does the heavy-handed, disciplinary Japanese system. When we contrast the role of trade unions in Western Europe with those in Japan, it becomes obvious why American employers and their business school allies are pushing the Japanese model of labor relations, rather than the West European one. The Japanese system is less democratic, keeps unions dependent upon joint government-industry collaboration, and largely excludes unions from the secondary and tertiary labor markets. In Western Europe, trade unions not only have their own political parties, they are very much a part of private enterprises' decision-making processes.

The European model also does more to harmonize technology's impact on the workforce and on society than does the Japanese model.

Our own observation tells us that while the European model promotes high-tech creativity and skills, the Japanese model tends to create high-tech coolies. When one looks beyond that one-third of the Japanese labor force that is employed in Japan, Inc., we note an almost total absence of trade unions and worker rights. In fact, the Japanese system of labor relations begets a caste system that, among other unattractive features, discriminates heavily against women.

Yet American managers, academics and media analysts are afflicted by the common malady of "Japanitis." There is gross over-simplification about all aspects of Japanese labor relations. Most American commentators, for instance, speak in terms of a rigid Japanese QWL model, when, in fact, there is no rigid model. There is a Fuzitsu Fanuc model, an oppressive Nissan model, several different Mitsubishi models, and dozens in between. American observers, particularly American managers, see one or two of these things in operation, then come back home and construct not what actually they saw but what they wanted to see.

If American managers really want to emulate the Japanese system, why don't they go the whole nine yards and adopt its more attractive features like job retraining and lifetime employment?

So when the question is asked, "What will it take to achieve greater labor-management cooperation," here's what we answer: It will take a new ethical commitment by Corporate America and all employers to bridle their hatred of trade unions, to subscribe to a decent code of behavior in the political economy and society, and to permit workers, through their unions, to enter into key economic decision-making processes at both the micro and macro levels.

Let us be frank about trade union rights in a democratic society. Workers' rights to organize are our only guarantee that we will be represented. Our bosses don't represent us. Economists, professors and other experts don't represent us. If you believe the current bunch of politicians represent us, you probably believe in the tooth fairy too. We have to represent ourselves.

The time is long overdue for this country to accept worker and trade union rights as unchallengeable human rights. Neither academics nor government nor employers can continue to ask labor for a love-in in the workplaces, for tax payments, wage and other concessions, support for austerity programs and declining living standards, then commit mayhem and rape against us outside in the political economy or inside the workplace itself. Their whining appeals for greater labor-management cooperation ring hollow when workers and their trade unions are condemned as "special interests," ignored and discarded when capital

and government abuse, misuse or abandon us in the name of minimizing costs and maximizing profits.

Neither we in the trade unions nor unorganized workers should
become sacrificial lambs in some grand business-government global
design. We in the trade unions have no duty to cooperate with hostile,
jaundiced employers and a hostile government and political leaders.
That's the route to class war, not to rebuilding our economy.

Labor-management cooperation must be a two way street. Cooperation must take place outside the work sites and workplaces, in the
domestic political economy and in the international trade negotiation
arena, or there can be no cooperation at all. That means putting trade
union representatives in key decision-making slots with management
and government representatives, too. Cooperation must come as a total
package in the form of an economic and social contract, inside and
outside the workplace,

That's what we call labor-management cooperation.

WAGE INVESTMENTS, NOT CONCESSIONS

If an employer will open his books and prove he needs help, and if
that help will save the enterprise, then concessions may be in order,
but if and only if the employer agrees to give workers something of
value in return for those concessions. None of that "business for the
sake of business and shareholders" crap, or job blackmail stuff. Slaves
had jobs. Any good supply-sider ought to tell you that if there's no
economic incentive to work, then why work?

In the IAM, we counter concession demands with what we call *wage
investment strategies* whenever our employers mismanage us into an
economic morass and out of a job and income.

What, you may ask, is the difference between a wage or benefit
concession and wage investments? The difference is workers stand to
gain something of value in return for temporarily foregoing or giving
back negotiated wage increases. We negotiate those concessions as loans
to the employer, to be paid back with interest; as deferred wage
increases; or as stock purchases with dividends. If we are asked to give
up something in the short run, and the employer opens his books and
proves his case, then we will work out an agreement, but we will also
insist on bargaining for something of bigger value in return over the
longer run.

At the same time, we insist that our investment be protected with
more than token representation in the corporate hierarchy and investment and decision-making processes. We want to bump heads with the
big boys upstairs in the boardroom and executive wing, as well as rub

elbows with the foremen and supervisors down on the shop floor and in the offices. That way, we can look after our investment, our jobs, our incomes and wealth, our livelihoods, just like bankers, suppliers, and prime customers all have their representatives on each others' corporate boards. If we invest our wages or other compensation in our employers, then we want to be on that corporate board, too, to protect our interest.

Our wage investment policy is predicated on three principles.

First, whenever we offer it, the employer must really need help and open his books to prove it.

Second, our members will get something of value in return for their wage investment over and above a job they already hold. Slaves had jobs. That's not enough. We're talking compensation plus a future return on investment, which is negotiable. While we recognize the long-term convergence of our members' pecuniary interests with those of shareholders, we are determined our members' jobs and incomes will not be used to subsidize the short-term interests of management, or the exclusive interests of investors, creditors, or any other group. We ask a fair *quid pro quo* for any burdens our members carry to keep the firm in business.

The third principle our wage investment policy is based on is that it will be negotiated by the IAM and implemented through the bargaining representative and collective bargaining process.

When we invoke this policy, we don't want to run the business, we just want the business to run.

Let me cite three outstanding cases from the airline industry where we carried out a flexible wage investment plan.

In 1984 Republic Airlines came to us with a financial and operating-cost problem and we sat down and negotiated a wage investment program in 1985 that saw us give up some short-term wages for stock purchases for about 2,500 of our IAM members and other Republic employees. When Republic and Northwest merged, our Republic members split $33 million for a healthy return on their initial wage investment.

The Republic case had a happy landing.

Our second wage investment case is at TWA. In April 1985, Mr. Icahn, who had just greenmailed his way into the TWA corporate cockpit, came to us for concessions. We offered and he accepted a wage investment package that cost each of our members $2 per hour and we gave up TWA's contribution to our supplemental pension plan for three years.

We thought we'd established a solid partnership with that sort of good faith cooperation and flexibility. But, alas, so far all we've received in return is confrontation, not cooperation. This wage investment case may be headed for a bumpy landing.

Our third wage investment case is at Eastern Airlines. It has received a lot attention over the past few years, so I won't trace its gory history in detail. Suffice it to say that when the IAM was faced with a job blackmail threat and concessions were demanded, we responded with our wage investment strategy. Between 1976 and 1986, Eastern employees contributed some $921 million to that carrier. In return for wage reductions, the unions at Eastern acquired a one-fourth ownership of the company. The unions even had representation on the board. But when inept management continued to run the company into the ground, we were out-voted on the board and eventually locked out of the boardroom.

It was behind those closed doors that Eastern sold out to Frank Lorenzo and his jerry-built Texas Air holding company. He bought Eastern for $660 million! Whether he paid with cash, stock or junk bonds is beside the point. The point is the purchase price was $260 million *less* than Eastern employees had invested in the company over the previous ten years!

Lorenzo promptly embarked on a union-busting strategy of whip-sawing his non-union carrier employees against our organized Eastern members in a tactic is similar to the double-breasting tactic used by employers in the building trades. Double breasting is a pernicious practice designed to circumvent contracts, and it should be outlawed. Lorenzo pitted his substandard and subscale Continental employees against our unionized Eastern members to force down Eastern's wage, hour and work standards.

That's a hell of a way to run an airline. As one more enlightened airline executive has noted, "An airline's future should not depend on its ability to take advantage of its employees."

We could not agree more.

The lesson to be learned from these three experiences is, simply, when we have worked with good-faith management, our flexible wage investment plan is successful. When management acts in bad faith, there is no way we can cooperate.

A couple of final comments on wage investments are in order. First, note that even if employees buy the enterprise, a union is still necessary, because the same old personnel problems of hiring, firing, promotion, discipline and grievances will remain, not to mention compensation and distribution of profits.

Second, while Employee Stock Ownership Plans (ESOPs) may be useful, they are no panacea. ESOPs are only good if workers aren't taking all the risks and aren't giving away their pension funds. Workers need guarantees against failure. The record of worker buyouts to avert shutdowns is not very promising to date. South Bend Lathe in Indiana, Rath Packing in Waterloo, Iowa, and Hyatt-Clark in New Jersey are recent notable failures. Lemon socialism is no replacement for good jobs.

Third, the lesson we've learned from the Eastern experience is that worker ownership is no guarantee that capital won't sell you out anyhow. If you're going the worker ownership route, then you had better have controlling financial interest and majority voting rights on the company's investment and strategy decisions.

FACING LABOR'S FUTURE

In the strictest sense, strict because it is mandated by law, our primary trade union purpose is to represent the best interests of our members in workplace matters which directly concern their wages, hours and conditions of employment. Our duty to represent in those matters takes place in an adversarial environment. Under recent and evolving labor law, we are subject to penalty, should we be charged with failing our duty to represent. So we are a closely regulated institution. If we seem overly cautious to some, it is because the rules we live by are strict and we never know when they may change, or what the next turn of the labor law screw may bring.

Outside the workplace, in the most liberal sense, we strive for economic and social justice in the political economy at large. Most of us do, anyhow. In the IAM, at least, our cause includes the notions of economic and social equality among all classes, races and the sexes. It also means the notion of extending democracy from the merely political to the economic. And that means a form of democratic socialism, just like that found among our NATO allies in Western Europe.

Should matters continue to move along the ruts of reaction, or along right-wing centrism's slow curve down and to the right economically and politically, then the day is not too far distant when U.S. workers will have to move to redefine their role in the political economy and society, just like the workers in Chile, Nicaragua, and Poland and South Africa are trying to do today, just as workers in Lowell, Massachusetts, did in the nineteenth century, and just like workers in depression-era big cities did in the 1930s. In the 1930s, we were suckered for a trade-off of power for money. We won't do it again. The potential always exists that our free trade unions will form an independent political party. We in the unions could transcend our current economic and political limbo simply by calling a convention, changing our Constitution, and declaring ourselves a political party. In redefining that role, workers will redefine the roles of employers and political parties, too. And that means redefining the role of government in a renewed quest for economic democracy and political egalitarianism.

We need to ask the key questions: Who owns and controls America and America's wealth? Who decides to invest it and how and where? Who's going to benefit from it all? Answers to questions like those will determine U.S. workers' credo and ethic for the next century and beyond. We believe that credo will reject the extreme individualism, fawning self-interest and outrageous cupidity so much in evidence now. We also believe the new collar workers' credo will reject political authoritarianism, corporate statism and fascism, however cleverly disguised, even when it comes with a feigned humility and an infectious smile, as it has during the 1980s.

Our free trade union credo must champion genuine cooperation among cooperative lateral interests, as opposed to competition between competitive vertical interests. And we must always protect and promote democracy and equality. Our shared materialism must be tempered by our understanding of humankind's innate decency.

Meantime, those of us who do have our trade unions will slug it out the best way we can, through collective bargaining, through organizing, through the political process, and through civil disobedience which has always been part of the U.S. political process. It is imperative that we throw off the blinders of apathy and the yoke of powerlessness that restrain us now.

We in the trade unions and those others among us participating in progressive struggles must never permit our good names or our organizations to contribute to the alienation and powerlessness that half the working class in the U.S. feels today. They are our friends and neighbors. The storm will pass. Our day is coming. When it does, we must be prepared to seize history and to right the wrongs that are weighing so heavily upon us as a civilized, free people.

We must put full employment back on the nation's political and economic agenda. We must be ready to change the regressive distribution of wealth and income, both at home and abroad. We must be prepared to make trade union rights universal human rights for the employed and the unemployed alike. We must have the vision, the courage and the plans for conversion to restructure our political economy away from war and poverty, toward peace and prosperity for all.

This means we must be prepared to use government in the public interest, rather than to protect profiteering private interests. That requires breaking up the current iron-clad phalanx of business, government and the judiciary aligned against worker rights and free trade unions. When all is said and done, it is a nation's labor policy that determines the kind of nation it is—the values of its society: democratic or dictatorial; high living standards or mere subsistence; class division and conflict or equality and fairness.

It is not this nation's constitutional values that must change. It is not the majority of the people's preference for economic and political democracy that must change. It is business and government leadership's attitudes and values that must change or must be changed.

The U.S. political economy and the workers, managers, and investors in it are best served by a labor policy that recognizes trade union rights as human rights; that provides for constructive intervention whenever and wherever the market system fails; and that does not apologize for helping the victims of the "free" market survive and gain fresh starts.

Believe me, there is a lot of poetry in achieving justice on the job through free trade unionism and the art of collective bargaining. The spirit of extending freedom from the political to the economic sphere encompasses the history of humankind's progress. This struggle to achieve economic freedom, alongside political freedom, is our struggle.

NOTES

1. Exposure rates are frightening. About one quarter of the workforce is exposed to at least one known cancer-causing agent as a regular part of the job. Some 3 million workers are exposed to benzene, 2.5 million to asbestos, 1.5 million to chromium, 1.4 million to nickel, and a half million to arsenic. In addition, some 800,000 clothing and textile workers are exposed to cotton dust's insidious brown lung, 1 million women of childbearing age are exposed at work to chemicals that cause birth defects and miscarriages, 2 million workers are exposed to carbon monoxide poisoning, and some 7 million are threatened with hearing loss because of excessive noise. While the Occupational Safety and Health Act of 1970 was excellent legislation, it has generally been implemented by hostile administrations which were responding to massive employer pressure not to enforce it. Under the Reagan administration, enforcement was further reduced. Currently OSHA has the capacity to inspect each American workplace once every half century.

Where we have state occupational safety and health laws, many of those states appropriate more money each year to preserve pheasants and wood chucks than they do to preserve workers' lives. Other states spend more money to prevent hog cholera than they do to prevent silicosis. And some hire more livestock disease inspectors than they do occupational safety and health inspectors. My point is not that pheasants shouldn't be preserved or that hog cholera shouldn't be prevented. My point is simply that human beings ought to be given at least equal consideration with animals in the scale of values implicit in official policy.

SEVEN

labor and politics

There's nothing in the middle of the road except yellow stripes and dead armadillos.

—Jim Hightower

Trade unions have long concerned themselves not only with bargaining wages, hours and conditions of work for members, but also with achieving real political democracy, equality of economic opportunity, economic security, and justice for all citizens. That required going beyond collective bargaining. That required political action.

For decades labor has fought the good fight against the likes of Richard Nixon and Ronald Reagan—the right wing's Yin and Yang— to keep their kind out of power, to keep their grubby mitts away from the public purse and to keep their bloody hands off the nuclear button. Put those pinch-nosed, self-righteous right wingers in power and they do it every time: make us urinate in a bottle while they pick our pockets and sell out democracy.

Whenever I hear a politician insist how honest, hardworking, patriotic and God-fearing he is, the first thing I do is put my hand on my wallet, because history and experience tell me that those who wrap themselves in God, flag and motherhood in loud tones are people who lie, cheat and steal on a daily basis.

But labor has always fought for something more, too.

Labor has fought for the American Dream for all Americans: a house, car, decent clothes, vacations, health care, education for the kids and retirement security for our senior citizens. We've fought for civil rights, human rights and women's rights. We've fought for clear air, clear water and a pollution-free environment. We've fought the war against poverty and want. We've fought for trade union rights. And for the past several years, we've fought along side the forces of peace and disarmament in this country, rather than support the madness of militarism and war.

After all the battles we've fought, after all the causes we've championed, our detractors say that labor is just another special interest group, just another big corporate dairy operator milking the public cow. We're told that labor is no more enlightened, no more idealistic and no more noble in spirit than the worst businessman or employer who ever ripped off a government contract, cheated on his income tax return, broke the labor laws, defied the civil rights laws, violated the pollution control laws, or tried to buy a politician's vote.

Know why our adversaries say that? Because they were on the other side: they were the guys who profited from exploitation, pollution, racism, sexism, poverty, and want. But it is deeper than that. Where they come from, by their own code of conduct and low-life standards, every decent cause winds up as a racket.

Our "special interest" is the future of America, not for ourselves alone, but for all Americans, born and yet to be born. Our "special interest" is fulfillment of the American Dream, not for some but for all.

Yet despite our traditions and our hard work in politics, the American trade union movement has been neutralized. We remain loyal to the rhetoric and sentiment of class struggle in days gone by, but have been tempted by the false lures of sharing power in the Corporate State and utterly dazzled by the prospect for international adventure in slaying the Communist paper dragon.

We've gone on practicing politics as usual while the world has been changing around us.

Do you remember when Ronald Reagan was considered a right wing extremist? Hell, by the time he left office he'd become a mainstream moderate. That didn't mean that Ronald Reagan had moved to the left, but it does demonstrate that there was a massive shift right by U.S. opinion molders—academics, corporate chiefs, media pundits, and political party leadership at the national level. At the top, the Democrats demonstrated how far they had moved to the right by their determination to compete for the same 26 percent of the electorate that the Republicans represent.

Someone must speak for the other 74 percent.

Someone must speak for that half of the American electorate that has chosen to boycott the last five elections.

The Democratic Party no longer speaks for them because it has mortgaged its vision and its ideals apparently for a handful of corporate cash.

There can be no doubt that the major stockholder in both the major parties is Corporate America. Through Political Action Committees

(PACs) and political contributions Corporate America has bought the only major political party it didn't already own. In fact, I don't know what's holding up the merger that usually follows this sort of corporate acquisition.

Perhaps they're a little worried about image. Perhaps they want to perpetuate the myth of two different and contending parties in this country. But when you next see the leaders of the Democratic Party in Congress falling all over themselves in their rush to introduce a classic corporate/Republican budget, you realize what a myth it is to call our political system a two-party system.

We need a political party in this country that represents the interests of the people, not the corporations. We need a political party that represents that half of America which chose to stay home last November, rather than prostitute their franchise. Make no mistake about it, our political system cannot survive with half of our people totally unrepresented.

The Democratic Party once represented the interest of workers, minorities, the poor and downtrodden in our society. It used to strive for economic and social justice in this country. But since a Democratic Congress unleashed the corporate PACs to corrupt our political system, so-called Democrats have been lining up in droves to gorge themselves at the trough of corporate contributions. They have moved from compromise to outright collusion with the corporate and monied interests that have *always* opposed the path of economic and social justice, which the Democratic Party used to be committed to.

So those among us who still support the ideals of economic and social justice find ourselves faced with two tasks. We need to create a political party which will articulate and follow those ideals. And we need to organize support for that party among the people of this country.

The key to the accomplishment of those tasks is grass roots organizing. We must organize amongst those 50 percent of our fellow citizens who are essentially disfranchised, and whose viewpoints, I am convinced, are predominately left of center. If we can motivate and mobilize those people we can build the political and financial base necessary to sustain a progressive party.

Perhaps we can make the Democratic Party once again a party which represents those people and those viewpoints. If not, then perhaps we will need to start a new party. That is exactly what the working people in Canada did. Faced with the identical situation of two major parties both articulating the same views, they formed the New Democratic Party.

CONSERVATIVES, LIBERALS, AND NEOLIBERALS

At the root of the poverty of American party politics are the illusions of our political ideologies, conservative, liberal, and neoliberal alike. Let us be faithful to the scientific method of inquiry and define our terms.

What is a conservative? Conservatives have three distinguishing characteristics.

First, a conservative believes in the religion of free enterprise and laissez faire economics—in the name of supply, demand and the mystical marketplace. Amen.

Excluding the new breed of entrepreneurial and high-tech spirits, the free enterprise faith is a bizarre hypocrisy. Those from Corporate America's supereconomy, who sit in elite secrecy as the Knights of the Business Roundtable, do not believe in free enterprise based on dog-eat-dog competition, with free and unfettered entry of new firms into their sectorial turf. Less than 800 corporations own and control two-thirds of all business assets in the country, conduct 70 percent of all business transactions and reap three-fourths of the profits. Down below, some 10 million firms snap and snarl over the remaining scraps of the business world. Clearly free enterprise isn't so free.

If you don't believe that, may I suggest you go out and start your own aerospace, automobile, bank holding, chemical, electrical equipment, light bulb, petroleum or gas, or shipyard company? Damn few can even get into farming and ranching these days—unless it's for hobby and tax-loss purposes.

A second conservative characteristic is that he or she favors strong or weak government, depending on what interests are being served. Ronald Reagan and Margaret Thatcher are classic examples of this schizophrenia.

They denounce as government "meddling" those policies which appear to move toward equalization of life's chances, income and class; or which attempt to make corporations accountable to employees, to the communities where they do business, and to the national interest. Conservatives appear to oppose all government assistance programs, except military contracts, corporate subsidies, bail-outs or guaranteed loans, tax breaks and tax incentives for big business and investors. But they advocate an authoritarian government role in the regulation of private morals, crime control, security surveillance, restrictions on dissent, suppression of left-of-center ideas, and the use of military intervention overseas to protect "our" interests.

Finally, a conservative is one who champions freedom of the individual in theory yet promotes property rights over human rights in practice. When the two values conflict as they sometimes do in labor and management relations and as they often do where Corporate America has foreign investments, conservatives protect property in preference to individual rights and sometimes at the cost of individual life.

Conservatives have to be reminded periodically that the ringing phrase in the Declaration of Independence reads:

> We hold these truths to be self-evident, that all men are
> created equal, that they are endowed by their Creator with
> certain inalienable rights, that among these are life, liberty
> and the pursuit of happiness.

The word is "happiness," not "pursuit of property."

A long time ago, the British commentator L. T. Hobhouse made this case against conservatives: "Liberty without equality is a name of noble sound and squalid result."

That case can be made today against George Bush and that minority of the electorate, who are responsible for elevating him into his present position as Chairman of the Board of the Corporate State. They personify the power of the rich to trade political rights, dignity and survival, in the market place, as though they were mere economic goods. Their every waking hour, every utterance and every legislative proposal seems to consist of clumsy attempts to manipulate the lives of the people for the private profit of business.

Governments founded on those values have risen and fallen throughout the course of history. They always have left in their wake the same squalid results: economic depression and deprivation, unemployment, human misery and excessive militarism burdening the backs of those who have the least to defend.

This much we know for certain: Ronald Reagan and George Bush's brand of conservatism will not save the country, with or without God and the Pledge of Allegiance in the classroom—assuming, of course, we're talking about saving the economy, rather than this piece of real estate called the United States of America. Even in the case of real estate, it seems highly improbable that Star Wars, if allowed to take its course, will preserve our geography.

So what of liberals?

What are the distinguishing characteristics of liberals? Outside of striped ties, button-down collars, penny loafers, foreign cars, two kids in bib overalls and flannel shirts, a shaggy dog, a mortgage the size of the state debt (there was a time when we would have said the national debt) and those interminable wine and cheese receptions, liberals, like conservatives, accept the basic structure and values of the capitalist system. The traditional liberal, however, has tempered his faith in the market system by supporting government intervention to curb some of the more flagrant abuses found there. Similarly, the liberal supports some restraints on the behavior and conduct of corporate enterprise. But the true liberal will always champion the rights of people over the rights of property, sometimes even at great personal sacrifice.

Liberals like to be logical. They like to set agendas, determine priorities, enunciate principles and exercise the power of deductive reasoning. To them, conservative simple slogans and syllogisms are void, silly and full of nonsense.

Once a liberal has mastered the mental logic of a proposition, he or she will stick with it but rarely will go out and objectively test reality to see if empirical evidence supports or warrants the position taken. Sometimes liberals get into trouble when they forget that just because something is logical, doesn't necessarily mean it's valid.

Free trade is a current example of this phenomenon. As a textbook exercise, free trade is perfectly logical. The real world of international trade, however, is a far cry from the textbook case. Our West European trade competitors do have industrial policies, their governments do intervene in domestic and international markets to promote exports; Japan does have protectionist practices that close its market to foreign producers; OPEC is a cartel; and U.S. multinational corporations do export capital and technology in huge amounts to our trade competitors—particularly to Europe—and in the case of technology for military production, the exports go to Japan.

Thus, U.S.-based multinational corporations are "the foreign competitor" in many instances. Most of that foreign investment is not placed in third and fourth world countries. Fully three-quarters of it— some $185 billion out of $225 billion—is placed in the advanced industrialized nations of Canada and West Europe. The IAM calculates that cumulative U.S. direct foreign investment abroad has cost our home economy 4 to 5 million jobs during the 1980s.

What's more, those multinational corporations and U.S. multinational banks control several hundred billion dollars in other currencies, through overseas subsidiaries that are not under the control of the Federal Reserve System, but can be brought back to the United States and entered into the money flows here, through speed-of-light intra-corporate electronic fund transfers. The Federal Reserve's tight money policy does not impede that access to money.

Liberals may not want to believe it, but U.S. multinational corporations and banks *do* play the floating exchange rate roulette wheel, and *do* have clever accounting systems that often work against the U.S. balance of trade, the current account balance and the value of the dollar. And, whether liberals want to hear it or not, U.S. tax laws *do* favor multinational corporations over small and medium businesses here at home; the tax laws *do* encourage multinational corporations to invest in other nations and *do* encourage multinationals to keep their profits abroad rather than bringing them home to plow back into the U.S. industrial base.

To conservatives and liberals alike, we advise they give up their free market ideology; look at reality; look at the exports of capital and technology from U.S. multinational corporations to our major trade competitors; look at the impact those transfers have on our own economy. Stop following the yellow brick road of an illusory free trade system.

We must rein in the international sovereignty of U.S. multinational corporations and their privatized capital. We must make them responsive to the national interest, rather than their own narrow self interest.

Before concluding this essay on ideology versus reality, let us look at a newly developed species. That's that animal called the neoliberal.[1]

What is a neoliberal?

That's someone who says he or she is a Democrat, or a liberal, but acts, behaves, looks and thinks like a Republican; a conservative with a social conscience, if it doesn't cost too much. On military matters, a neoliberal is a superhawk that talks about strengthening and modernizing "conventional" forces, while "building down" nuclear weapons. In foreign policy, a neoliberal is often a chickenhawk, who favors intervention with armed force, if we can be certain victory will be quick and easy. This creature gets queasy, though, if the intervention or invasion looks like it could become something expensive and protracted. It's not the principles of sovereignty or international law, mind you. It's the loss of money and blood, and the awful reality that maybe we've become a "shadow empire."

Neoliberals are the ones who keep harping about new ideas to rejuvenate the nation, but trot out the same old conservative ideas to do it: austerity and sacrifice for workers, government incentive systems and privileges for investors and employers. In other words, free enterprise for the vast majority, with socialism for the rich and powerful few. Neoliberals, by the way, do not like this kind of rhetoric. They think it unsophisticated and doesn't fit the real world.

Neoliberals need to learn that the real world is a big place. There are a lot of people in it. Damned few of them have ever gone to college or inherited their parents' estate and investment portfolio.

However, neoliberals are developing some distinguishing characteristics. They believe in the gambler's spirit of small business entrepreneurs. They would sack the smokestack industries and put all the workforce and capital formation eggs in the sunrise, high-tech industrial sector. Robots, the microchip and computers are their industrial symbols—that's why they were called "Atari Democrats" in the early 1980s, before Atari moved to Southeast Asia. Like traditional liberals, neoliberals see the logic of a thing, and go for it. The fact that they haven't really observed very carefully, or thought through thoroughly, the possible consequences of a high-tech industrial policy as a lone stratagem, doesn't deter them.

For example, neoliberals apparently don't concern themselves with questions like:

Do robots buy cars, homes, ride airplanes or eat out?

Nor have neoliberals taken into account, that, unlike the automation of the 1960s, which was electro-mechanical and impacted on factory assembly lines almost exclusively, the new technology of this era is semiconductor microcircuitry and is being applied to the service sector as well as the manufacturing sector. Labor is being displaced in both sectors simultaneously. This has enormous consequences for workers that the invisible hand of the free market simply cannot facilitate— except to the end of an unemployment line. Few, if any, neoliberals have ever been there. And if they haven't been there, then it doesn't exist. The neoliberal's sense of history goes back to about 1965. Creation began the day they achieved political awareness.

Neoliberals are mostly an ignorant lot who've never worked in production or maintenance, know little or nothing about collective bargaining, and have never sat on either side of the bargaining table. It doesn't appear they've ever met a payroll on their own, either.

Neoliberals do not trust the federal government or federalist solutions to problems, because they've never experienced a federal government that did work or *did* help solve economic and social problems. The only Administrations they've seen in action have been the anti-federal ones: Richard Nixon's, Gerald Ford's, Jimmy Carter's, Ronald Reagan's, and now George Bush's.

They are gullible as hell. They've never heard about old Joe Kennedy warning JFK that "all businessmen are sons of bitches." Neoliberal lambs think they can lie down with corporate lions. And right now, they're feeding from corporate PACs. They'll take union money, too, but more and more they're looking to our employers. And we all know our employers never "give" anything. They only know how to buy and sell.

Neoliberals' historical blindside is their flaw.

If they had a well developed sense of history and some hands-on experience in the real world of trade, commerce and work to match it, then, one suspects, we'd find about half the neoliberals in the ranks of traditional liberals and half in the conservative ranks, depending upon the affinity of each for people or for property.

Neoliberals are often seen flying Japan, Inc.'s flag, touting that country's autocratic and dual labor market. Like right wingers and conservatives, neoliberals think free trade unions are great in Poland, but we don't need 'em in America. Civil rights groups, human rights groups, women's rights groups, and trade unions are "special interests," say neoliberals.

And isn't it strange, how the dictionary is being rewritten? From time immemorial, "special interest" has been a term to depict narrow, private, profit-motivated, self-serving business and financial interests control and manipulation of government; private interest at the expense of public interest. Today, non-profit human and public interest groups are labeled "special interest."

Instead, neoliberals and conservatives alike suggest that licensed thieves, thugs and free enterprise pirates are today's champions of the public interest and common good! Our salvation lies out there among the Hunt Brothers, Lee Iacocca, Ruppert Murdock, Frank Lorenzo, and H. Ross Perot. Corporate bad is good. Television's J. R. Ewing is our role model.

Believe that stuff and you'll end up losing your life savings in pyrite mines.

So those of us who have worked long and hard in the Democratic Party, who have stuck with it through thick and thin, who deliver for it year after year, in spite of the obstacles, odds and snobs, who know what the Democratic Party stands for, and who it represents—we say to the neoliberals, "Stuff it!"

CAN POLITICAL PARTIES GO BANKRUPT?

When American politics is awash with corporate cash, it may seem funny to talk about the bankruptcy of our parties. But I don't mean financial bankruptcy. Both the Republican and Democratic parties have tapped Corporate America's treasury. With some honorable exceptions, it's the best bunch of office holders that money can buy.

What I mean in asking this question is whether our parties have become morally and ethically bankrupt. Can they be bankrupt of ideas? Let us explore the answer and what we can do about it.

We don't need to spend a lot of time talking about the Republican Party. We know what their values are: that property is more important than people, that the business of government is to make the world safe for monopolistic corporations and the rest of the Fortune 500, and that the government should regulate the lives of the poor and working people, but never restrict the abusive power of Corporate America. The neutron bomb is the ideal Republican weapon. It destroys people but leaves property intact.

Republicans represent Corporate America and the filthy rich and always have within living memory. Corporate America owns the Republican Party lock, stock and cash register. Republicans don't have an identity crisis like the Democrats do.

Twenty or thirty years ago, the Democratic Party thought of itself as the party of the New Deal and the Fair Deal, the party of Franklin Roosevelt and Harry Truman. That was the way that John F. Kennedy thought of the party. That was the basis for the New Frontier and the Great Society. It was the working people's party, striving for a fairer deal for all Americans, regardless of race and sex, a party that tried to achieve basic economic rights for all.

There are still plenty of Democrats who believe in those traditions. I'm one.

But the party itself has changed. The Democratic Party was devastated by its presidential defeats in the 1970s and 1980s. Those campaigns left it short of money and woefully short of ideas. Its inability to stand up to Republicans has led many Democrats to ape the Republicans. That may be right if it is restricted to areas such as fund raising, organization, candidate schools, direct mail lists, and other tools of the political trade, but it is dead wrong if it extends to the principles and ideology of the party. It is perhaps all right to have a wealthy banking lawyer as head of the Democratic National Committee. It is dead wrong to advocate the same ideals as the banking community.

Today we have a lot of Democrats who think they ought to represent corporations and those perched on top of the economic pyramid. These are gentrified Democrats. They are dandies who chase fads, trends, and corporate PAC money. They accept the myths of Corporate America as if they were the gospel. They quarreled with Reagan only over details of his policies instead of fighting tooth and nail against the whole disastrous program. We all know Reagan's program could not have passed without their votes.

It is not enough for Democrats to say they have a social conscience, and then tell us they are fiscal conservatives. Fiscal conservatism has long seen to it that there is never enough money to make good social democratic programs work. Adopt the rhetoric and starve the program, that's fiscal conservatism. All those fiscal conservatives, Democrats and Republicans alike, are free wheeling big spenders when it comes to the Pentagon and the military budget. They are penny pinchers when it comes to people, but prodigals when it goes to the Pentagon.

The fundamental fact of life today in our political economy is that there is little or no difference between Democrats and Republicans when it comes to matters of economic policy. The median income of delegates to the Democratic National Convention in 1980 was $37,000 plus—just a little under the Republican $43,000 figure. That puts the leadership of both major parties in the top 4 percent of the nation's income receivers. The capital gains crowd is calling the shots in both camps. Both parties continue to blab a blind and babbling faith in the free market mythology. They do it even when events and reality force them to abandon it, as happens regularly. No one in their right mind would say that the Pentagon operates on the principles of the free market. Nor does the oil and gas industry. It wasn't the free market that bailed out the Chrysler Corporation. And sure as hell it isn't the free market that is bailing out mismanaged savings and loan associations. The free market doesn't set interest rate levels in this country. The Federal Reserve and a tight little band of big bankers control the supply of money and credit and determine interest rates.

The only markets that are "free" in this country are those for capital and labor. That means that capital is always free to pull up stakes, shut down the plant, pack up its bags, transfer investments and technology overseas and move out on us, leaving workers and whole communities stranded in the wake. The free labor market means that you are then free to stand in long unemployment lines.

We've had enough of the so-called free market. And we've had enough of those Democrats who join their erstwhile Republican opponents in promoting the free market rip-off.

The strength of the Democratic Party has always been its concern for the little man, its concern for the disadvantaged in our society. We cannot, and should not, turn our backs on them now. We should be proud of our heritage and not ashamed of it.

We cannot compete by trying to out-Republican the Republicans. We cannot compete by shedding our heritage in order to move to the center. We cannot compete by espousing the values and ideals of Corporate America. We cannot *win* by shifting to the right.

The political party system today is increasingly like a two-headed calf. One head is labeled "Democrat" and the other "Republican," but the message each head bawls is often the same.

That message is that what's good for those who reside at the top of the economic pyramid is also good for those who dwell below the pyramid's peak. What's good for the rich and a few nation-sized corporations is also good for family farmers, workers, and the poor, who support those at the top of the pyramid. Feed the bulls of Wall Street so the sparrows on Main Street can eat.

Now that's bull. The trouble has always been that none of the good ever trickles down—save in time of war when we exchange the lives of our young people for the temporary profits of war.

The two-headed calf feeds at the corporate trough on the promises of free market economics and preaches the virtues of holy trinity of free enterprise, but all it really passes on to its laboring constituents is crap and hot air.

Year in and year out for as long as I can remember, the Democrats have been coming to the unions—usually after they picked the Party's national chair, the state chair, and the candidates for public office—to ask for our money, our votes and our workers. We've always produced, even when the going was rough. Labor has supplied the backbone and muscle the Democrats have asked for, whether the candidate was a dog, a dead horse or a winner. We've stuck by the Democratic Party through thick and thin.

All we asked in return was that the Party, its candidates and elected officials and office holders represent at least some of our interests on some of the issues. We never asked for a 100 percent voting record, or even in most cases, consultation prior to a vote. But we did expect that in a crunch, when an issue was up that could literally mean life or death to trade unions as viable institutions in a Democratic society, when an issue was so clearly drawn that our enemies on the right and our employers presented a united axis against us, in those cases we had a right to expect that Democrats would line up on our side of the issue, and give us that critical vote we sorely needed.

Former Iowa Democratic Chairman Lex Hawkins used to say, "Vote Democratic so you can live like a Republican." That had a lot of appeal to many people. But, damn it, he said *live* like a Republican, not think like one, not believe like one, not vote like one.

But a funny thing started happening in the 1970s. Democrats not only dressed and lived like Republicans, they started thinking they had arrived—they began talking like Republicans! And when the corporate PACs were unleashed in 1974 by a Democratic Congress, those conservative spots began to get bigger and bigger.

The Campaign Finance Act of 1974, which gave legitimacy to corporate corruption of the political process and which spawned mushrooming corporate PACs and New Right money machines, has enormously facilitated our Ship of State's swing to the right. This rightward swing has not emanated from the grass roots. It has been commandeered by those at the top of the economic and social order. That single Act of Congress has permitted the voters' franchise to be sold to the Corporate State.

The retreat to the right, at first by slow and stubborn compromise, became a rout, as compromise became outright collusion with the corporate and monied interests that have *always* opposed the path of economic and social justice, which the Democratic Party, on paper at least, and the trade unions are committed to.

Now Corporate America is not just spreading its big bucks around evenly to be nice guys. Corporate America never gives away anything. It just buys what it wants.

Even liberal Democrats have moved to embrace or be embraced by the probusiness lucre and succor. Here's the way Representative Douglas Bosco (Democrat, California) stated it for the *Wall Street Journal* (December 18, 1985, p. 54), after the plant closing bill was defeated: "Members are broadening their views about where they can get contributions, and both Republicans and Democrats sometimes feel it's worthwhile to be amenable to both sides." In other words, to hell with the merits of the issue; to hell with economic and social justice; to hell with ethics and morality. Go with the flow. Go with Big Money.

Whatever happened to those candidates who took their philosophy and principles seriously and went out to preach the gospel and create the issues and lead the public opinion polls, rather than follow them? That's what the Democratic Party needs right now: leaders, not followers; principles, not PR posturing; feeling and reason united; not smooth mouthed economic jargon and social gobbledygook.

The time is ripe for the Democratic Party to reassert its traditional values, regroup its coalition and reassert its traditional populism and progressivism. It is time to do our level best to restore the Democratic Party to its role as the workers' party, as the party of the people, a party of peace and prosperity, not war and poverty.

The working people of this country inside and outside the trade unions are fully entitled to an open discussion of the issues. We are not getting it from the Democrats. It is no service to democracy to have two major parties spouting the same line, serving the same corporate masters. This country doesn't need two Republican parties.

If we in the trade unions are going to achieve our goals in politics, we have to ask Democratic candidates who talk and think and vote like corporate Republicans why we should answer their call for help. When the Republicans are giving the country away to the corporate bankrollers, it is not enough that Democrats promote a few cosmetic liberal reforms to provide temporary solutions to old grievances and problems, but do nothing to restructure and change the fundamental causes which created the problems in the first place. It is not enough that some Democrats will feign a political left jab with an empty buzz word like "neo-liberalism."

Democrats used to offer us a half loaf rather than a whole loaf. We are realists. We could live with that. Then it became a slice of bread. Then it was God damned crumbs. And now they tell us, "Let them eat cake."

We resent being told we have to support the Democratic Party because there's no place else to go.

We do have some place else to go.

We can stay home on election day and boycott the electoral process, which a majority of voters across the country are doing—because no one is articulating their viewpoint, which I believe is left of center— or we can begin to build our own progressive party with a hard-core trade union constituency.

IS A LABOR PARTY A VIABLE ALTERNATIVE?

This isn't the first time that the major political parties have become wholly owned subsidiaries of the corporate and financial interests. It happened in the nineteenth century when the Republican Party—which began as a Third Party in the 1850s—achieved its goal of abolishing slavery and gave up its reform ideas to become a party of Corporate America. It happened again after World War I in the days of Harding, Coolidge and Hoover, when employers were running rampant with their American Plan and were praising Mussolini for his union-bashing tactics and stress on "efficiency" (interchangeable with "productivity") in all things economic. Things got so bad that in 1924 the Democratic Party nominated a lawyer for banker J. P. Morgan and the Standard Oil Company to be its presidential nominee. For the record, his name was John Davis. But the Democrats couldn't be more Republican than the Republicans in those days, either. Davis lost the Presidency convincingly, with barely a quarter of the vote.

Farmers and workers—those who actually produce in our society— have repeatedly formed third parties to press their demands when the two old parties became too sclerotic. Hard times were the incubator of farm-trade union alliances. Hard times forced farmers and trade unions to form the Greenback Party in the 1870s and 1880s, William Jennings Bryan's Populist Party in the 1890s, Eugene Debs's Socialist Party in early 1900s, and North Dakota's Nonpartisan Political League, Wisconsin's Progressive Party, and Minnesota's Farm-Labor Party in the 1920s. Those groups were not tiny, sectarian splinter parties; they were realistic alternatives to the two-headed calf.

Before World War I, Eugene Debs's Socialist Party was the main alternative for workers to Democratic and Republican Parties. It elected thousands of office holders at the local level both in industrial cities and across the farm belt, and the western mining and timber regions.

Eugene Victor Debs, who had headed the American Railway Union, had an abiding faith in the inevitability of human progress. Whatever his reverses and setbacks—and they were many and severe—he never relinquished his ideals, never gave up his goals, never narrowed his scope and vision and never apologized for propagating his faith or exposing and criticizing his enemies.

Debs equated his struggle for socialism with opposition to despotism of every stripe—foreign and domestic, economic and political, government and corporate (the two were and still are indistinguishable), racial and sexual, right, left or center. He realized that democratic socialism *is* the real alternative to Stalin-style communism and Nazi-style capitalism. Both those totalitarian systems feared and purged strong democratic socialist movements and free trade unions as a first order of business.

Much to Debs's credit, he didn't run around the union halls or the country reciting passages from Karl Marx or Lenin or Leon Trotsky. He didn't engage in academic debates or choose sides in some distant revolution. His was a practical bread-and-butter socialism, born of a passion for fairness and the need for workers to survive, above a bare subsistence level.

He was the epitome of the good, ordinary man driven to greatness and unwanted martyrdom by the meanness of selfishness rampant in his time. When the big monied interests dragged the United States into World War I, Debs cut through the false simplicity of knee-jerk chauvinism and jingoism and the patently fraudulent economic and political arguments for the war framed by the power elite and packaged by its kept media managers. The Socialist Party opposed the war. The Government threw Debs in prison for sedition. In 1920 he polled a million votes running for president on the Socialist ticket—from a federal prison cell.

But patriotism is a powerful force even when manipulated by monied interests that fly their flags of convenience.

World War I saw the break up of the Socialist Party into three parts. (1) The Communist Party wing emerged as a small but influential force in some Finnish, Slavic, and Jewish fraternal organizations and among garment workers, coal miners and metal working unions. (2) The Socialist Party itself remained a power in some localities: Milwaukee; Reading, Pennsylvania; Montana; Sioux City, Iowa; and other western and Great Plains locales. (3) The remainder of the SP deserted in favor of major parties and local electoral movements that emphasized loyalty to the war cause and concerned themselves with immediate needs of working people.

The most important of those local movements was the Nonpartisan League created by Socialists in North Dakota. The NPL called for state-owned banks and grain elevators and pushed a farmer-labor coalition. In 1916, the NPL caucused in both Republican and Democratic Parties of North Dakota. It won seventy-two of ninety-seven Republican seats in the Legislature and fifteen of sixteen Democratic seats. The NPL passed the Workers' Compensation Law, Mine Safety Law and restricted injunctions on strikes.

The success of the North Dakota NPL spread to Minnesota where Machinist Thomas Van Lear was elected Mayor of Minneapolis. Farmers and labor then united in the Nonpartisan League to throw Republican hegemony into confusion as "Steel Republicans" and "Grain Republicans" fought each other over who should foot the bill for the Farm-Labor programs. Nonpartisan Leaguers invaded major party primaries. Farmers won with rural constituencies but labor couldn't overcome commercial media and business combinations in cities.

In 1922, the Minnesota NPL moved toward a new party, based on trade unionists and farmers. The new Minnesota Farm-Labor Party's platform focused on labor's needs but candidates were from the farm movement. It won 38 percent of the vote and elected a U.S. Senator. During the next three years, the Minnesota Farm-Labor Party worked out a party structure that distinguished itself from Democrats and Republicans, based on individual dues payers, unions and cooperatives, and ward clubs with proportional voting power. Biennial conventions made policy binding on candidates.

In the same period, a serious effort was made to put together a national alternative party. In 1922, the rail brotherhoods, coal miners, machinists and needle trades formed the Conference for Progressive Political Action to promote public ownership of rails and mines and to elect friends of labor to Congress. In 1924 the Minnesota Farm-Labor Party invited like-minded organizations all over the country to form a national Third Party. Gompers and the AFL fiercely attacked the idea, but the meeting gave rise to Progressive Party and Wisconsin Senator Robert M. LaFollette's candidacy for president in 1924.

LaFollette supported labor's demands but rejected the idea of a Labor Party. LaFollette held that the "American way is to run as an independent individual, not to form a class party." The AFL endorsed LaFollette, but its support was cautious. The Progressive Party received 16 percent of the vote in 1924 and carried only Wisconsin. It collapsed after the election.

The strength of the third party movement, which waned during the Coolidge-Hoover "prosperity" years, surged again with the coming of the Great Depression. The League for Independent Political Action (LIPA) was formed in 1928 to promote a Labor Party. By 1935, LIPA efforts produced a wave of demands by trade union local and state central bodies, and by railroad, textile and needle trades unions to form a Labor Party.

But by that time the New Deal was underway and the Democratic Party was moving from its business orientation to enact part of Labor's program. While local labor parties were established in a number of communities including New York City, the AFL's Nonpartisan Political League, which was established in 1936, and the New York Labor Party both endorsed FDR in 1936. Labor's marriage to the Democratic Party had begun. That was the end of LIPA and Labor Party movement.

Like many marriages of convenience, this one proved surprisingly durable. The unions provided the party with manpower and support; the Democratic Party put Labor's goals on the political agenda. In some states, the unions *were* the party. Very few labor leaders backed the occasional third party candidate, like Henry Wallace's Progressive Party in 1948.

The non-partisan movement in Dakota, the Democratic Farm-Labor (DFL) party in Minnesota and the Progressive Party force in Wisconsin sustained prairie state populism throughout the Great Depression era, through World War II and the post-war decades of the 1950s and 1960s. The legacies of those alternative movements were personified by the late Senator Hubert H. Humphrey and yet today by North Dakota Senator Quentin V. Burdick and his junior colleague Senator Kent Conrad.

The North Dakota and Minnesota experiences stand as the most successful alternative party movements in modern times in the United States. Both gave voters a clear choice. There was none of that masquerading, where conservatives wrapped themselves in Democratic garb and mouthed "radical" rhetoric, while preserving the status quo.

The importance of that early Farm-Labor honesty was seen in voter participation. Throughout the 1920s, during Harding, Coolidge and Hoover "prosperity," voter participation nationwide fell below 50 percent. But in Minnesota and North Dakota, between 90 and 95 percent of eligible voters went to the polls.

There is a simple powerful message in that experience for the Democratic Party today. The message is: Be honest! Don't take the majority of Americans for turkeys. We're farmers and working people, caught up in the machinations of private interests in a global economy. We watch your hands not your lips. We can usually tell when establishment politicians and middle-of-the-roaders—fence straddlers—are lying. It's when their lips move. We watch what they do, not what they say.

We've had enough of the politics of deceit.

We've had enough of the politics of sameness.

We want no more Democrats with Republican spots—liberals practicing fiscal conservatism.

And that's what the Farm-Labor Coalition was all about: an honest-to-God clear progressive alternative to the bland and homogenized politics of deceit.

But since corporate money has flooded the political arena after 1974, the marriage between the unions and the Democratic Party has fallen on hard times. The party's subservience to free-spending corporate PACs, its retreat on the old issues and its failure to address emerging issues have forced us to look at the alternatives. We're tired of lesser-of-evils, tired of business-as-usual, and tired of those at the top of the economic pyramid calling the shots.

As we consider the issue of an alternative to this two-headed calf of a party system, there are some conclusions to be drawn from historical experience with third parties.

1. When nationwide voter participation is low because major parties represent the same corporate constituency, then the move for an alternative party can enlist great numbers and receive sympathetic hearing.
2. Success of alternative parties comes at local and state levels, but at the national level, vested interests and fear of losing pull it apart. The attraction that such parties have for fringe elements and groups also tends to destroy or weaken their credibility, and the commercial media never fail to define such movements as extremist.
3. War and the threat of war historically have chilled alternative party movements and driven dissidents back into the compromising fold of major parties, as their patriotism and loyalty were called into question.
4. Trade union leaders at the international and national federation levels have no zeal or pioneering spirit for alternative party movements. Sometimes it seems that "a half of loaf is better than a whole loaf" is an absolute given. They prefer to settle for crumbs from the existing parties rather than taking the initiative to organize a better alternative.

The current alternative parties leave much to be desired. The Libertarian Party is what the Republican Party used to be: isolationist, anti-government, self-reliant and individualistic. It represents a smug, selfish middle-class and upper middle class, with a spattering of the new rich, business types.

The socialist parties that run candidates are generally sectarian groups of political theologians who stopped thinking once they read the bible according to Stalin or Trotsky or Mao or Castro. An exception may be the Socialist Labor Party, an old romantic group left from days of Daniel De Leon at the turn of the century.

Democratic Socialists of America (DSA) is not a political party at all, but a caucus within the Democratic Party to provide a left-of-center influence. DSA combines reform politics with some socialist economic principles and looks to Western European Democratic Socialist Parties for a role model. While it is attempting to make trade unions the core of a coalition with intellectuals, students, women, and minorities, its success is relative and limited to major eastern cities. Only some unions—the IAM, UAW, AFSCME, and ACTU—give it much support. To be really successful, DSA needs to come out of its ivory tower and organize at the grass roots, possibly in coalition with Jesse Jackson's Rainbow Coalition or some similar organization. Michael Harrington has laid out the road map. We need only to mobilize and get on track.

The last serious third party electoral effort was the Citizens Party in 1980. It was a well-intentioned group of intellectual activists and frustrated Democrats. It was reform-minded rather than Socialist-minded and emphasized individual rights and civil liberties. The Citizen's Party correctly diagnosed the causes of the current political economy's failures and had a platform and policies that squarely met the emerging issues.

Its leaders, however, were novices and innocents when it came to nuts-and-bolts politics. They put their organization together with a relatively closed group of thinkers, articulated their platform, then said, "Come join us."

Let's face it. You can't organize from the top down. Even if you are the Messiah, no one will recognize you as such.

If none of the above offer a viable alternative party, where are we at this point in time?

I am tempted to compare these times with those that led to the Progressive Party in 1924. The failures of both major parties are obvious. Their leaders are dull, uninteresting, and myopic. Big business dominates both. Both pay lip service to peace while preparing for war. Both are captives of the corporate and financial interests.

One of the political parties, at least, ought to come down from the mountain and represent the interests, needs and aspirations of the producers of this great country—the workers, the farmers, the educators and other productive citizens.

Otherwise, farmers and labor may be forced to repeat history and forge another political alliance outside the two major parties. The trouble is, there aren't that many small family farmers left.

Still, don't smirk at that idea. All our NATO allies have strong Democratic Socialist parties and, in the Scandinavian countries, the trade unions practically run the governments. They have higher wage levels, higher per capita incomes, higher standards of living, cradle-to-the grave social welfare and educational programs, less unemployment and less inflation than we do. And they're beating our socks off in foreign trade.

You don't have to go to Europe either. In Canada, the trade unions have provided the constituency for the New Democratic Party which has significant influence in Parliament and runs some provincial governments.

The Canadians use a different metaphor than we do in characterizing the sameness of the Liberal and Conservative Parties. They say they have white cats and black cats. White cats are liberals. Black cats are conservatives. For years and years all the farmer mice and all the worker mice voted for either the white cat or the black cat. And they switched back and forth. They would even change one white cat for another white cat or one black cat for another black cat. Finally, they started voting for spotted cats and calico cats.

But nothing changed. The big got bigger. The rich got richer. The poor got poorer and the weak got weaker. The cats got fatter, and the mice got eaten.

The Canadians finally asked a few years ago, what makes the difference whether we vote for a white cat, a black cat, or a spotted cat?

All cats eat mice!

So the Canadian workers and some of the farmers and main street business people formed their own political party—the New Democratic Party which is a democratic socialist party. And they have put together an impressive string of successive victories in provincial and local elections and in the Parliament.

They've already put the blocks to exploitation and price gouging by the major oil companies—Pig Oil, as we call it—by creating a national energy agency.

They have a national health care service that is second to none in quality and quantity. No one goes without health care in Canada. Even the U.S. citizen visiting there can get all the health services he or she may need if stricken by illness or accident. But when American citizens get sick in America, it's cash on the barrel head at the toll gate, or lie down and die!

Canadian doctors get mad now and then and strike for higher fees, but at least those doctors admit they have an overriding public duty to perform and collective bargaining is just part of the process to adjudicate their role in fulfillment of that duty.

Meanwhile, south of the Canadian border here in the United States, the two-headed calf continues to dominate our political system. But it's not even feeding the sparrows; it's just passing gas.

Maybe it is time to consider the Canadian route. To rebuild America we may have to take the labor party route just like the unions in our NATO allies and most other free world industrialized countries did long ago. We have to tell our pinto Democrats with the spreading conservative spots that if they want to think and act and vote like Republicans, then move over to their side of the aisle. For our mission is not simply to change riders on political horses; it is to change our system of political economy itself.

WHERE AMERICA STANDS

There is a firm foundation for progressive politics in America. Poll after poll, survey after survey, post-election analysis after post-election analysis over the past two decades have shown that the American people are deeply concerned with Corporate America's control of government.

In the mid 1970s, when we were experiencing the depths of the Nixon-Ford economic recession, pollster Peter Hart probed the attitudes and sentiments of ordinary Americans. He learned some valuable things: 58 percent of the people thought that Corporate America dominated and determined policy in Washington, D.C.; 57 percent of the people believed the Democratic and Republican Parties alike favor Big Business; and 41 percent of the people favored trying things which have not been tried before to change our economy.

The lesson here is that Big Business, not Big Government, is the people's nemesis—the reverse of what we are told so often by the media owned by Big Business.[2]

A free press is a wonderful thing—especially for those with the money to own it and buy access to it.

In 1984, the labor movement pulled out the stops for Walter Mondale. Not only did he lose, he lost by one of the largest margins in American history. We have spent some time since then trying to figure out why and what lessons we should draw from the defeat of this honest, upright, direct, and competent friend of labor.

In the labor movement, our hypothesis was that Mondale's defeat reflected the failure of his campaign strategy, not rejection of the Democratic Party or its traditional coalition of working and middle class Americans, who sought to protect and advance the interests and rights of society's economically and socially disfranchised. To test this hypothesis, we enlisted Washington pollster Vic Fingerhut to conduct an election day exit poll. That poll focused on that 25 percent of Democrats who voted for Ronald Reagan. Those Reagan Democrats provided the President with 20 percent of his total vote. He could not have won without them.

Here's what those Democrats who voted for Reagan in 1984 told us in that election day exit poll:

- 75 percent agreed that "government should do more to protect ordinary Americans from the power of banks and big corporations."
- 84 percent said that "business, labor and government should do more cooperative planning to solve problems of foreign competition." In other words they are receptive to economic planning and an industrial policy.
- 83 percent agreed that "government has a responsibility to see that every able-bodied person in the country has an opportunity to work."

Nearly three-fifths of those Reagan Democrats said the features that still attract them to the Democratic Party are its commitment to "working people," "the average person," and "fairness."

The oxymoron is that 73 percent of those Reagan Democrats said Reagan, rather than Mondale, appeared to be the candidate who showed he was more in the Democratic tradition of Roosevelt, Truman and Kennedy. Only 8 percent of them identified Mondale with those Democratic heroes. Half of them—49 percent—identified Mondale with Jimmy Carter.

The bitter irony is that when Mondale chose to base his campaign on traditional Republican issues—reducing the deficit and balancing the budget—he lost votes wholesale. Reagan, of course, did just the opposite and spent the last half of the campaign pretending he was FDR, HST or quoting JFK. He suckered 25 percent of the Democrats. But that was enough. And that's where Republicans get the idea they can permanently switch—realign—those sucker Democrats into the Republican/Right Wing ranks.

In other words, Democrats for Reagan didn't know what the hell they were voting for. They bought the campaign rhetoric, the 30-second commercial, the 10-second TV news sound bite. Democrats for Reagan thought that he—not Mondale—was in the mold and tradition of FDR, HST and JFK. Of those Democrats who voted for Reagan, nearly 80 percent believed the federal government should do more—not less—to curb the power of corporations and banks, to promote and assist economic and industrial growth, to guarantee full employment and job opportunities for all willing and able to work. In short, our exit polls showed Democrats who fell for the ploy that Reagan was FDR reincarnate want the federal government to be a strong friend, not an enemy, of the people.

The valid conclusions to be deduced from the results of the 1984 Election Day exit poll are that the Democratic Party can only grow and prosper if it maintains its traditional populist and progressive principles and if it sells itself through the dialogue of the populist idiom and progressive ideals. Those exit polls showed the Democratic Party can't win by trying to be more Republican than Republicans or by trying to out-right wing the right wingers. Democrats have to move left, not right, to win back defectors and to move that huge political nonparty of nonvoters into the voting booths. Nonvoters don't vote because the economic pablum served up by both parties over the years doesn't move them or represent their interests.

The day after the 1986 elections, Fingerhut/Madison Opinion Research, Inc. polled a representative cross section of those who had voted. Fingerhut found that 74 percent of voters who chose Democratic Senate candidates said they did so because the candidate, "stood up for the elderly, family farmers and ordinary working people." What's more, supporters of Republican Senate candidates said the same thing. Significantly, only 32 percent of the voters who chose Republican Senate candidates said they did so because the "candidate was a traditional Republican who backed cuts in government programs and who favored reducing regulation of big business!"

If two-thirds of the Republican supporters think their party represents ordinary working people and only one-third mentions the Party's traditional pro big business, anti-government bias, no wonder conservative and right wing theologians are now sending up all sorts of populist trial balloons of their own. This means Democrats have one hell of an opportunity to develop and launch a full scale populist campaign. We need Democrats in high position to fight the good fight in our behalf. And it will gain them votes, not cost them votes.

We all know that in 1984, if Democratic Party regulars had voted for Walter Mondale by the same proportion union households and members did—57 to 43 percent—Walter Mondale would have been elected president. Similarly, according to Peter Hart's 1984 election night poll, union voters voted 70 percent Democratic in Senate races and 67 percent Democratic in House of Representative races.

In 1986, union voters voted 66.9 percent Democratic in Senate races; 72.4 percent in House races; 70.4 percent in Gubernatorial races. Overall, union voters voted 70 percent Democratic. In the voter population at large, Democrats received only 51 percent of the vote in Senate, House and gubernatorial races. Only Black and Hispanic voters gave proportionally stronger support to the Democrats than did trade unionists.

Analyses of the 1988 elections show much the same results as those of 1984 and 1986. Exit polls conducted by the major media networks and the AFL-CIO showed union members and union household voters supported the Dukakis-Bentsen ticket by better than three to one. Willie Horton didn't get the trade union vote in 1988; neither did phony flag-waving patriotism. Wavering conservative and middle-of-the-road Democrats obviously fell for those crass Bush ploys, but the overriding majority of trade union voters did not. Labor's pro-Democratic support was even greater than three to one in Senatorial and House of Representatives contests in 1988.

None of this poll data suggests to me that Democrats can gain anything by moving away from their traditional constituency toward becoming more "business-Democrats," more centrist or moderate, or more "neoliberal." Every time they try to win elections by talking and acting like conservative Republicans, they make chumps of us in the trade union movement. Trying to act and talk like a conservative didn't work for Jimmy Carter in 1980. It didn't work for Walter Mondale in 1984. And it didn't work for Michael Dukakis in 1988.

Throughout the entire 1988 Presidential ordeal, among all candidates, only Jesse Jackson addressed the real issues, stirred the common people's enthusiasm and played to traditional Democratic Party values. But for racism, Jesse Jackson would have been the people's choice in 1988. Clearly, his message and values delivered a clarion call to Democrats and nonvoters to join their hearts and minds in an effort to throw off the yoke of right wing conservatism that still presses so heavily on so many. Too bad that Dukakis didn't espouse Jackson's principles before the last two or three weeks of his campaign, after it was a lost cause. That his belated effort to pick up the Jackson campaign did spark his final drive stands as testimony that a progressive liberal constituency—a democratic socialist constituency—is out there, waiting to be called into action.

It is my belief that a progressive candidate from the left, who doesn't waffle and doesn't break out with conservative spots of fiscal fever or militarism could keep faith with the Democratic Party faithful and could attract a majority of the biggest party of all—the nonvoters' party—in 1992 and beyond.

People simply aren't a bunch of illiterate political nerds, as conventional wisdom too often implies. As in the elections of the 1920s, there was simply no candidate articulating their views, and hence, meriting their confidence. The same has been true in the presidential elections of the 1980s. Carter in 1980, Mondale in 1984, and Dukakis in 1988 first began to pick up votes when they began to sound like real liberal Democrats in the final weeks of their campaigns. There is a large progressive constituency, with a trade union and worker core, if Democratic candidates at all levels would only appeal to it.

Outside the esoteric confines of Congressional Committees and the special interest politics of Washington, compromise, centrism and middle-of-the-roaders have little coin of credibility.

It is precisely for this reason that the Democratic Party must now decide whether it will make the trade unions and working people the core of its constituency, and hence its beneficiaries, or whether it will continue to play to those in the upper income brackets.

If ERA, gun control, abortion, and red baiting among other moral majority issues are the only issues to distinguish Republicans from Democrats, then the time has arrived for progressives and trade unions either to take over the Democratic Party or to form an alternative genuinely social Democratic Party.

We are at that watershed.

We cannot afford—there is no need for—a Democratic Party mired in anti-federalism, fiscal conservatism, free market mythology and rampant militarism. Republicans, Conservative Democrats and middle-of-the-roaders are all coming from those cramped quarters.

Whatever direction Democrats take, trade unions and their progressive allies cannot accept the argument that the way for Democrats to rebound from their repeated presidential disasters is to become more conservative.

If we want to win, shift left not right.

Be progressive not reactionary.

As Arthur Schlesinger put it in 1988, "For Democrats, me-too Reaganism will spell disaster." The Democratic Party must decide whose side it is on. The peoples' side—or corporate and monied interests side? "Fidelity to party convictions is not political suicide," Schlesinger says. And I agree.

The future of the Democratic Party, then, remains in its commitment to provide economic opportunities and security to working men and women and their sons and daughters of the younger generation. That means a continued commitment to trade unions. They're not only good for Poland, they're good for the USA, too.

I've said it before and say it again: America doesn't need two Republican Parties. It does need a good solid peoples' party to challenge the existing Republican and conservative right wing order.

BUILDING A PROGRESSIVE COALITION

So this is the environment in which we find ourselves as we prepare to enter the next century. In our great democratic experiment, fiction has become reality; up is down; over is under; poverty is progress; war is peace; the rich are getting richer, the poor poorer, and the middle class is on the skids.

We are caught between the tweedledee of Republican conservative reaction and the tweedledum of the Democratic shift right. Corporate America is the majority stockholder and broker in both major political parties.

To get out of this dilemma, we have to use defensive and offensive tactics simultaneously. First we have to join forces with our friends inside and outside the trade union movement, circle the wagons and defend what is left of the FDR-HST-JFK-LBJ legacy: unemployment benefits, OSHA, Trade Adjustment Assistance, educational opportunity and job training, food stamps, civil rights, human rights, voting rights, senior citizen rights, and trade union rights. There is room in this defensive strategy to conduct our share of legislative guerrilla warfare, and we may even win a couple of big ones in the short term. National health care and child care are two immediate possibilities.

Second, now is the time to take a long look down the road and start now to build an offense that will give us credibility and dividends in the years ahead. In the Machinists Union we have developed a grass roots political education and political action program. This program is designed to deliver legislative and political issues to our members *at the place where they work.*

There is nothing so rare as a new idea, and this idea, quite frankly, has been borrowed from our Canadian brothers and sisters. The New Right is out there every day. They work in coalition with the single-issue nuts and the moral majority. They meet regularly with Corporate America's political and legislative operators. They own a chunk of the media and they have cowed the rest to run their errands for them. They think they have God, guns and money all on their side.

We know they have guns and money. Lots of money. Somehow, we don't accept the notion that God will permit his only begotten son, Jesus Christ, the Prince of Peace, to make his return to earth as a lily-white, blue-eyed flag waving American, ready to nuke the world into oblivion.

Right now, these extremists have the grass roots field to themselves. Neither the Democratic Party nor the trade unions have the communications apparatus or the financial resources to match the New Right.

Therefore, if we're going to get our members involved in the political game, and get them to join the fray on our team, then we've got to take the issues to them where it counts—in the workplace. The IAM grass roots educational program is a common sense, relatively inexpensive way to overcome the media black-out of our philosophy and viewpoint, and at the same time a way to produce tangible results in the voting booths and with our legislative program.

At the grass roots level, we can follow that time-honored trade union principle: agitate, educate, mobilize and organize. Seize every opportunity to mobilize. Point out every flaw and injustice. Expose every cover up and corruption. Promote every measure of equality and justice.

The third road forward that we in the trade unions must travel is the Coalition Road. For a dozen years now, we have been building a new progressive alliance between the unions, minorities, women, students, environmentalists, churches and citizen action groups.

Since only about one-fifth of the U.S. labor force is organized, trade unions members are in a minority status. We realize that while a few corporate directors may, by themselves, influence or even dictate the course of our lives and livelihoods, the Ship of State and our political economy, we in the trade unions can no longer, alone, counterbalance our employers' might. We are, therefore, building bridges from our parochial interests to the interests of the community at large and its variety of constituencies. These bridges span the common interests ordinary people have on pressing issues of the day, gives them empowerment, and ennobles their purpose.

One of these coalition groups was the Citizen/Labor Energy Coalition, which was composed of some sixty organizations around the country. It was a grass roots organization which educated and developed programs to counter the ill effects of the International Oil Cartel, natural gas deregulation, and the arbitrary and capricious behavior of local and monopolistic private utilities. It also lobbied in the Congress, state legislatures and public utility commissions. Subsequently it has expanded its activity to encompass a broader range of issues including hazardous and toxic waste disposal and clean water and now is tackling the high handedness of high prices in the insurance industry. This coalition now calls itself Citizen Action.

Such coalitions are bridges to the future and they are taking us in new directions. We believe they will lead to control of corporate be-

havior and to a peaceful, full-employment economy. But as we build
our progressive coalitions, as we strive for reason in an age of cynicism,
remember that liberal reforms for social and economic problems provide
temporary solutions to conservative caused grievances. But they do not
structurally transform the fundamental causes, which created the problems in the first place.

When the Corporate State's Road To Ruin has run its course—when
the crash comes—as history and common sense tells us it will—then
the trade union movement in coalition with its friends will stand ready
with a program to plug in and help put America on a true democratic
course.

A POLITICAL PLATFORM
FOR LABOR IN THE NINETIES

Many Democrats and all the media keep telling us that the Democratic Party's dilemma is that New Deal liberalism is dead. A new
program is needed, these critics say, to meet the times and challenges.
They are right about our needing a new program, but they're wrong
about what it is.

And they are wrong about the New Deal. Some Democrats are
obviously more comfortable with their newly found fiscal conservatism
and anti-union biases than they are with an expanding economy, guaranteed jobs, fair taxes and real wage gains for workers, but just because
they don't talk about these real economic problems doesn't mean they
don't exist.

The old, enduring economic problems of this country have never
been solved—not in the forties, fifties or sixties. New Deal solutions
never were fully implemented. Too often, workable solutions were
compromised through the legislative process to the point that they
became unworkable. More often New Deal–type programs were starved
and underfunded.

If we in the trade unions want to recover the Democratic Party
from the neoliberals, fiscal conservatives and other trendy types who
have never done a day's physical work in their lives, it is imperative
that we launch a progressive counter-offensive. We can do that by
adopting a two-track political program.

First, the hard path. We must organize much like a political party
at the state and local levels. That's where the action is. In targeted
states and Congressional Districts, we can move our members into
precinct, county and state central committee levels, with an eye toward
influencing the party at those levels. In this process, we can reach out
to our friends and allies. We can work with ADA members, DSA,

students, environmentalists, Senior Citizens, Citizen Action, SANE/ Freeze, and state and local public action groups. They're out there— ready, willing and waiting. At those levels, we can redefine the party platform, then recruit and select candidates to run on that platform and bind them to it.

The second track is the soft path. We must adopt a comprehensive economic and social program to Rebuild America, by adopting the social democracy models found in Canada, Europe, and, to a lesser extent, Japan.

In that program, we will have to be both negative and positive. Our negative program would emphasize the overwhelming power and might of Corporate America and the Business Roundtable. We have to expose the social irresponsibility of "respectable" conservatism, and the anti-democratic, moral bankruptcy of the right wing. Much of this we're already doing in our own separate ways. We need to coordinate our information and focus with intensity on the issue. The Bush Administration, I suspect, will be of considerable unwitting help during the next four years. Otherwise, multinationals, Big Oil, Big Banks and military jingoism, not to mention the KKK and the book burners, will feed our negative campaign.

Our positive program must be one that sympathizes with the every-day economic and social plight of ordinary Americans.

First, government that is bought and paid for by a few powerful and private entities is not a free government and cannot provide freedom of choice to its people, either in the marketplace or in the political realm. A government that is corporate dominated cannot be expected to conduct itself in the public interest or the best interests of the nation as a whole.

Mark well the definition of fascism: "a philosophy or system of government that advocates or exercises a dictatorship of the extreme right, typically through the *merging of state and business leadership.*"[3] Merging state and business leadership is precisely what the Reagan/ Bush government in the United States is all about. Merging state and business leadership is what the Mulroney government in Canada is all about. And merging state and business leadership is the aim of the Canada-U.S. Trade Treaty which is laying the groundwork for the North American mega-economy.

The number one item on any Democratic agenda must be reform of the campaign contribution laws. We must stem this unholy flood of money from corporate and trade association PACs that is corrupting our political system. We must advocate and enact public financing for all federal elections. We cannot expect elected officials to represent the interests of the people when they have to depend on corporate largesse to be elected and re-elected.

Second, our positive program must provide a vision of hope based on four economic rights: the right to guaranteed employment, the right to guaranteed real income gains, the guaranteed right to organize on the job and bargain collectively, and the right to peace and prosperity.

Under these four broad rights, we can distribute all the specific issues we're concerned about: education, job training and retraining, public ownership and investment, the new technology, economic reconstruction, fair taxes, fair trade, repeal of Taft-Hartley 14(b), plant closing protections and automatic union recognition, safe and sane energy policies, secure retirement and pensions, economic planning, and campaign finance reform.

We must present a program to put America back to work. Unemployment is the greatest scourge of our economy. It is a flagrant waste of our most valuable resource, human beings. It brings with it a whole train of social problems. Every time unemployment goes up so does the incidence of spouse and child abuse, alcoholism, homicide, and admission to mental facilities as well as the economic costs.

The Democratic Party must offer more than the promise of a short term economic upswing. We must reaffirm all that we have accomplished in the past, and point the way toward a better future. That future must be based not only on a return to economic prosperity, but on the promise of a new era of social and economic justice. We must confront the reality of corporate power and force it to serve the interests of all the people, not just the wealthy.

We need a national system of health care in this country. We need improved unemployment compensation and occupational safety and health laws. We need improved pensions and old age care programs. We need child care programs for working parents that have affordable, decent, and humane standards for kids entrusted to them. We need laws regulating capital mobility and the economic and social chaos it causes.

This nation needs a targeted industrial policy—just like our international trade competitors have. Corporate America says we can't have those things, that we can't afford them or that they'll wreck our economy. But Corporate America is lying to us. Our Democratic Socialist allies and trading partners have them and their economies are outperforming ours.

If Corporate America can live with the types of program I have mentioned overseas, then they can damn well live with them here.

A left-of-center program would call for some publicly owned entities in supplying the basic necessities of life: energy, food, housing, transportation, and health. It would also call for some nationalization of banking, primary metals and strategic minerals, and some secondary industries. Direct and targeted public investment in these industries would provide yardstick competition for monopolistic private enterprise and would give the consumers and workers a handle on investment and pricing policies now held exclusively by a few corporate executives and boards of directors. Economic planning by a few private, profit-oriented firms would be influenced by the public sector. Nowhere in our economy is the need for public control and direction greater than in the military-industrial complex.

At the same time there would remain the need for improved New Deal-type programs in taxation, education, and income maintenance. The idea is to redistribute wealth and income away from the top of the economic pyramid where it is now concentrated, toward those at the bottom and middle. The idea is fairness of economic opportunity for all.

It is not the government bureaucracy that hassles most people every-day, but the private corporate bureaucracies where we pay gas and utility bills, doctor and hospital bills, insurance bills; where we stand in grocery check-out lines and pay a dear price for bread and meat; where kids can't afford to go to school and can't get jobs except in the military; where wives work to help make ends meet—and the household budget is always in the red. "Let's get the Corporate State off our backs" can be our cry. People will respond to that.

If spotted Democrats don't like all this, let them move to the other side and stay there.

To make the program work, we will need to conduct continual organizing and educational programs. Above all, we're going to have to come up with the means to utilize television and the other mass media on a broad scale, sustained for the long term.

Our opportunity is that we can lay aside our old shibboleths, throw off our old bonds and trappings of homogenized politics and laissez faire economics, and develop an alternative program for a viable po-litical economy, featuring peace, prosperity, and social and economic justice for all, rather than penury, poverty and war and the threat of war that have plagued my lifetime.

NOTES

1. As for those who call themselves neoconservatives, there's nothing new about them. The New Right is simply the old conservatives and old right wing hooked on the same hoary hypocrisies as of yore.

2. Perhaps the most outrageous piece of disinformation spread by the radical right is the claim that the media is "liberal." Working journalists may be, but they don't determine what story to cover. In point of fact, it is the unions and the civil rights, human rights, and community interest groups that have legitimate complaints and grievances against corporate media's biases. Most of us don't even have access to corporate media; we couldn't get it if we had the money to buy access. Let's face it, in this country, the free press ain't so free either, particularly if it's access you want. Networks, stations, wire services, and local print monopolies do the choosing and selecting. And they do it by their own rules. As usual, the Golden Rule prevails: he who has the gold makes the rules.

3. *The American Heritage Dictionary of the English Language* (Boston: Houghton Mifflin, 1980). Italics added.

EIGHT

American labor in the twenty-first century

The mass of mankind has not been born with saddles on their backs, nor a favored few booted and spurred.

—Thomas Jefferson

Every four years we elect a president. The bands play. The TV cameras roll. The candidates utter their platitudes on motherhood, apple pie and the flag as if they were Moses returning from the Mount. "Vote for me," they tell you in their thirty-second TV ads, "and you can feel good about America." Grandchildren run endlessly across sunny yards to waiting grandfathers. There's no smog and pollution, no shut plants or unemployment lines, no slums, no homeless. It's a new day, a new dawn.

But when the sun rises the morning after the election, the TV ads vanish like early morning mist, and we see again the harsh realities that the candidates ignored.

It is a reality of great inequality. Remember the example cited earlier? If blocks representing the individual income of each American were stacked against the 853-foot high Transamerica Pyramid in San Francisco, 98 percent would lie at the base, less than one foot off ground level. The remaining 2 percent would stack to the tip of the spire.

That's economic reality in America. It's an income pyramid with few at the top and all the rest of us at the base. The peak of the pyramid is narrower and the base broader today than it was fifteen years ago.

But if our blocks represented dollars of wealth instead of people, the pyramid would be inverted. Those 2 percent at the top own the bulk of productive wealth in this country: Through it, they control those mammoth corporations that stand astride the economy like elephants among ants.

It is those corporations that have brought us massive capital flight and disinvestment that undermine the economic security of all working Americans. It is those corporations that engage in the unbridled merger mania that drains investment capital from productive uses. It is that top 2 percent who profit from the index options, currency futures, and the like that have turned Wall Street into Las Vegas East. And it is the economic elite that purchases compliant politicians through channeling almost infinite amounts of money into the political process to persuade you on election day that you should "feel good about America" and ignore the poverty, the loophole-riddled tax system that favors the wealthy, the subsidies for giant corporations, and the stagnant or declining real incomes for everyone but a few corporate chief executive officers and independent professionals.

Unless we make major changes in the direction of socioeconomic policy, this harsh social and economic reality will continue to exist in the twenty-first century. Indeed the trends since 1973 and especially since Reagan was elected in 1980 are toward greater inequality: greater income and wealth for the few individuals at the top of the pyramid, growing poverty for those at the bottom and a shrinking middle class as the deindustrialization of America, carried out by the speculators and the big corporations, pushes increasing numbers of Americans from economic security to the edge of poverty.

This is not a law of nature. This is not a product of an "invisible hand" moving in our political economy. Instead it is the result of conscious decisions that benefit the wealthy few at the expense of the rest of us.

It doesn't have to be that way. This is not Chile. This is not Poland. This land does not belong to those few and privileged economic Pharaohs perched on the peak of the economic and social pyramid. This land is our land! We can fight for our jobs and our livelihoods. We can revolt against the politics of greed, meanness and retrenchment.

We've had enough of this ship of fools running our lives aground. We've had enough of the assumptions and theories of the free market and free trade. We've had enough of trickle-down economics. We've had enough of the reincarnation of Harding, Coolidge and Hoover by Republicans and Democrats alike.

We've had enough of the Corporate State's unisex politics; enough of Tweedledee and Tweedledum heading our political parties and voters' ballots.

We've had enough of politicians who promise full employment but deliver over millions into unemployment and low-wage underemployment, who promise prosperity but give us depression, who promise economic and social equality but give us class warfare.

We've had enough of those who promise us a dream but give us a nightmare.

Why do we tell farmers not to plant when a quarter of the world's people doesn't get enough to eat and millions in our own country are malnourished? Why do we force tens of thousands of building trades workers to mark time in the unemployment lines while there are homeless people in the streets and millions of young families can't find adequate housing? Why do we provide tax subsidies to big corporations to shut down plants and liquidate our manufacturing base while millions of our fellow citizens are in need of the goods those plants can produce? Why does our political economy produce growing misery for some and hardship for many amid great wealth for a privileged few?

It doesn't have to be that way.

There is no law of God or nature that tells us "Go thou and be avaricious. Strip thy neighbor of his property. Lie, steal, cheat, and commit income tax fraud." That isn't the basis for a good society—or, for that matter, any society at all. That's the recipe for civil strife.

Our task is to reorganize our political economy so it serves the interests of all the people, not just the wealthy few.

If we're going to rebuild America along fair and just lines, we have to set our clear and unmistakable objectives.

Franklin Roosevelt's New Deal programs have served this nation well for fifty years. They built our bridges and highways, built our water supply and electric energy systems, gave us public ground transportation and airway services, and brought the crass and callous behavior of big businesses under some form of public control.

Harry Truman's Fair Deal extended the New Deal and helped this nation build and improve our hospitals and health care facilities; the Fair Deal gave a new impetus and placed a new emphasis on education and training.

The brief glory of John F. Kennedy's New Frontier not only conquered space, but it also launched the great Civil Rights victories of the 1960s; committed the federal government to providing the basic necessities of life to all our citizens; and took the initial and, to date, the only steps toward abolishment of nuclear weapons.

"Neither dead nor red," JFK said, "but alive and free." And he had us on the route to peace and prosperity.

The tragic demise of Lyndon Johnson's Great Society was a result of the Vietnam war. His Great Society domestic programs did not fail us. Monuments to the success of his domestic economic and social programs dot the landscape of America. Colleges and universities were rebuilt and expanded with his aid to education programs. Community hospitals and health centers were modernized and expanded. His war on poverty cut the poverty rate in this country in half. The infrastructure of the nation continued to be built, expanded and modernized under the Great Society.

And under all those programs, taxes were more fair than they have been since Nixon. The rich, the wealthy, and the corporations all came closer to paying their fair share under those Democratic governments than they have since then.

If we're going to rebuild America the way we want America to look, then we cannot go back to the old economics of the pure free market and free trade as conservatives seek to do. We cannot rebuild America by instituting the law of the jungle's "might makes right" and a world in which the king of the beasts is the greedy corporate cat.

In order to rebuild America, we must go beyond the New Deal, the Fair Deal, the New Frontier, and the Great Society. We must remake that system so that it serves the needs of the people, rather than corporate might.

Let us make labor's objectives clear to ourselves as well as to those politicians who solicit our contributions, our votes and our support.

Our objectives must be these: (1) the right of each individual to rewarding employment in a full employment economy; (2) an equitable distribution of wealth, income and the political power derived therefrom; (3) industrial democracy in the workplace, with the absolute right of employees to form trade unions, bargain collectively with employers over terms and conditions of employment, including the right to participate at the highest enterprise and national planning levels, in investment decisions which may impact upon our lives and livelihoods; and (4) the pursuit of peace as a priority and complementary goal of all of the above.

In a nation and world of finite natural resources, it is clear that massive numbers of people are, and are going to be in need of the basic necessities of life. The current depletion of our resource base, primarily by narrow and powerful private interests, is undermining our productive capacity and potential for sustained economic growth. In little more than 200 years, our North American continent has been mined, stripped, and depleted of its vast natural resources by the unfettered "invisible hand" of the so-called "free" market.

We can no longer rely on those private interests to act in the majority of the people's interests. They cannot be trusted to do the people's business. It is time to go beyond the New Deal and to restructure our political economy. This will require a leveling of the economic pyramid and making the crooked straight. It will require hacking out of the free market jungle a road toward peace and prosperity for all.

That's the American Dream. And that's what trade unionism in the 1990s must be all about: commencing the urgent task of rebuilding America.

BASIC RIGHTS MUST BE BASIC GOALS

Rebuilding America requires common sense—a quality that has been uncommon among policy makers in recent administrations. Instead of seeking to provide good jobs and good pay for all Americans, government economic policy makers have worshiped at the Shrine of the Phillips Curve—the Golden Calf of orthodox economists—that uses mass unemployment and the misery of the unemployed as a tool to fight inflation. Instead of seeking greater economic equality, with all the good that that brings in a democratic society, they have used the power of government to make the rich richer and the poor poorer and more numerous. Instead of promoting a more democratic economy, they've encouraged an attack on trade union rights and an unprecedented concentration of economic power through corporate mergers and acquisitions. Instead of promoting peace and disarmament, the United States government has undertaken an unparalleled peacetime program of military spending that has brought the government to the precipice of economic disaster; that spending has provided security for the profits of defense contractors, but not for the American people. And they cloak all these policies that serve the wealthy few at the expense of the vast majority of Americans in patriotic rhetoric and flag waving.

The time has come for us to stop being cowed by those legions of bought-and-paid-for corporate economists ensconced in the universities who testify before Congress and the media on the virtues of unemployment, poverty-level wages, and authoritarian workplaces. That's nonsense, not common sense, as every American worker knows. Unemployment and poverty have no virtue—except maybe as a way to re-educate some of those orthodox economists, so they can understand firsthand of what they speak. And as for those flag wavers who gush about Star Wars and first strike capacity, that's nonsense too. Show me a reactionary zealot who is raising hell about foreign policy, morality and patriotism, and I'll show you a crook damned near every time. Nonsense is nonsense even when the speaker is a professor or a president.

Our basic goals are common sense.

The Right to a Good Job

The right to full employment opportunity for every American of working age seems so fundamental that we shouldn't have to dwell on the issue. It is fully consistent with the nation's commitment to the work ethic. Yet each time the issue has been brought before the Congress—in 1946 with the Full Employment Act and in 1978 with the Humphrey-Hawkins bill—full employment as a national priority and a job for everyone as a guaranteed right has been rejected and compromised.

Worse, official government policy declares unemployment is necessary to combat inflation. For two decades we've used high unemployment to combat inflation. We've had mini-recessions, mild recessions and severe recessions. We've sacrificed the unemployed and their families on the altar of fighting inflation and managing the economy. All we have to show for it are declining real incomes for American workers and their families, a growth in poverty-level jobs, and the wasted lives of nearly 10 million people marking time in the ranks of an army of unemployed.

Trading unemployment for price stability is like burning down the barn to get rid of the rats. We lock up people who practice arson as a rodent control policy. Those who promote the conscious use of unemployment to manage the economy are even more destructive. As a national policy it is hypocritical, bankrupt and bereft of intelligence. It is long past due for this nation to commit, absolutely and unequivocally, to full employment as its number one priority.

The Right to a Fair Share

The right to a fair share of the national income and wealth is acute. One sixth of the American people live below the government's artificially low poverty line. Another 15 percent live on the marginal edge of poverty. That means nearly one-third of our people are ill-fed, ill-housed, ill-clad, and have little or no access to decent health and dental care. Inflation in the basic necessities of life—energy, utilities, transportation, food, housing and health care—is twice the inflation rate for non-necessity items. That cruelly compounds inflation's impact on those Americans.

Real after tax income for individuals is at the same level it was in 1967. There has been no real gain for two decades. Household real after tax income may have risen, but that's because more wives and other family members are working to make ends meet. When two or more people are required to maintain a standard of living formerly supported by one person, that is not progress. It is retreat.

At the top of the pyramid, just one percent of the people own and control 35 percent of the nation's wealth. At the bottom, 60 percent of the people own only 8 percent of the wealth, and that primarily consists of consumer durables, such as cars and refrigerators. In terms of financial assets, such as stocks, and bonds, the maldistribution of wealth is even more skewed.

These inequities in income and wealth distribution constitute a social stratification that seriously impairs the functioning of democracy. Wealth means economic power and power means politics. Given our auction block system of campaign fund raising, it is small wonder so many politicians are beholden to so few wealthy people and corporate interests. But even if we correct the campaign financing system, there remain the discrimination and stigmata attached to those who do not share meaningfully in the nation's wealth and income.

We must guarantee an opportunity to all Americans to share in the national affluence at least at a modest level. The right to a fair share for all Americans is an important goal.

The Right to Participate in Economic Decisions

The third basic right would guarantee to every American worker the right to organize and participate in private and public investment decisions affecting his or her life and livelihood.

There is no place in this country where the hypocritical norm of preaching democracy and practicing autocracy is clearer than in the workplace. Frankly, I've never understood why, as a nation, we've always extolled the virtues of democracy in ringing terms and then willfully, methodically and even ruthlessly denied democracy to most people in the one sphere of their lives that counts most and should mean most—their place of work. It seems to me that, in terms of conflict resolution in the world of work, democratic values are not only essential, they provide the means and tools to resolve conflicts.

On the other hand, when one surveys the long history of labor and capital in this country, it is obvious that we as a nation do not practice what we preach.

Workplaces are communities. They are not simply places where people go to carry out assigned tasks in exchange for a wage or salary, albeit that is the primary consideration for those of us who are not endowed with unearned incomes and inheritances.

The sense of community in the workplace can only be experienced by being part of it. That is why so many behavioral scientists, who make a great fetish of analyzing and studying work and workers on the job, miss the camaraderie, the folklore, the genius and the *humanity* of the community of people, that make up the workplace.

The workplace community, like any other community, has its own group dynamic, its hierarchy of needs, its structured interpersonal relationships, its rituals, its enforcing codes, mores and taboos. Behavioralists' attitudinal surveys of workers at work, particularly in manufacturing industries, are generally useless, because they tell us nothing about the people in a given workplace as a collective group. They perceive automatons and drones. They portray boredom and monotony and ignore the phenomenon of *schmooze*.

Schmooze is simply the manner in which workers add creativity to those jobs that may look like drudgery, to ward off boredom and exhaustion. Joking and wisecracking are part of it. Figuring out new ways to do the same job also is often part of it. Covering for a fellow worker who may be having a rough day is part of it. In manufacturing, the pressure for more production goes on without relief, and devising ways and means to slow down speedups can also be a part of schmoozing.

Schmoozing is often ingenious and always creative. It is the way workers get some control over the work pace and make life interesting in the workplace. Its importance to the health of individual workers and to productivity should never be underestimated. It takes the solemnity out of demanding and tedious work and contributes to the spirit of the community. Playfulness often is an important element in work satisfaction. Its absence, I have noted from long experience and observation, leads to work alienation and the phenomenon of the lonely crowd.

Democracy in the workplace builds on that community through collective bargaining. The contract that results is a bilateral agreement between your workplace community and your employer that regulates your wages, hours, working conditions, work rules, job classifications and job descriptions. It is sanctioned by the law of the land and until the Reagan era enforceable in the courts. In a society committed to adversarial relationships, collective bargaining is a democratic tool and democratic institution without equal in settling disputes in the workplace. It is designed to avoid conflicts and to bring about resolution of conflicts. Fully 98 percent of all collective bargaining contracts are negotiated successfully without resort to strike action. The common cold causes more lost time than do strikes.

The alternative to collective bargaining in today's world of work are paternalism or despotism—the latter of which can be either benevolent or malevolent.

Paternalism is alien to us because it requires a system of conduct that deprives workers of their adulthood. It is inimical to the concepts of enablement and self-reliance. In the community of work, we are all workers with different functions, but the difference in functions should not define our social privileges or our securities and insecurities. Paternalism rests on the notion of privilege and security, to be dispensed in a way not unlike the master-slave relationship. Robbed of their adulthood, workers are forced to seduce, in a manner of speaking, employers for favor, privileges and security. Instead of collective bargaining, paternalism means individual begging.

Despotism—no matter whether benevolent or malevolent—is the very antithesis of democracy. Its rigidity and fixed values impress on workers that the condition they find themselves in is somehow ordained by some form of predestination. It is grounded in fear, and paralyzes people into inferiority and servility. It destroys the sense of community and smothers the individual's innate desire to be communal, creative and self-reliant.

The American business community has never accepted the principle of democracy in the workplace.

That is more evident today than it was ten years ago. We witnessed the antidemocratic wrath of employers, in 1978, when Labor Law Reform legislation was before the Congress. Since then business after business, corporation after corporation, has persistently and systematically violated workers' legal rights and protections.

They do it in many ways. They tell workers if they form a trade union, they will shut down and move the plant away. They tell them if a union is formed, there will be a strike and violence. They tell them they will be replaced by people standing hungry in the unemployment lines. And they fire them for union activity, to make certain the chilling effect takes hold.

But even before workers try to organize, employers hire psychiatrists, psychologists, behavioral scientists, lie detector peddlers and lawyers to prevent any possibility of democracy coming into their workplaces. These hired specialists call themselves management consultants. But they are really cold-blooded union busters. In the hiring process, they use screening tests to eliminate workers who might be sympathetic to organizing. They invade their privacy by asking very personal questions about their religion, their creed, their affiliations with other organizations, the history of their families and work records. Anyone who exhibits a previous trade union membership, who has underdog empathy, or a good social conscience is denied employment, because he might be a potential trade unionist.

They want only the fearful, the docile, the ignorant or the selfish to inhabit their workplaces. And they want increased productivity, too! They can't have it both ways.

Our goal must be to strengthen employee rights to participate and to organize themselves in the workplace.

The right of workers to organize into trade unions for collective bargaining must be an absolute one—an *a priori* assumption for an enterprise to do business and for workers to sell their labor.

Beyond the right to organize, workers and communities must have a voice in corporate investment decisions that have an impact on them. The runaway employer must be held accountable to those who have served him faithfully and dependably. The mobility of capital and flight of technology can not much longer be permitted unrestrained license.

Our most fundamental message must be that the people should have a voice in the economic decisions which affect them. It should be our position that we want to extend the same rules of democratic participation which supposedly govern the political life of this nation, to the economic life of this nation; that we aim to break the domination of our economy and our society by the corporate interests; that we want a political party that represents the workers, the minorities, and the disadvantaged in our society. We must convince the people of this country that a viable alternative exists to the control of our economy by that small group of people who enjoy most of the wealth created by that economy.

The Right to Peace

The fourth basic right of every American is to enjoy the fruits of peace.

The Department of Defense employs 3.5 million people to plan, prepare and wage war—a war with no winners. But there is not a single individual working for the Federal Government to plan and prepare for peace. Three-quarters of the interest paid on the national debt is war related, stemming from government borrowing to pay for current military programs and defense production, past wars and veteran programs and programs outside the Defense Department, justified on grounds of national defense. Austerity is mercilessly applied to employment, health, education, welfare and social security programs, but the Defense Department is bloated with funds that it has trouble spending despite buying every imaginable weapon and some unimaginable and unworkable ones too.

In spite of ever-escalating defense budgets in pursuit of a first-strike capability in the arms race, we still have no first-strike capability, and, far from achieving national security, we have only obtained greater insecurity. In an age of missiles rivaling the speed of light, each tipped with nuclear holocaust, first-strike capability is a figment of the Mad Scientist's imagination, be he American, Russian or any other nationality.

We must stop the nuclear madness, pursue disarmament negotiations with vigor, and plan the conversion of defense production to meet human needs.

THE PATH FORWARD

What sort of structural changes are needed to achieve these goals?

It is clear that nothing short of comprehensive economic planning will stem the decline of the nation's industrial base and move us ahead to full employment, peace and prosperity. A warfare state, based on the service economy and high-tech information revolution, simply isn't getting us where we want to go.

If we're going to substitute the power of the people for the power of Corporate America, then those parts of the market system that are not working in the public interest—that are impairing our four basic rights—will have to be altered, changed or discarded in spite of vested interests and corporate prerogative. That means confronting the Corporate State and all its might. As Franklin D. Roosevelt said over fifty years ago, "The country needs, and, unless I mistake its temper, the country demands bold, persistent experimentation."

FDR preserved the system. Now it is out of whack and malfunctioning again. This time the animus is global in nature and structure. That means something more must be done than fine tuning the market system, with reliance on corporate prerogatives and priorities, if we're going to make the economy serve the people.

What is required is coordinated economic planning.

Coordinated Economic Planning

The idea of economic planning is hardly new in America. We used it with great success to mobilize the economy for World War II. We had a War Production Board then to determine priorities and allocate resources.

We need a similar agency for socially useful peacetime production.

During World War II we had mandatory price and profit controls. We didn't need wage controls, because trade unions knew they couldn't demand more than the treasury held. In return for wage restraint, workers were guaranteed real wage gains. The economy was inflation proof.

We need similar mandatory controls on all forms of income today, with a guarantee that workers' real incomes will be permitted to rise incrementally each year.

We had a War Manpower Board and War Labor Board in those days, too.

In short we had a finely-tuned, centrally directed, efficient and relatively fair economy.

Our troubles began, when we returned to the so-called "free market" and let Corporate America take over the planning in its closed board-rooms. If we are to have administered prices, as we do anyway, it is better that they be set in the public interest rather than by oligopolists and monopolists.

At the heart of our industrial policy program is a requirement that the business community enter into an economic and social contract with labor and the government, in exchange for the considerable public assistance and monies, pension funds and tax concessions that it already receives. That economic and social contract would be expressly written into every public assistance law and grant providing federal assistance or tax concessions to business. It would be negotiated into every contract, treaty and trade deal involving interstate and foreign commerce.

The economic and social contract would commit business enterprise to a code of conduct and behavior befitting a democratic and humane society preparing to enter the Twenty-first Century. It would specify that business beneficiaries of federal monies and assistance (1) agree to abide by and support the civil rights and human rights, including women's rights, that are the laws of the land, (2) agree to uphold and enhance international and national fair labor and wage parity standards, (3) agree to abide by and improve international and national workers' safety and health laws, (4) agree to meet and promote international and national environmental protection standards and laws, (5) agree to accept as a universal human right the right of workers to organize and bargain collectively, without adversarial intervention in their petitions, and (6) agree to use direct federal subsidies, assistance and tax concessions for investment in the domestic industrial base and economy. This economic cooperation is a three-lane highway involving business, labor and government in achieving shared goals. For it to work, business and government must recognize and cooperate to achieve labor's goals and objectives, for workers themselves and society as a whole.

U.S. businesses are now receiving and benefiting from some $600 billion worth of cumulative taxpayer largesse and concessions. Beyond six figure executive salaries and bonuses, rising corporate profits, and accelerating incomes derived from excessive interest rates and an astronomical federal debt, all the people are currently getting for this $600 billion business welfare program is a deindustrialized, deunionized, dehumanized and polarized economic and social system.

If a business enterprise—if any employer—cannot or will not agree to these fundamental, fair and civilized rules of conduct in exchange for taxpayer and worker assistance, then we say let that business sink or swim by its own animalistic and predatory code of "Social Darwinism." The rest of us are going to play by different rules.

We reject the notion that private capital is sovereign—either at home or globally. The people are sovereign. And the exemplary way to exercise their sovereignty is through a binding economic and social contract with business and government. We need to extend the democratic franchise from the purely political to matters economic, too.

For those who may say this nation cannot afford to base its economic activity on the itemized principles of an economic and social contract, then we say take a look at those countries who are beating our socks off in the trade game. Trade unions are much stronger, wage and compensation levels higher, environmental protections and worker safety and health standards stricter, business taxes greater, and over the long run inflation and unemployment levels much lower than our own.

We don't buy into the Reaganite notion that American workers must reduce their level of living to the world's least common denominator in order to compete in world commerce. Rising living standards, not exploitation of cheap labor, creates markets, provides economic and social stability, and ensures peace and prosperity. That's just as true here at home as it is in the Third and Fourth Worlds. We have to discard the antiquated principle of the sovereignty of capital and industry; to go beyond the New Deal, New Frontier and Great Society programs; to skip yesterday's corporate liberalism. We have to offer the American people and American workers an economic and social contract that will include them in the control, ownership and decision-making authority of the nation's economy.

Rebuilding America

In 1983, the International Association of Machinists presented our program for rebuilding America.[1] Unfortunately, given the retrograde movement in America since 1983, it is even more necessary today than it was then. It calls for the rehabilitation and development of our inner cities; for establishing a domestic investment and production policy; a foreign trade policy; an energy policy; creating national health services;

and developing a fair tax policy. Its parts are integrated. None is addressed without consideration of the others. All point to full employment with no phoney trade-offs.

We would achieve our goals through ten major innovations.

First, we would legally redefine a corporation doing business in interstate and foreign commerce as an entity operating for the convenience of the public and in the public interest. The Good Book says that the Lord created Adam and Eve, not that He created the modern corporation. The corporation was created by human law and it can be reshaped by law. As a matter of fact, precedent for this redefinition of the corporation is found in North Dakota Statutory Law. Corporations engaged in interstate and foreign commerce would be federally chartered, and that charter contains an economic and social clause that would require labor participation in corporate investment, planning and policy decisions.

Second, we would require that economic and social clauses be included in legislative acts, treaties and all private and public international trade agreements as well as corporate charters. All federal assistance to private enterprise and state and local government would be contingent upon their subscription to, in writing, an economic and social contract that would contain five basic clauses that would commit them to upholding and implementing civil rights, human rights, worker trade union rights, safety and health and community environmental protections, and the payment of an economic and social dividend into a federal investment reserve fund.

Third, a national and international industrial and investment strategy agency would be established. It would include a Labor Industrial Sector Board composed of thirty-two Basic Industrial Sector offices from aerospace and automotive through machine tool, railroads and down to offices for steel and utilities. It would have within it a federal Domestic Investment and Production Office, to be chaired by a trade unionist, who, with the advice and consent of the Senate, would appoint a representative for each of thirty-two basic industrial sectors to design and direct a coordinated national economic and trade strategy. The Labor Industrial Sector Board would be the nation's primary research, fact finding and policy recommendation arm for both international trade and domestic commerce. Academic and business representatives would also serve on the governing board of this independent agency.

Fourth, a national development bank would be created. It would have windows for international trade and for domestic purposes. Behind the domestic window might be other windows for regional, state and local or industrial sector purposes. The governing authority for all such financial institutions would include democratically elected representatives from geographical, user, consumer and public constituencies.

Fifth, we would establish an International Trade Office, and all trade negotiations, government and private, would be coordinated through that office. Each government sanctioned trade negotiating team would be required to include trade union negotiators.

Sixth, in the case of capital mobility and plant closures, for whatever reason, our IAM proposal calls for local due process public hearings before shutdown and transfer of operations. Both citizens of the community and directly affected workers could petition for a local due process hearing to force a runaway company to show cause why it could not remain operating profitably in that community. The hearing board would be impaneled from the American Arbitrators Association. Corporate records could be subpoenaed. If a firm failed to show cause, it would be permanently enjoined from closing, moving, and laying off workers. Violation of the injunction would come at the risk of impoundment, communalization or nationalization.

Seventh, to get a grip on the sovereignty and mobility of corporate capital at the international level, a multinational corporation monitor would watch-dog and publicly report on the activities, behavior and conduct of U.S.-based and foreign-based multinationals.

Eighth, with respect to military contracting and production, our IAM program would require workers and community representatives to work with corporate management in designing and periodically updating a full employment peace plan, to coordinate, prioritize, and reconcile a realistic military industrial policy with civilian industrial priorities and requirements. In effect, our economic conversion program (see Chapter 4) would reassert the constitutional authority of civilian rule over the military.

Ninth, our technology control proposal (see the Technology Bill of Rights in Chapter 5) would ensure that labor cost savings and profits stemming from technology induced productivity increases would be shared with workers and their communities, and not accrue solely to management and shareholders.

Finally, we would establish a Federal Investment Reserve Fund to accompany the more comprehensive industrial development strategy. The purpose of this Fund is to provide a pool of collective savings for business and industrial development. Outside of worker-owned pension funds, there is no pool of collective savings available for investment on a nation-wide scale today.

In our national plan, money for the Fund would come from requiring corporations and businesses doing business in interstate and foreign commerce to pay an annual economic and social dividend from after-tax profits. The Fund would recycle those dividends into business and industry through stock purchases. The objective, however, would not be to maximize return on investment or to speculate on an individual firm's economic performance or to speculate on the stock market as a gambling casino.

The purpose of the Federal Investment Reserve Fund would be to make stock purchases according to national priorities, as determined by the needs of the nation's industrial development. As a shareholder in those corporations and businesses, the Fund would then have greater potential for influencing the corporate decision-making process and corporate behavior. The Fund, where necessary, could purchase private firms that may need to be reorganized under private, public or community ownerships.

Surpluses earned by the Fund would add to its working capital or could be distributed to the general treasury. In any case, the Federal Investment Reserve Fund would provide a means for Corporate America to contribute to the economic stability and viability of the American economy by establishing a collective savings pool, which would backstop its own failings and shortcomings and help prevent further decline of our industrial base, and promote our export industries' development.

What we propose is to take economic and social decisions away from an exclusive, private domain of powerful and often invisible corporate officers and government accomplices, and to share them with the workers and the people. That would be democratic in principle, cooperative in ethic, and fair and equitable in results.

The IAM program is not an economic planning blueprint. What it calls for is constructing a framework within which economic planning at local, state, regional and national levels, and among the various industrial sectors, can be coordinated and conducted with proper democratic safeguards to prevent the process from becoming over-centralized, over-bureaucratized, over-regionalized or over-privatized.

The IAM's goals call for us to link our idealism and pragmatism in a realistic program to overcome the impediments to a more democratic America. In the long term such policies are a realistic alternative to the dog-eat-dog policies of Corporate America which have beggared many to enrich a few.

Exploring the Economic and Social Contract

The economic and social contract between labor and the public on the one hand and the corporations on the other which is at the heart of the IAM proposal would reshape the relation between corporations, their workers, the community, and the country.

Let me illustrate how it would work.

Assume the Boeing Corporation receives a research and development grant and contract from the Pentagon to design, test, evaluate and produce a new intercoastal and inland waterway hydrofoil. During the negotiations and deliberations for this grant and contract, the Boeing Company and the Pentagon would be required to negotiate into each an economic and social clause that would give the people of Seattle, where the work would be done, and the Boeing workers doing the work something of value in return for receiving this lucrative taxpayer-paid grant and contract.

The economic and social contract would bind Boeing to a code of conduct and behavior befitting a democratic and humane society preparing to enter the twenty-first century. That economic and social contract or clause would specify that Boeing, as the primary benefactor of federal monies and resources, agree to abide by and support civil rights and human rights, including women's rights, that are laws of the land and that may be contained in international accords, conventions and treaties, to which the U.S. government is signatory.

If Boeing should later move production of the hydrofoil to another country, the economic and social contract would bind the company to negotiate an economic and social clause into its deal with the foreign entity that would uphold and enhance international and national fair labor and wage parity standards. The economic and social contract would bind Boeing to abide by international and national workers' safety and health laws. The economic and social contract would specify that Boeing agree to meet and promote international environmental protection standards and national environmental protection laws and standards.

The economic and social contract would stipulate that Boeing use any direct federal subsidies and tax incentives for investment in the domestic industrial base and economy, unless that assistance is specifically designed for foreign investment, in which case negotiation of all the elements of the economic and social contract would still be binding on the company in making its deal with the foreign entity.

In the event that federal monies and resources or any worker resources, such as pension funds, are committed to the company's hydrofoil project, or workers are asked to make any wage or labor concessions in order to get the grant and contract, then the economic and social contract would stipulate that Boeing agree to, as an undisputed human right, the right of its workers to organize and bargain collectively, without adversarial intervention in their petitions to organize and bargain.

The reality incidentally is that Boeing *did* have such a hydrofoil grant and contract, and the research, development, testing, and evaluation were done in Seattle. But when it was ready for production, the company moved it to Indonesia, where unions are outlawed. Meantime, some 11,000 Boeing employees were unemployed and on indefinite lay-off status in Seattle.

Investing Employees' Pension Funds

One of the areas in which employees have a right to immediate action is in the investment of their pension funds. Pension funds are the largest single source of investment capital in the United States, and we are just beginning to discover their power.

It was long assumed that investment of pension funds was best left to traditional financial institutions and experts. Only they, it was held, could prudently place pension fund monies in a manner which would achieve a high rate of return and avoid undue risk at the same time. For many years the courts implied that pension funds belonged to the employers, not the employees. Later rulings, however, by the courts and the Internal Revenue Service have determined that pension funds are deferred income and belong to the workers. Therefore employees should be entitled to have a hand in the management of what is, after all, their money.

Most managements, however, resist this interpretation and may even insist it is "their" money and the corporation or employer must manage it. Their rationale is that the money simply accumulates in a fund and does not belong to the employee until he qualifies for it in some respect. It should also be noted that more often than not, management doesn't even try to rationalize its position. It simply maintains that union people cannot possibly know anything about "financial matters," or they say, "We pay for the pensions; therefore, until the pension is received, it's our money to control and use."

For those not easily intimidated by employers and their legal hired guns, there is plenty of room to maneuver in the limbo of pension fund management and control, and, at the same time, fulfill the fiduciary responsibility and prudent man obligation.

Like every other union, the IAM fully subscribes to the principle that pension funds must be managed and invested for the exclusive benefit of covered members. That is first and foremost our rule.

Normally, pension funds, in seeking high rates of return, are concerned not only with present yield, but with future earned income meeting demands on the system. The quest for high yield and future income is tempered by concern for risk. In fact, risk is often considered more important than return.

The risk argument is one that inevitably is thrown in our faces whenever social investments are broached among professionals. But when we consider that, according to one 1975 study, roughly 60 percent of private pension fund assets were in corporate common stocks and 20 percent in corporate bonds, and then look at the roller coaster history of the stock market, employees have a right to ask what is more risky than investing their funds in Corporate America. What prudent man would exercise full fiduciary responsibility by investing his money in the recent stock markets?

The risk argument is too often a smokescreen to cover the financial community's fear of losing its vested interest in the control of employee pension funds. These funds have been held captive by professional investors for a long time on the grounds that only they were capable of being prudent in investing employees' money.

But this overemphasis on corporate stocks and bonds undermines their prudence. In fact, when we see government-guaranteed security issues such as the Government National Mortgage Association (Ginnie Maes), Federal National Mortgage Association (Fannie Maes) and Federal Home Loan Corporation (Freddie Macs) yielding rates of return as high as or higher than corporate stocks and bonds, then we are almost forced to conclude that it is fiduciarily irresponsible and imprudent not to invest pension funds in those public securities. They are safe—100 percent guaranteed—highly liquid and easy to purchase.

The clinching argument in favor of those government securities is that they serve socially useful purposes, as opposed to the purely private profit motivated purposes of the corporations. Money raised from Ginnie Mae issues support the national housing market, a good deal of which is targeted into low income and economically depressed areas. Fannie Mae issues support the needs of poor and middle income urban dwellers, while Freddie Macs play much the same role in the conventional uninsured mortgage housing market.

Contrast those constructive social purposes with the destructive role of corporations which use employee pension funds to flee from unions, by running away overseas or to low wage right-to-work states. Corporations also use employee pension funds to escape environmental standards and taxes. When we look at the track record of Corporate America during the 1970s and 1980s, responsible trade unionists have to conclude that, in too many cases, they have been financing their own destruction.

While there is need for caution in using pension funds for social investment purposes, there is nothing in the law that says those funds have to be turned over to a few giant banks and insurance companies to be loaned to 50 or 100 giant multinational corporations. An employee can enjoy the exclusive benefit of his pension fund only if he has a job secure enough and long enough to collect his deferred income pension. There is nothing that requires him to finance his own job loss. As Randy Barber and Jeremy Rifkin's remarkable book *The North Will Rise Again* (Boston: Beacon, 1978) suggested, trade unions can use pension funds to influence corporate behavior, for democratic and socially useful purposes.

In the current anti-union climate, for example, we could invest our pension funds in pro-union companies only. We can refuse to invest in corporations with poor occupational safety and health and environmental records; refuse to invest in corporations with poor equal employment opportunity records; refuse to invest in corporations systematically exporting technology and jobs overseas; refuse to invest in corporations exploiting human rights in Third World countries; refuse to invest in corporations doing business in apartheid South Africa, as many of us are now doing; refuse to roll over and play dead while our pension funds are consumed as tools in leveraged buyouts and predatory corporate takeovers. In a world of moneychangers, if sweet reason won't win for the cause of economic and social justice, maybe our money can buy it.

Such was the case in 1977 when the Machinists Union through the IAM Pension Fund, a jointly administered plan, sent word to Manufacturers Hanover Trust Company, to which was delegated the responsibility for investing the Fund's assets, that unless the J. P. Stevens[2] official sitting on Manny Hanny's board of directors was removed therefrom, the IAM Pension Fund monies would be removed from that bank's tender care and placed elsewhere. Since we were talking about roughly $200 million, the bank decided to act. That was a relatively simple power play, based on the accurate assumption that "money talks." Carried to its ultimate source of power, that play would have been backed by a majority vote of the Fund's trustees, who represent equally the Machinists and the employers.

Private pension funds can be used for solid public purposes and, in my book, should be. Only tradition and a great con game has kept pension funds in the control of the private sector giants.

Rethinking Production in Our Culture

We also need a cultural revolution in how we think about work. For too long we have denigrated productive labor. Business schools stress finance, not production. Apprenticeship programs have been starved for support, despite the shortage of many categories of skilled labor.

Television programming systematically glorifies white collar jobs no matter how menial, while blue collar workers are depicted as prejudiced buffoons. (This last is a vicious calumny; you'll find far more racial and ethnic prejudice in the country club and the corporate boardroom than on the factory floor.) In this environment, even craftsmen encourage their kids to look down on their parents' skills and to opt for a college education devoid of any concept of how goods are actually produced.

As a result, we have a surplus of people who know how to write research papers, apply for foundation and federal study grants, talk learnedly about a host of highly specialized disciplines and theories, but they can't find jobs and do not know how to stop a running toilet, fix a leaking faucet, replace a broken light switch, or identify anything on an automobile more complicated than the gas tank cap.

We are a nation of industrial illiterates.

I do not wish to appear to be a blue-collar snob, but the time has arrived when society must give priority to manpower programs which may combine plumbing and steamfitting with poetry and philosophy; which will permit political science and sociology majors to learn how to be mechanics, machinists and tool and die and pattern makers, too, and vice versa.

In other words, we must learn how to work with both our hands and our minds. That requires respect for all productive work, both physical and mental. It requires a conscious societal effort at life-long education that uses part of the surplus from technological improvements to improve the skills and the knowledge of all Americans.

Americans suffer from a kind of philosophical Taylorism: that we should know how to do one thing and one thing only. In Europe, craftsmen and laborers have a keen interest in things political and poetic, in knowledge for the sake of knowledge, as well as their primary economic and occupational pursuits, but there is a lack of interest in books, the arts, music and philosophy in the American workplace. That may have served us well enough when technology changed more slowly, but it has served us badly in recent years as the speed of change has accelerated, and it will serve us very badly indeed in the next century. As someone has said, "Training is for monkeys; education is for people." It is education that will permit workers to be creative, adaptive, and competitive in the global political economy.

Vision and Reality

It's a long road from the America of Ronald Reagan and George Bush—of each grabbing for his neighbor's share and the devil taking the hindmost—to the America that organized labor has always sought. Since the origins of the labor movement, unions have sought to achieve collectively a fairer, more equitable order in the workplace and in the larger society. There have been detours, side tracks, and leaders of limited vision, but labor's goal has always remained that shining city on the hill where there are good jobs for everyone in a fair society in which all participate in economic as well as political decisions. In that city, there is dignity for all work and all workers, and none enrich themselves by speculating in the misery of others. That is the basis for a good society and for a peaceful world.

An unclouded vision of this shining city is of little value if you are sinking in quicksand in the swamps of Corporate America. Labor needs to continue to put its own house in order as the AFL-CIO began so notably with its analysis *The Future of Work* (1983) and *The Changing Situation of Workers and their Unions* (1985). This self-examination of the union movement and of our environment was crucial to modernize labor's strategy to reach the unorganized in the service sector and among new entrants into the labor force including women and immigrants. It is also crucial to understanding and responding to new abuses, whether through the multinational corporations' disinvestment in America, through merger mania's burdening American business with dangerous levels of debt, through the multiplication of carcinogenic and other toxic chemicals in the workplace, or through Corporate America's enthusiasm for polygraphs, drug tests, genetic tests, and computer and telephone monitoring in the workplace. When they read George Orwell's *1984*, too many of our corporate executives adopted Big Brother as their role model.

Labor's message to the American people must be consistent and clear. It must stress equitable policies designed to insure that everyone in this country enjoys the blessings of the unparalleled wealth which we have created. We must stand for such fundamental ideas as tax reform that more fairly distributes the tax burden and does not allow the rich to shirk their obligations. We must stand for a system of national health care which provides medical services based upon need, not upon ability to pay. We must stand for a policy that invests American capital in America. We must stand for policies that halt the flood of American money, technology and jobs to overseas locations. (Let us be very clear on this point. We fully support economic aid to, and investment in, the developing economies of the Third and Fourth worlds. But fully 75 percent of overseas investment by American companies goes into already industrialized countries, and it is those already industrialized countries that are currently buying America. We must remember we have economically underdeveloped areas in this country, too.) We must stand for policies which rebuild our industrial base and regenerate our cities. We must stand for policies that provide safe, renewable energy at reasonable prices, and which are not designed to fatten the already swollen coffers of the multi-national oil companies. We must stand for a safe, renewable energy policy that drastically reduces our dependence on imported oil at the risk of war, and will avert depending on potentially disastrous nuclear energy.

We must stand for policies which will freeze and then reverse the insane arms race promoted by Corporate America. We must stand for programs that invest our wealth in ways which produce usable commodities and not weapons which can only ultimately ruin us all. We must show the people that national security is better served by restoring that economic and social strength which has always been America's greatest asset.

And we stand for a new bread-and-butter legislative agenda. We must stand for health insurance for all workers now. Our younger workers—female and male—have little or limited access to the full range of health care services. Today most young people have little chance for home ownership. We need a new home ownership program for them. Working parents need maternal and paternal leave and access to affordable, reliable child care. Auto and home insurance costs too often preclude saving money and eat into basic family budgets. And if OPEC gets its way again, we will all need utility rate and fuel cost containment protections.

In the current economic madness, most working people can expect to change jobs and careers several times over during their working lives. That's what new technology, international trade, reorganized work places and the service economy are bringing about. Under these circumstances, we need an education program like the G.I. Bill for everyone. To put a floor under the general wage decline we need an immediate increase in the minimum wage that would provide an annual income above the poverty level, and we need to index the minimum wage to the cost-of-living index. We must sustain our efforts for clean water and for controlling toxic chemicals inside the workplace and toxic wastes outside.

Let's spend the money it takes to build our safe energy base and to rebuild our crumbling roads, bridges, airports, rail systems, and ports and harbors. Let's spend the money it takes to educate our kids properly and to educate, train and retrain our unemployed and underemployed people—in schools, in colleges and in apprenticeship programs. Let's quit building more high-cost weapons and build more low-cost houses.

Let's invest in America! Let's produce in America so we can Buy American. Let's preserve and strengthen our civilian industrial and manufacturing base, so we'll always have a military industrial base, if and when we need it.

Let's quit exporting capital, technology and jobs and start importing those economic planning and industrial policy programs our trading partners are using to beat us in the trade game.

We need to preach the concept of worker rights. Worker rights mean economic rights: the right to a job that pays more than poverty wages; the right to full employment; the right to another job and income, when management fails, goes belly up, sells us out, spins us off, leaves town and leaves us stranded on the beaches of despair. Worker rights mean fair trade, not "free" trade. Worker rights mean job security. Worker rights mean taking from the greedy and helping the needy; helping the poor get off welfare rolls and on to payrolls rebuilding America.

Worker rights mean no Big Brother in the workplace: no bugs, no spooks, no hidden cameras, and no hired spies to watch, harass and intimidate us on our jobs. Worker rights mean safety and health rights in the workplace. No more operating unsafe butcher machines; no more breathing lung-withering fumes; no more cancerous chemicals silently killing us on the job. No more death and disease—no more murder in the workplace!

Worker rights mean civil rights, minority rights, women's rights outside in our work-a-day world *and* inside in our workplace world. Worker rights mean economic rights on the job and in the community. Worker rights mean jobs with justice.

Worker rights mean trade union rights: the right to free and fair elections for union representation; the freedom from fear of employer threats and punishment; freedom from fear of government-backed bosses putting us out of business in a deregulated union-free environment. Worker rights mean throwing out union-bashing legal racketeers and the right to rebuild our lives and our workplaces with justice and dignity on the job.

In short, worker rights mean an expansion of individual freedom and of collective rights.

We need to integrate this worker rights agenda in a general democratic effort to rebuild America.

Rebuilding America means restructuring the way decisions are made about money, investment, technology and what is going to be produced.

Rebuilding America means taking control and ownership of our basic natural resources out of the hands of private monopolists and putting it under the direction of the public interest. The poorest child in the South Bronx has more right to a return on investment in the oil shales of western public lands than does Exxon, Gulf or Mobil.

Rebuilding America means replacing the absurdities of the market place and the excesses of private, profit-motivated behavior with coordinated economic planning.

Rebuilding America means committing ourselves to the goals of full employment, to a progressive distribution of wealth and income, to the guaranteed right of trade unions to grow and prosper, and an end to the madness of the arms race.

We offer this agenda for worker rights and economic reconstruction to the Democratic Party which has been labor's home since the New Deal. That party is at a cross roads. Either it is going to return to its natural constituency and champion the cause of rebuilding America, along with those individual rights and civil liberties we all hold dear, or it is going to continue its futile attempt to imitate the Republican Party.

If it does the former, we'll try to help it do so. But if it chooses the latter, then we better prepare to go the Canadian route that led to the New Democratic Party north of our border: a democratic socialist party with a trade union core and a citizens' action constituency.

AMERICAN LABOR IN THE TWENTY-FIRST CENTURY

When I took over the reins of the Machinists Union in 1977, this century was only three quarters done. Today we stand on the threshold of its last decade, and we can not only chart the history of the century but also make some reasonable projections about the next.

Our destiny as members of the national and world labor force is not to promote a nation and world divided between haves and have-nots. Our destiny is not to become bound to an interventionist foreign policy that supports conquests by imperial multinational corporations. Our destiny is not to become willing serfs of global corporate sovereigns nor to consummate a master-servant relationship with our employers. Our destiny is not to deliver our minds, skills, and talents for the sake of keeping our employer in business, no matter the sacrifices and indignities that may be incurred. Our destiny is not work for the sake of a job or work alone. Slaves had jobs.

Nor is our destiny to experience a holocaust of technological unemployment and underemployment while systems designers and systems analysts, microprocessors, robots and flexible manufacturing systems shove us out of our workplaces and into the ranks of a useless army of unemployed, or into the lowest paid service sector slots that coddle the rich and swell the ranks of the working poor.

Our destiny is not to match the world's lowest economic, political and social standards. Instead our destiny is to raise those wretched standards so those who are exploited will become liberated and be able to buy and consume that which they produce.

Our destiny is not to surrender our American birthright to the unilateral authority of capital, corporations or their instruments of economy and politics. Instead our destiny is to coalesce as members of the labor force and launch a determined offense to secure, once and for all, our "inalienable right to life, liberty and the pursuit of happiness."

A long time ago, the U.S. Supreme Court declared that human labor was not an article of commerce to be bought, sold and buffeted about in the marketplace. We in the labor force, from the least paid to the highest paid, from the most menial to the most skilled, have a natural right and legal right to deny and resist the coercive power of private capital and the Corporate State when they seek to trade our dignity, our livelihoods, and our survival in the market as though we are mere economic goods or chattel slaves.

As we sail into the twenty-first century on the good ship America, our struggle to achieve those four basic objectives—a society with good jobs for everyone, a fairer distribution of income and wealth, democracy in the workplace, in a peaceful world—will harmoniously be achieved. First, each American will have a right to rewarding and munificent employment in a full employment economy, while sharing the fruits of labor-saving technology with increasing amounts of paid leisure time. Germany and Finland already have pushed their workweek standards to 37.5 hours. Full employment through a reduced worktime and a shorter workweek must be made new national commitments.

Our second objective would naturally follow from meeting the full employment objective. It is an equitable distribution of wealth, income and the political power derived therefrom. In order for a political economy to be strong, fair, and just, wealth and income must be equitably distributed to provide each citizen with an "inalienable right," as Jefferson put it, to the basic necessities of life. And as we build toward the twenty-first century, those basic necessities must be expanded to include employment, education, energy, food, health care, shelter and transportation. Food, clothing and shelter are necessary, but they are no longer enough.

Any individual denied access to just one of those basic necessities, for whatever reason, runs a race on the road of life at a staggering disadvantage. If denied more than one of those necessities, the notion of pulling oneself up by one's bootstraps becomes sheer nonsense. Let those who preach it go try it themselves. Poverty is no more character-building and virtuous than are extreme wealth, power and privilege.

As we enter the next century, a fair tax system, of course, would support a fair and equal distribution of wealth and income. That precludes the subversion of our federal income tax system by those corporate entities and private persons residing at the pinnacle of the economic pyramid. Those who have the most to defend, do the least and pay the least to defend it. Those who do the defending and pay for the defense have little or nothing to defend. Somehow that strikes me as inimical to the best interests of a democratic society. Without going into the numbers of this distorted public revenue system—and its attendant but misdirected spending priorities—it is easy to see that we have converted a half-hearted welfare state into a full-fledged warfare state. What we have come to witness is "inverted socialism" running amuck under the guise of free enterprise. We have every imaginable corporate subsidy for every corporation that is "too big to go bankrupt." Corporations have socialized their losses but they keep their profits private. We have socialism for the rich but dog-eat-dog capitalism for the poor.

All this greed, inequality, injustice and hypocrisy must change if our democracy is to survive passing through the sound barrier into the twenty-first century.

The best guarantee of that change is our third objective: securing trade union and employee rights in the workplace, in the enterprise, and in the political economy. Trade union rights are human rights in America as well as Poland. Despots from time immemorial have repressed and forbidden trade unions, except insofar as they might be manipulated into becoming accomplices and tools of ruling authority and power—whether that authority is governmental or private.

There has been no major change in our concept of collective bargaining since enactment of the National Relations Act in 1935—over half a century ago. The typical collective bargaining contract still provides for the same four fundamental features (1) recognition clauses, (2) grievance procedures, (3) wages and working conditions, and (4) seniority rights. Innovations which have extended the scope of bargaining are limited to pension, health and welfare benefits and supplemental unemployment benefits, both of which come under the fundamental wage and working conditions clause.

As we view the behavior of the Corporate State, it is apparent that existing labor law and bargaining limitations have yielded a disequilibrium in which corporations have outflanked unions both nationally and internationally.

Restoring the equilibrium requires extending the scope of bargaining nationally to include a measure of worker control over corporate decisions concerning manpower, investment and the organization of production. It is possible this control can be shared with the public at large through an economic and social contract for business and industry—a move which I believe is inevitable, particularly with respect to monopolistic and oligopolistic industries. But in the meantime, it may take the form of co-determination agreements, board-of-director representation, or outright employee ownership, such as we see in European countries today. Some union leverage on corporation decision making is already beginning to take place through the use of pension fund placements, but existing ERISA law prevents full exercise of this lever.

Federal legislation could also extend and expand the scope of bargaining beyond the four fundamentals. That would be the rational, sensible and democratic path. I am no seer, visionary or clairvoyant, but if we fail to extend the scope of bargaining then I predict that the twenty-first century will be marked by intense efforts on the part of labor and trade unions to puncture the management prerogative and proprietary information shields.

Congress will be called upon to redefine national labor relations policy in a broad social context, which will make corporate behavior accountable to workers, communities and the national interest—to the common good, if you please.

The American labor movement must also come to grips with the reality of international economics in labor relations in the twenty-first century. There can be no mistake about the impact of multinational corporate behavior on labor relations. The multinational corporation is unchecked, respects no boundaries or flags, and is answerable only to a few individuals who sit on governing boards of directors and a few government officials whose favor must be curried in collaboration toward grand designs and strategies. Multinational corporations are entities unto themselves, transcending the power and sanctions of national governments. The runaway shop is a international phenomenon. The flight of capital and technology is a feature of the multinational corporation. Violations of human rights and worker rights, through indifference toward or in contempt of, democratic and social values are a corollary of their proliferation. Trade unions can neither check their power and mobility nor effectively bargain with them—even in the four traditional areas of collective bargaining. Existing labor relations policy is bankrupt with respect to the behavior of multinationals.

As the twenty-first century approaches, it is essential that workers from different countries, who toil for the same employers, design ways and means to collaborate in collective bargaining. In the twenty-first century, international strikes and boycotts may become the rule, rather than the few faltering exceptions we have witnessed so far. International tribunals and agencies may be forced to develop codes of conduct governing corporate behavior and may be forced to piece together an international labor relations policy, which heretofore has received scant attention.

Thus, the twenty-first century will witness first attempts to establish labor-management dispute settlement procedures on a global basis. Voluntarism is already feebly forcing these issues into the international dialogue, but voluntarism will fail as it inevitably does. Strong sanctions will have to be written into an international labor code and into respective national codes. Trade union representation and participation in international agencies, such as the International Monetary Fund, the World Bank, and Regional Development Banks, which have heretofore been the exclusive domain of academics and business and management personnel, will become essential.

As I see it, the alternative to these developments is continued aggression by the Corporate State around the globe and eventual indentured servitude and subjugation of billions of ordinary working people.

Finally, achieving full employment, a fair and equitable distribution of wealth and income, and the guarantee of free trade union rights for employees would mean little, unless we can wean our political and economic systems from dependency on the warfare state.

We are all citizens of the world. But in time of nuclear overkill and speed of light nuclear delivery systems, controlled by distrustful and paranoid military and political leaders on all sides, we are all prisoners of war, hostages of technological tyranny, and potential victims of thermonuclear homicide.

We see our destiny as the pursuit of the American Dream, not in the isolation of selfishness and misanthropy nor in the craven fear of xenophobia; but rather in coalition with those who perceive our peril and our decline through the anxieties, injustices and misery among and all around us.

By thinking globally and acting locally in concert with our fellow citizens, we in the nation's workforce can help liberate ourselves and humanity from the bondage of ideological and technological terrorism.

As Spaceship Earth spins silently through the heavens into the twenty-first century's tenuous time zone, we must assert and do these things and more. First class world citizenship during our ride is not a private privilege but a public right for everyone.

Let ordinary working people the world-over vow we will not be left at the docking station. We are on board. We know where we're going and how to get there. Ours is the long and noblest of journeys toward genuine economic, political and social democracy. It is time to take control of our destiny.

NOTES

1. For the full text of the proposal, see *Let's Rebuild America* (Washington: IAM, 1983).

2. J. P. Stevens was at that time the most notorious labor law offender in the country.

sources

This volume has been edited from speeches delivered to a variety of audiences between 1977 and 1988. The principal talks that form the bodies of individual chapters are identified by their titles (if any), audiences, places and dates of delivery.

INTRODUCTION

IAM Staff Conference, Cincinnati, Ohio, September 8, 1978; Ron Chernow, "Wimpy," *Mother Jones*, January 1979, pp. 57–63. *Current Biography*, February 1980, pp. 38–41; "Life, Liberty and the Pursuit of Happiness in the Reagan Era," National Adherent Forum, Atlanta, Georgia, April 15, 1982; Robert G. Rodden, *The Fighting Machinists* (Washington, D.C.: Kelly Press, n.d.); Community Church, Boston, Massachusetts, March 16, 1986; *Proceedings, 32nd Grand Lodge Convention, International Association of Machinists and Aerospace Workers*, April 26, 1988, pp. 153–161; and interview with John Logue, September 1, 1988.

CHAPTER ONE

IAM Staff Conference, Cincinnati, September 6 and 8, 1978; Institute of Politics and Public Affairs, Kennedy School, Harvard University, Cambridge, MA, November 28, 1979; Opening and Closing Remarks, 30th IAM Grand Lodge Convention, Cincinnati, September 2, 1980; "Why We're Losing the Trade War," College of Wooster Foreign Policy Association, Wooster, Ohio, January 13, 1983; Opening and Closing Remarks, 1984 Grand Lodge Convention, Seattle, September 17 and 25, 1984; American Political Science Association, August 29, 1986; IAM Electronics and New Technology Conference, Orlando, Florida, December 2, 1986; Opening and Closing Remarks, 100th Anniversary Convention, Atlanta, April 26 and May 5, 1988; and "Economic Patriotism in a Global Economy," Indianapolis Economic Club, Indianapolis, Indiana, December 8, 1988.

CHAPTER TWO

Americans for Democratic Action, Washington, D.C., September 17 and 18, 1977; Testimony before the Subcommittee on Employment, Poverty and Migratory Labor of the Senate Committee on Human Resources, Washington, D.C., September 27, 1977; Third Annual Convention, Citizens Action Coalition of Indiana, Indianapolis, Indiana, November 5, 1977; "Managing the Future," University of Minnesota Corporate Executive Seminar on Strategic and Long Range Planning, Minneapolis, Minnesota, January 16, 1978; "Labor, Trade and the Economic Arsenal," American Institute Panel, Scottsdale, Arizona, November 21, 1978; The 1979 Eugene V. Debs/Norman Thomas Award, New York, New York, June 6, 1979; "Direct Foreign Investment and Productivity," Industrial Relations Association of Detroit, Detroit, Michigan, November 8, 1979; The Community Church of Boston, Boston, Massachusetts, March 29, 1981; Statement before the Committee on Ways and Means, U.S. House of Representatives, on the President's Tax Proposals, March 31, 1981; "Conflicting Interests in Reindustrialization," Massachusetts Institute of Technology, Cambridge, Massachusetts, April 13, 1981; University of California, Berkeley, California, May 12, 1981; "When Reagan Economics Fail," Evansville Chamber of Commerce Labor and Management Committee, Evansville, Indiana, September 25, 1981; "The Role of Trade Unions After Reaganomics Fail," Kenyon College, Gambier, Ohio, March 29, 1982; "Life, Liberty and the Pursuit of Happiness in the Reagan Era," National Adherent Forum, Atlanta, Georgia, April 15, 1982; "What Kind of a Country?" IAM Southwest Territory Staff Meeting, San Francisco, California, July 7, 1982; IAM Electronics and New Technology Conference, Seattle, Washington, September 21, 1982; International Metalworkers Federation, First World Aerospace Conference, London, England, October 13, 1982; "Our Crumbling Economic Pyramid," Cleveland Engineering Society, Cleveland, Ohio, October 28, 1982; "Two Headed Calf," National Farmers Organization, Louisville, Kentucky, December 8, 1982; California Consumers, San Jose, California, April 9, 1983; "A Modest Proposal," U.S. Air Force ICAM Industry Days Conference, New Orleans, Louisiana, June 8, 1983; IAM New Technologies Conference, December 5, 1983; "The Declining Middle: Judging Industrial Policy's Success, IUD Legislative Conference, Washington, D.C., January 25, 1984; "Technological Tyranny," Cornell University Economic Dislocation Conference, Washington, D.C., April 9, 1984; "Industrial Policy: An Alternative to Corporate Welfare," IUD Industrial Policy Conference, Seattle, Washington, June 4, 1984; Labor Education Department of the University of Arkansas at Little Rock, Wagner, Oklahoma, October 21, 1984; Cleveland Club, Cleveland, Ohio, October 26, 1984; "The Big Lotto Ain't Delivering the Goods," House Education and Labor Committee Hearings on Full Employment, Chicago, Illinois, September 4, 1985; IAM Electronics and New Technology Conference, St. Louis, Missouri, September 25, 1985; Alabama AFL-CIO, Montgomery, Alabama, October 14, 1985; "America and the World," New Directions Conference, Washington, D.C., May 3, 1986; American Political Science Association, Washington, D.C., August 29, 1986; Pioneer Valley Central Labor

Council, AFL-CIO, Chicopee, Massachusetts, March 7, 1987; "A Time for Activist Government," Commonwealth North, Anchorage, Alaska, November 10, 1987; and Danville Area Community Service Council, Danville, Illinois, June 10, 1988.

CHAPTER THREE

"U.S. Trade Unions in the Current Domestic and International Economic Scenes," Washington, D.C., September 30, 1977; "Managing the Future," University of Minnesota Corporate Executive Seminar on Strategic and Long Range Planning, Minneapolis, Minnesota, January 16, 1978; Joint Meeting of the NAM International Trade Subcommittee and International Economic Affairs Committee, Washington, D.C., November 9, 1978; "Labor's View of Multilateral Trade Negotiations," Brookings Institution, Washington, D.C., March 6, 1979; "Trade and the Dollar: Coping with Interdependence," National Town Meeting, Washington, D.C., March 15, 1979; International Metalworkers Federation, Seattle, Washington, May 22, 1979; "How Can Employment be Maintained and Unemployment be Fought in Industrialized Countries Without Resorting to Protectionism?" International Metalworkers Federation Congress, Washington, D.C., May 27, 1981; "Looking for a Democratic Socialist Strategy in the U.S. Trade Union Movement," Conference on World Systems of Labor and Production: Challenges to Social Democracy in the 80's, Hobart and William Smith Colleges, Geneva, New York, May 13, 1982; "The USS Economee," Purdue University, Lafayette, Indiana, March 29, 1984; "Problems from Unfair and Illegal International Trade Practices," U.S. House of Representatives, House Energy and Commerce Committee, Washington, D.C., February 27, 1985; and "America and the World," New Directions Conference, Washington, D.C., May 3, 1986.

CHAPTER FOUR

"The Need for Economic Conversion," Coalition for a New Foreign and Military Policy, Washington, D.C., April 6, 1978; Press Conference on Budget Priorities, Washington, D.C., January 25, 1979; "The Arms Race vs. the Human Race," Reversing the Arms Race Conference, Pasadena, California, October 22, 1979; Institute of Politics and Public Affairs, Kennedy School, Harvard University, Cambridge, Massachusetts, November 28, 1979; Opening Remarks, 20th IAM Grand Lodge Convention, Cincinnati, Ohio, September 2, 1980; Reverse the Arms Race Symposium, American Association for the Advancement of Science, Toronto, Canada, January 6, 1981; "We Can't Eat Bombs," Cleveland City Club, Cleveland, Ohio, March 13, 1981; "Borrowing from Western Economies," National Law Center, George Washington University, Washington, D.C., October 22, 1981; "Life, Liberty and the Pursuit of Happiness in the Reagan Era," National Adherent Forum, Atlanta, Georgia, April 15, 1982; "The Economics of Peace," Janesville Area Community Council, Janesville, Wisconsin, September 17, 1982; Economic Conversion Conference, Swedish Metal Workers

Union, Gothenburg, Sweden, March 2, 1983; Unitarian Universalist Association National Workshop, Washington, D.C., April 25, 1983; "Economic Links of Defense Spending," World Affairs Council, Los Angeles, California, August 29, 1983; "Toward a Rational Foreign Policy," Labor and Industrial Relations Colloquium, University of Illinois, Urbana-Champaign, Illinois, November 18, 1983; IAM Electronics and New Technology Conference, St. Louis, Missouri, September 25, 1985; Star Wars Action Forum, San Francisco, California, January 18, 1986; "America and the World," New Directions Conference, Washington, D.C., May 3, 1986; Indiana University and Purdue University, Indianapolis, Indiana, May 19, 1986; Trinity Conference, Santa Fe, New Mexico, June 27, 1986; Testimony before the Subcommittee on Economic Stabilization of the Committee on Banking, Finance, and Urban Affairs of the U.S. House of Representatives, Washington, D.C., September 15, 1987; and "A Time for Activist Government," Commonwealth North, Anchorage, Alaska, November 10, 1987.

CHAPTER FIVE

Massachusetts Americans for Democratic Action, Boston, Massachusetts, March 12, 1978; Testimony before the Subcommittee on Energy of the Joint Economic Committee, Washington, D.C., March 16, 1978; Testimony before the Environment, Energy, and Natural Resources Subcommittee of the Government Operations Committee, U.S. House of Representatives, Washington, D.C., June 14, 1978; International Chemical Workers Union Convention, Las Vegas, Nevada, October 5, 1978; International Conference on Science and Technology, New York University, March 28, 1979; "Three Reasons Why We Oppose Nuclear Power," Committee for Jobs and Safe Energy, Harrisburg, Pennsylvania, March 28, 1981; "Nuclear Power and Technological Totalitarianism," SEIU Local 660, Los Angeles, California, May 8, 1982; IAM Electronics and New Technology Conference, Seattle, Washington, September 21, 1982; "Robots and New Technology," IRRA Southwest Chapter, Kalamazoo, Michigan, April 4, 1983; "A Modest Proposal," The U.S. Air Force ICAM Industry Days Conference, New Orleans, Louisiana, June 8, 1983; "Cleaning up Reagan and his Colorado Crazies," IUD/Environmental Network Convention, Aspen, Colorado, June 30, 1983; "Can We Control Technological Tyranny?" East Hartford Association for Human Services, East Hartford, Connecticut, November 17, 1983; "Technological Tyranny," Cornell University Economic Dislocation Conference, Washington, D.C., April 9, 1984; IAM Electronics and New Technology Conference, St. Louis, Missouri, September 25, 1985; Georgia Tech, Atlantic, Georgia, September 26, 1985; and "Technology's Unfulfilled Promises," Labor Center Conference on Union Strategies for a High Tech Era, University of California at Los Angeles, Los Angeles, California, November 5, 1987.

CHAPTER SIX

Testimony before the Subcommittee on Employment, Poverty and Migratory Labor of the Senate Committee on Human Resources, Washington, D.C.,

September 27, 1977; "Managing the Future," University of Minnesota Corporate Executive Seminar on Strategic and Long Range Planning, Minneapolis, Minnesota, January 16, 1978; "Blue Collar Workers and Quality of Working Life Programs," draft of article for Viewpoint Magazine, August 1, 1978; Detroit Area Chapter, Industrial Relations Research Association, Detroit, Michigan, December 6, 1979; "When Reagan Economics Fail," Labor and Management Committee, Evansville Chamber of Commerce, Evansville, Indiana, September 25, 1981; "Labor Management Relations in the Reagan Era: The 'New' Industrial Relations," Foundation for Student Communications, Dallas, Texas, November 23, 1981; "Labor's Proper Role in the New Economics," Western Michigan University IRRA Conference, Grand Rapids, Michigan, March 8, 1982; Midwest-Southern Region, UCLEA Professional Council Conference, St. Louis, Missouri, December 2, 1982; Georgia State University, Marietta, Georgia, May 5, 1983; "'We'll Cooperate, If . . . ,'" Graduate School of Business, Columbia University, New York, New York, June 6, 1983; "What's Happening in Labor Law?" Labor Law Section, Los Angeles County Bar Association, Los Angeles, California, January 17, 1984; "If You Can't Write a Novel, Live One," Montgomery College, Rockville, Maryland, October 24, 1984; Case Western Law Forum, Case Western Reserve University, Cleveland, Ohio, February 1, 1985; 12th Annual Seminar on Collective Bargaining, Cleveland State University, Cleveland, Ohio, November 14, 1985; Vanderbilt University, Nashville, Tennessee, November 21, 1985; Rutgers University, New Brunswick, New Jersey, December 6, 1985; Presidential Classroom, Washington, D.C., March 13, 1986; IUD Legislative Conference, Washington, D.C., April 17, 1986; "The Future in Labor Relations," FEI Glenmore Distilleries, Hilton Head, South Carolina, May 8, 1986; Seventh Annual Lowell Conference on Industrial History, National Park Service, U.S. Department of Interior, Lowell, Massachusetts, October 30, 1986; IAM Electronics and New Technology Conference, Orlando, Florida, December 2, 1986; Northeast Ohio Chapter of the Industrial Relations Research Association, Cleveland, Ohio, May 20, 1987; "Labor Looks at 'New Management,'" *Management Review*, July 1987, and "Managing Modern Capitalism," Kent State University, Kent, Ohio, November 3, 1988.

CHAPTER SEVEN

"Labor Movement Challenges to Contemporary Problems," Vassar College, Poughkeepsie, New York, February 12, 1979; "A Socialist Response to the Current Economic Crisis," Democratic Socialist Organizing Committee, Georgetown University, Washington, D.C., March 9, 1979; Humanist Society of Metropolitan New York, New York City, December 10, 1979; Catholic University Chapter, National Lawyers Guild, Washington D.C., March 18, 1980; "Politics Today and Alternative Political Parties," Labor Education and Research Center, University of Massachusetts, Amherst, Massachusetts, October 15, 1980; Acceptance of Eugene V. Debs Award, Eugene V. Debs Foundation, Terre Haute, Indiana, November 1, 1980; "The Changing Power of Unions and Corporations in our Political Life," Hofstra University, Hempstead, New York, November

15, 1980; The Farmer-Labor Association, St. Paul, Minnesota, December 13, 1980; Closing remarks, Machinists Non-Partisan League Planning Committee, Washington, D.C., January 29, 1981; "Reagan's Road to Ruin," 1981 IAM Legislative Conference, Washington, D.C., March 23, 1981; Iowa Fourth Congressional District Democrats, Des Moines, Iowa, May 2, 1981; Fifth National Convention of the Democratic Socialist Organizing Committee, Philadelphia, Pennsylvania, May 25, 1981; "Lobbying Reaganomics Style," National Students' Association, George Washington University, Washington, D.C., February 27, 1982; "Two Headed Calf," National Farmers Organization, Louisville, Kentucky, December 8, 1982; "On Conservatives and Liberals," Commonwealth Club of California, San Francisco, California, January 28, 1983; Southern California ADA Chapter, Santa Monica, California, January 29, 1983; Wisconsin Action Coalition, December 3, 1983; "Counterforce Coalition: Rebuilding America," IAM Legislative Conference, Washington, D.C., January 24, 1984; Machinists Non-Partisan League, Chicago, Illinois, February 5, 1984; Southeast Pennsylvania Chapter of ADA, Philadelphia, Pennsylvania, March 25, 1985; Community and Labor Coalition, Binghamtom, New York, May 14, 1985; Montgomery County Democrats, Washington, D.C., January 13, 1986; Machinists Non-Partisan League Planning Committee Meeting, Hollywood, Florida, February 2, 1987; Western States Caucus, Democratic National Committee, Phoenix, Arizona, March 27, 1987; Opening Remarks, IAM Legislative Conference, Washington, D.C., May 4, 1987; MNPL Planning Committee, New Orleans, Louisiana, February 1, 1988; IAM Transportation Conference, Hollywood, Florida, November 16, 1988; and "Creeping International Fascism," British Columbia Labor Federation Convention, Vancouver, Canada, November 30, 1988.

CHAPTER EIGHT

United States Senate Committee on the Judiciary, Subcommittee on Citizens and Shareholders Rights and Remedies, Washington, D.C., November 22, 1979; "Labor Movement Challenges to Contemporary Problems," Vassar College, Poughkeepsie, New York, February 12, 1979; "The Pyramiding of America: Labor Relations in the 21st Century," Richmond Virginia, April 3, 1979; "Four Basic Rights for Americans," Rural America Conference, Washington, D.C., June 26, 1979; Commencement Address, Wilmington College, Wilmington, Ohio, June 8, 1980; "Eurosocialism and America," Institute for Democratic Socialism, Washington, D.C., December 5, 1980; Fifth National Convention, Democratic Socialist Organizing Committee, Philadelphia, Pennsylvania, May 25, 1981; Solidarity Day III rallies in Florida, Iowa, and California, September 5, 1983; "Beyond the New Deal: An Economic and Social Contract," National Democratic Party Platform Committee, Washington, D.C., June 12, 1984; Rutgers University, New Brunswick, New Jersey, December 6, 1985; Pennsylvania State University, University Park, Pennsylvania, April 9, 1986; Machinists Non-

Partisan League Planning Committee Meeting, Hollywood, Florida, February 2, 1987; "Labor's Emerging Agenda," Department of Labor, Atlantic City, New Jersey, November 24, 1987; MNPL Planning Committee, New Orleans, Louisiana, February 1, 1988; and Jobs with Justice rally, Atlanta, Georgia, April 30, 1988.